Appalachian Trail Guide to New Hampshire and Vermont

Appalachian Trail Guide to
New Hampshire and Vermont

Fifth Edition

The Appalachian Trail Conference
Harpers Ferry
1988

Cover photo: Kancamagus Pass,
White Mountains, New Hampshire

Published by the Appalachian Trail Conference
P.O. Box 807
Harpers Ferry, West Virginia 25425

Fifth edition
Printed in the United States of America

ISBN 0-917953-22-3

Contents

Maps

The following maps are included with this guide. (All maps show roads, lakes, and peaks.)

Key Map: Shows the order of strip maps.

New Hampshire

Map 1. Mahoosuc Range: Grafton Notch (Maine Highway 26) to Androscoggin Valley (U.S. Route 2)
Map 2. Presidential Range: Androscoggin Valley (U.S. Route 2) to Crawford Notch (U.S. Route 302)
Map 3. Franconia: Crawford Notch (U.S. Route 302) to N. H. Highway 25
Map 4. Hanover: N. H. Highway 25 to Connecticut River (Hanover)

Vermont

Map 5. Ottauquechee: Connecticut River (Hanover and Norwich) to Sherburne Pass (U.S. Route 4)
Map 6. Killington Peak: Sherburne Pass (U.S. Route 4) to Danby-Landgrove Road
Map 7. Bromley Mountain: Danby-Landgrove Road to Arlington-West Wardsboro Road
Map 8. Glastenbury Mountain: Arlington-West Wardsboro Road to Mass. Highway 2 (North Adams, Mass.)

Abbreviations

E...east

ft. ....foot or feet

Mass.....................................Massachusetts

mi. ....mile or miles

N...north

N.H. ....New Hampshire

P. O. ....Post Office

RMC ....Randolph Mountain Club

S...south

Vt. ....Vermont

W...west

yd./yds. ....yard/yards

Notice to all Trail Users

The information contained in this publication is the result of the best effort of the publisher, using information available to it at the time of printing. Changes resulting from maintenance work and relocations are constantly occurring and, therefore, no published route can be regarded as precisely accurate at the time you read this notice.

Notices of pending relocations are indicated. Inasmuch as maintenance of the Trail is conducted by volunteers and maintaining clubs listed in the guidebooks, questions about the exact route of the Trail should be addresssed to the maintaining clubs or to the Appalachian Trail Conference, Washington & Jackson Streets, Post Office Box 807, Harpers Ferry, West Virginia 25425-0807. Telephone: (304) 535-6331. *On the Trail, please pay close attention to*—and follow—*the white blazes and any direction signs.*

Responsibility for Safety

It is extremely important to plan your hike, especially in places where water is scarce. Purify drinking water drawn from any source. *Water purity cannot be guaranteed.* The Appalachian Trail Conference and the various maintaining clubs attempt to locate good sources of water along the Trail but have no control over these sources and cannot, in any sense, be responsible for the quality of the water at any given time. You must determine the safety of all water you consume.

Certain risks are inherent in any Appalachian Trail hike. Each A.T. user must accept personal responsibility for his or her safety while on the Trail. The Appalachian Trail Conference and its member maintaining clubs cannot ensure the safety of any hiker on the Trail, and, when undertaking a hike on the Trail, each user thereby assumes the risk for any accident, illness, or injury that might occur on the Trail.

Enjoy your hike, but please take all appropriate precautions for your safety and well-being.

How to Use This Guide

The table of contents indicates the information contained in the first five chapters. Trail data follows; first for New Hampshire, then Vermont.

Trail data are presented for both directions so travelers may avoid having to reverse directions mentally. Trail description is written for travel in the opposite direction.

The Trail data have been divided into 19 sections, separated by highway crossings or other geographical features. The sections generally include more than a day's travel, and sometimes cover as many as three or four days.

In this guide, descriptions of the southernmost Trail section in Maine and the northernmost in Massachusetts have been added for the hiker's convenience.

The data for each Trail section are divided into three parts. The first part includes general information, needed primarily for planning. This material is arranged under individual headings in the following order:

Brief Description of Section
Road Approaches
Maps
Shelters and Campsites
Regulations
Supplies and Services
Public Accommodations

The detailed "Trail Description," the actual guide to the footpath, follows. Data are given first for the Trail hiker walking south on the Trail, then for the hiker walking north. A column of distances on the left gives the mileage from the start of the section to points of importance along the Trail section. Each point (generally, stream crossings, shelters, summits, or important turns) is described, followed by directions on how the Trail goes to the next point.

Eight "strip" maps, based on U.S. Geological Survey topographic quadrangles at a scale of one inch to one mile, are included with this volume. A key map, at a scale of one inch to eight miles, gives an over all view of the Trail in New Hampshire and Vermont, the location of major points of interest, and the location of each strip map. These nine maps give a quick look at the route and supply further information on the Trail. In each section, other maps are also listed.

The Appalachian Trail

The Appalachian Trail (A.T.) is a continuous, marked footpath extending 2,100 miles from Katahdin, a granite monolith in the central Maine wilderness, south to Springer Mountain in Georgia along the crest of the Appalachian Mountain range.

The Trail traverses primarily public land in 14 states. Virginia has the longest section with 552 miles, while West Virginia has the shortest, almost 26 miles along the Virginia-West Virginia boundary and a short swing into Harpers Ferry at the Maryland border. The highest elevation along the Trail is 6,643 feet at Clingmans Dome in the Great Smokies. The Trail is only slightly above sea level at its crossing of the Hudson River in New York.

Trail History

Credit for establishing the Trail belongs to three leaders and countless volunteers. The first proposal for the Trail to appear in print was an article by forester Benton MacKaye of Shirley, Massachusetts, entitled,"An Appalachian Trail, a Project in Regional Planning," in the October 1921 issue of the *Journal of the American Institute of Architects.* He envisioned a footpath along the Appalachian ridgeline where urban people could retreat to nature.

MacKaye's challenge kindled considerable interest, but at the time most of the outdoor organizations that could participate in constructing such a trail were east of the Hudson River. Four existing trail systems could be incorporated into an A.T. The Appalachian Mountain Club (AMC) maintained an excellent series of trails in New England, but most ran north-south; the Trail could not cross New Hampshire until the chain of huts built and operated by the AMC permitted an east-west alignment. In Vermont, the southern 100 miles of the Long Trail, then being developed in the Green Mountains, were connected to the White Mountains by the trails of the Dartmouth Outing Club.

In 1923, in the Harriman-Bear Mountain section of Palisades Interstate Park, the first section of the A. T. was opened by a number of area hiking clubs, that later formed the New York-New Jersey Trail Conference.

The Appalachian Trail Conference (ATC) was formed in 1925 to stimulate greater interest in MacKaye's idea and coordinate the clubs' work in choosing and building the route. The Conference remains a nonprofit educational organization of volunteers dedicated to maintaining, managing, and protecting the Appalachian Trail.

Although interest in the Trail spread to Pennsylvania and New England, little work was done until 1926, when Judge Arthur Perkins of Hartford, Connecticut, began persuading groups to locate and cut the footpath through the wilderness. His enthusiasm provided the momentum that carried the Trail idea forward.

The southern states had had few trails and even fewer clubs. The "skyline" route followed by the A.T. was developed largely within national forests. A number of clubs were formed in various parts of the southern Appalachians to take responsibility for the Trail there.

Judge Perkins interested Myron H. Avery in the Trail. Avery, charman of the Conference from 1931 to 1952, enlisted the aid and coordinated the work of the hundreds of men and women who brought the Trail to its completion on August 14, 1937, when the last section (the ridge between Spaulding and Sugarloaf mountains in Maine) was opened.

After the Trail was initially completed, the encroachments of highways, housing developments, and summer resorts caused many relocations, and the problem of maintaining its wilderness character became more severe.

At the eighth biennial meeting of the Appalachian Trail Conference, in June 1937, Conference member Edward B. Ballard proposed a plan for an "Appalachian Trailway" that would set apart an area on each side of the Trail, dedicated to the interests of those who travel on foot. This plan was adopted by the Conference.

Steps taken to effect this long-range program of protection of the Appalachian Trail culminated first in the execution on October 15, 1938, of an agreement between the National Park Service and the U.S. Forest Service for the promotion of an Appalachian Trailway zone through the relevant national parks and forests for a distance extending one mile on each side of the Trail. Within this zone, no new parallel roads would be built, or any other incompatible development allowed. No timber cutting would be permitted within 200 feet of the Trail. Similar agreements, creating a zone one-quarter mile in width, were signed with the states through which the Trail passes.

Three decades of work—and encroachment—later, Congress established a national system of trails and designated, as the initial components, the Appalachian Trail and the Pacific Crest Trail. The National Trails System Act directs the secretary of the interior, in consultation with the secretary of agriculture, to administer the Appalachian Trail primarily as a footpath and protect the Trail against incompatible activities and the use of motorized vehicles. Provision was also made for acquiring rights-of-way for the Trail, both inside and outside the boundaries of federally administered areas.

In 1970, supplemental agreements under the act—among

the National Park Service, the U.S. Forest Service, and the Appalachian Trail Conference—established the specific responsibilities of these organizations for the initial mapping, selection of rights-of-way, relocations, maintenance, development, acquisition of land, and protection of a permanent Trail. Agreements also were signed between the park service and the various states, encouraging them to acquire and protect a right-of-way for the Trail outside federal land.

Slow progress of federal efforts and lack of initiative by some states led Congress in 1978 to amend the National Trails System Act. The amendment, known as The Appalachian Trail Bill, was signed by President Jimmy Carter on March 21, 1978.

The new legislation emphasized the need for protecting the Trail, including acquiring a corridor, and authorized $90 million for that purpose. With less than 150 miles unprotected by 1988, this project is expected to be completed by 1991.

Appalachian Trail Conference

In 1984, the Interior Department formally delegated to the Appalachian Trail Conference the responsibility of managing the A.T. corridor lands for the public. In several states, similar pacts are progressing concurrently with the federal program. After completing the acquisition program, the Conference and its clubs will retain the primary responsibility for maintaining and managing the Trail.

The Conference also publishes booklets and supplies information on constructing and maintaining hiking trails, official A.T. guides, and general information on hiking and trail use. in general. Membership dues range from $18 to $30.

The affairs of the Conference are managed by a volunteer Board of Managers, consisting of a chair, three vice chairs, a treasurer, a secretary, a corresponding secretary, and 18 members, six from each of the three regions of the Trail: New England, mid-Atlantic, and southern.

The membership of the Conference consists of organizations that maintain the Trail or contribute to the Trail project and individuals. ATC membership includes a subscription to *Appalachian Trailway News*, published in March, May, July, September, and November, and 15-percent discounts on publications and merchandise. The Conference also issues a newsletter, *The Register*, for Trail maintainers.

Membership forms and a complete list of publications, with current prices, are available by writing the Appalachian Trail Conference, P.O. Box 807, Harpers Ferry, W. Va. 25425, or calling (304) 535-6331. The office is open 9 a.m. to 5 p.m. (Eastern time), Monday through Friday, and weekends from April through October.

Maintaining Clubs

Three member clubs of the Appalachian Trail Conference maintain the Trail in New Hampshire and Vermont. The Appalachian Mountain Club (AMC) and the U.S. Forest Service maintain the Trail from Grafton Notch, Maine, south to Kinsman Notch. The Dartmouth Outing Club (DOC) maintains the Trail from Kinsman Notch south to Vt. 12. The Green Mountain Club (GMC) maintains the sections from Vt. 12 south to the Massachusetts-Vermont state line. Each club has volunteer Trail workers, summer crews, and caretakers who maintain the A.T., shelters, and campsites.

The AMC is a nonprofit volunteer organization of almost 30,000 members, founded in Boston in 1876. It was established as a literary, scientific, educational, and charitable corporation for the purpose of "exploring the mountains of New

England and adjacent regions, both for scientific and artistic purposes and in general to cultivate an interest in geographical studies."

Over the past century, the club has published numerous maps and guidebooks as well as the periodical *Appalachia*; supported numerous efforts to preserve and conserve the natural mountain landscape in the northeastern United States; supported ongoing research into recreational impact on and management of the New England outdoors; and developed an extensive system of shelters, trails, and mountain huts. The AMC maintains about 300 miles of trails, 120 miles of which are part of the A.T.; 16 backcountry shelters and tentsites; and 10 huts in the White Mountain National Forest. For more information on the club, please write or call Appalachian Mountain Club, Pinkham Notch Camp, P.O. Box 298, Gorham, N.H. 03581, (603) 466-2721 or 5 Joy Street, Boston, Mass. 02108, (617) 523-0636.

The DOC, the oldest college outing club in the United States, was formed in 1909. The cabin and trail division of DOC maintains about 125 miles of trails, 75 of which are part of the A.T., and 10 shelters. The club also publishes several maps and guidebooks for hikers. For more information on the club, write or call: Dartmouth Outing Club, Robinson Hall, Box 9, Hanover, N.H. 03755, (603) 646-2428.

The GMC was formed in 1910 to establish and sponsor the Long Trail, one of the oldest long-distance hiking trails in the United States, predating the A.T. The Long Trail extends some 263 miles from Massachusetts to the Canada. Along its length are 70 shelters and campsites. The Long Trail and its nearly 175 miles of side trails, compose a 440-mile system. (The southern 97 miles of the A.T. in Vermont coincide with the Long Trail.) The GMC's main purpose is to protect, manage, and maintain the Long Trail system. The club also publishes several guidebooks and the *Long Trail News*. For more information, write or call Green Mountain Club, Box 889, Montpelier, Vt. 05602 , (802) 223-3463.

The Route of the Appalachian Trail in New Hampshire and Vermont

The Appalachian Trail enters New Hampshire from the east at the Maine-New Hampshire state line, 14.4 miles from Grafton Notch in Maine. It follows the Mahoosuc Range to the Androscoggin River, a few miles east of Gorham, and then traverses the Carter-Moriah and Wildcat ranges to Pinkham Notch in the heart of White Mountain National Forest. The Trail swings northeasterly, climbing Mt. Madison, and then south along the crest of the Presidential Range. Continuing west through Crawford Notch, the A.T. climbs Zeacliff, Mt. Guyot, South Twin Mountain, and Mt. Garfield. The Trail moves southward along the Franconia Range, leading west across Franconia Notch to Kinsman Pond. The Trail then turns south again across the Kinsman Range to Kinsman Notch at the base of Mt. Moosilauke.

After a steep climb of Mt. Moosilauke, the A.T. heads south over Mt. Cube, Smarts Mountain, and Moose Mountain to Hanover. It then strikes west across the Connecticut River.

From Sherburne Pass, the Trail heads south once again, along the main crest of the Green Mountains, often through Green Mountain National Forest. In this section, it coincides with the Long Trail of the Green Mountain Club for 97 miles to the Massachusetts-Vermont state line.

The Trail enters Massachusetts on East Mountain, four miles north of North Adams, Massachusetts.

Use of the Trail

Advice and Precautions

The hiker who uses the Appalachian Trail for more than day-hiking needs a thorough understanding of the Trail and should study the introductory parts of this guide carefully. Hikers planning an extended trip should write or call the Appalachian Trail Conference (ATC), P.O. Box 807, Harpers Ferry, W. Va. 25425-0807, (304) 535-6331 for advice and suggestions on long-distance hiking.

Except in the White Mountains, the Appalachian Trail in New Hampshire and Vermont is not in wilderness. From most elevations, towns or roads can be seen. If the route is lost, steady travel and persistance will probably bring the traveler to a highway. However, a poorly planned or ill-advised trip can result in unpleasant experiences and a night unintentionally spent in the woods.

The ruggedness of the terrain and the exertion required to walk the Appalachian Trail in New Hampshire and Vermont should not be underestimated. Do not travel here without adequate preparation, equipment, and physical conditioning.

All travelers in the New England woods should exercise extreme care with campfires or smoking.

Trail Marking

The Appalachian Trail is marked for travel in both directions. The marks are white-paint blazes about two inches wide and 6 inches high on trees (or poles) and rocks. Above timberline a series of cairns identifies the route. In some areas diamond-shaped A.T. metal markers are found.

Two blazes, one above the other, signal an obscure turn,

route change, or warning to check blazes carefully. Consult your map and this guide.

When the route is not obvious because of the terrain, normal marking procedure is to position the blazes so a hiker standing at one blaze will always be able to see the next one. When the footway is unmistakable, blazes frequently are farther apart. A hiker who has gone a quarter-mile without seeing a blaze should retrace his steps until he locates a blaze and then check to ensure no turn has been missed. Since the Trail is marked in both directions, if no blaze is visible on the route ahead, a glance back may locate blazes for travel in the opposite direction, reassuring the hiker he is still on the Trail

Side trails from the A.T. to water, viewpoints, and shelters usually are blazed in blue paint. Intersecting trails, not part of the A.T., are blazed in a variety of colors.

If the marked Trail differs from the guidebook description, a relocation has been made recently. The Trail was probably relocated to avoid some hazard or undesirable feature or to remove it from private property. If hikers use the old trail, they may be trespassing on private property, and generating ill will toward themselves and other Trail hikers.

Water

Water is found at frequent intervals along the Appalachian Trail in New Hampshire and Vermont. Carrying a canteen may seem unnecessary but is advisable. Dehydration increases fatigue. The exertion required in hiking combined with the possibility of water shortages might mar an otherwise enjoyable experience.

Although the A.T. has many sources of clean, potable water, any water source can become polluted. Most water sources along the Trail are unprotected and consequently very susceptible to contamination. All water should be purified by boiling or chemical treatment before use. The hiker should take particular care to protect the purity of all water sources. Never wash dishes, clothes, or hands in the water source. Make sure food and human wastes are buried well away from any water source.

Weather

New England weather changes rapidly, especially in the mountains. During summer months, the hiker can expect both hot and humid and cold and rainy days. Rain should be expected on all trips, and several rainy days in a row are common. If adequately equipped for wet conditions, the hiker can travel all parts of the Trail, except sections above treeline, at any time of the summer in any weather. (Occasionally, fords and stream crossings become hazardous due to high water. Waiting for the water level to lower is advisable.)

In addition to the generally damp soil in New England's hardwood and coniferous forests, many old roads used for the Trail have a growth of swale grass. Heavy dew, a frequent occurrence, makes for wet travel in the morning. The hiker should be able to waterproof footgear.

Above timberline, bad weather often makes travel unsafe. Weather conditions of arctic severity can be encountered at higher elevations, even in summer. Publicized incidents of lost and injured travelers on the Presidential Range illustrate the serious dangers that can be encountered. Travelers here should be prepared physically and plan their hikes carefully. Adequate clothing and equipment are essential. No one should continue hiking if storm warnings have been issued.

The season for travel on the Appalachian Trail in New

Hampshire and Vermont extends from May to November. The cooler, clearer weather and more satisfactory footway conditions during August, September, and October make these months preferable for travel.

At high elevations, snow is common in October and may occur earlier. When walking in late fall along alpine ridges, such as in the Presidential Range, the hiker should be prepared for winter conditions.

Late in the season, those hiking the entire Trail from Georgia to Maine may want to go directly to Katahdin from Vermont and hike back south to complete the Trail. This would prevent a hiker from getting caught in an early Maine winter and arriving at Katahdin after Baxter State Park had closed for the season.

Snow and winter conditions are to be expected from November through April in New Hampshire and Vermont. The potential winter hiker should plan on encountering extended periods of severe cold (temperatures below zero Fahrenheit), extremely high winds, deep snow (requiring skis or snowshoes), shelters filled with snow, and cabins and huts closed for the winter. Deep and drifting snow also make the Trail and its blazes exceedingly difficult to find. Any hiker planning winter travel on the Trail should first travel the route during summer.

Special equipment and training are needed for winter hiking and camping in New England. The rewards are great, but the hardships many. Hikers are warned not to underestimate the preparations necessary for a winter trip.

The Wind-Chill Factor

Wind Speed (mph)	*Actual Temperature (°F)* 50	40	30	20	10	0	−10	−20	−30	−40	−50
	Equivalent Temperature (°F)										
0	50	40	30	20	10	0	−10	−20	−30	−40	−50
5	48	37	27	16	6	−5	−15	−26	−36	−47	−57
10	40	28	16	4	−9	−21	−33	−46	−58	−70	−83
15	36	22	9	−5	−18	−36	−45	−58	−72	−85	−99
20	32	18	4	−10	−25	−39	−53	−67	−82	−96	−110
25	30	16	0	−15	−29	−44	−59	−74	−88	−104	−118
30	28	13	−2	−18	−33	−48	−63	−79	−94	−109	−125
35	27	11	−4	−20	−35	−49	−67	−82	−98	−113	−129
40	26	10	−6	−21	−37	−53	−69	−85	−100	−116	−132

This chart illustrates the important relationship between wind and temperature.

Getting Lost

Hikers should not proceed more than a quarter-mile (1,320 feet or roughly five minutes of hiking) without noticing a north blaze or other Trail indicator (see page 10). If none is found, retrace your course until an indication of the Trail appears. The cardinal mistake behind unfortunate experiences is insisting on continuing when the route seems obscure or dubious. Haste, even in a desire to reach camp before dark, only complicates the difficulty. When in doubt, remain at the location, to prevent straying farther from the route.

Hiking long distances alone should be avoided, and if undertaken, requires extra precautions. A lone hiker who suffers a serious accident or illness might be risking death if he has not planned for the remote contingency of isolation. Your destinations and estimated times of arrival should be known to someone who will initiate inquiries or search if you do not appear when expected. On long trips, reporting your plans and progress every few days is a wise precaution.

A lone hiker who loses his way and chooses to bushwhack toward town runs considerable risks if an accident occurs. If he falls helpless away from a used trail, he might not be discovered for days or even weeks. Lone hikers are advised to stay on the Trail (or at least on a trail), even if it means spending an unplanned night in the woods in sight of a distant electric light. Your pack should always contain enough food and water to sustain you until daylight, when a careful retracing of your steps might lead you back to a safe route.

Navigation

The compass variation, or declination, in New Hampshire and Vermont varies from 17 degrees at the Maine line to 14 degrees at the Massachusetts line. In other words, true north varies from 14 to 17 degrees to the right of the compass pointer, depending upon the location of the hiker. This considerable variation should be taken into account when the hiker orients himself or his map. The exact compass declination at different points along the Trail is shown on each map with this guide.

Equipment

The basic equipment rule is: never carry more than you need.

Some items should be with you on every hike: *The A.T. Data Book*; guide and maps; canteen; flashlight, even on day trips; whistle; emergency food; tissues; matches and fire starter; multipurpose knife; compass; rain gear; proper shoes and socks; spare, warm, dry clothes; and a first-aid kit.

We advise taking the time to consult periodicals, books, employees of outfitter stores, and other hikers before choosing the equipment that is best for you.

Distress Signals

An emergency call for distress consists of three short calls, audible or visible, repeated at regular intervals. A whistle is particularly good for audible signals. Visible signals may include, in daytime, light flashed with a mirror or smoke puffs; at night, a flashlight or three small bright fires.

Anyone recognizing such a signal should acknowledge with two calls—if possible, by the same method—then go to the distressed and determine the nature of the emergency. If more aid is needed, try to arrange it.

Most of the A.T. is used enough that a person who is injured can expect to be found. However, if an area is remote and the weather bad, fewer hikers will be on the Trail. In this case, it might be best for the injured to study the guide for the nearest location where people are likely to be and to attempt to move in that direction. If it is necessary to leave a heavy pack behind, be sure to take the essentials, in case your rescue is delayed. In bad weather, a night in the open without proper covering could be dangerous.

Pests

Black flies, mosquitoes, and "no-see-ums" (midges) are prevalent in New Hampshire and Vermont from May through August.

Hikers who have never experienced the dense clouds of black flies common in June are forewarned: they make life in the outdoors miserable. Wet or rainy weather will prolong the black-fly season. Fly-proof tents are essential for a good night's sleep. Even then, the tiny no-see-ums sometimes slip through mosquito netting. Several good insect repellents are on the market, but, in periods of heavy fly hatches, they are not very effective.

In the mountains, most insects disappear with the cooler evening temperatures. Black flies usually disappear by the middle of September, but can continue into October.

Poisonous snakes are rare along the Trail in New Hampshire and Vermont.

Poison ivy does grow here but is uncommon at the Trail's higher elevations.

Parking

Because of the possibility of theft and vandalism, travelers are cautioned not to leave cars unattended overnight in remote locations or on the roads noted in the individual sections of this guide. Leaving cars near a home is recommended, if permission can be obtained.

Publications

The Appalachian Trail Conference, as part of its charter to serve as a clearinghouse of information on the Trail or useful to hikers, publishes a number of books other than guides, and also sells books from other publishers.

A complete list of the publications and merchandise available from ATC appears bimonthly in the *Appalachian Trailway News*, the magazine for ATC members, or can be obtained by writing ATC at P.O. Box 807, Harpers Ferry, W. Va. 25425, or calling (304) 535-6331.

ATC members receive a 15 -percent discount on publicatons and most merchandise sold through the Conference. Proceeds from sales help underwrite the costs of A.T. maintenance and Trail-corridor management.

Those seeking basic information about hiking and equipment might consider joining one of the hiking clubs connected with ATC or consult the following books:

The Complete Walker III, by Colin Fletcher,
Alfred A. Knopf, Inc., New York, 1984, 670 pp.

Backpacking Equipment Buyer's Guide, by William Kemsley, Jr., and the Editors of *Backpacker Magazine*, Collier Books, New York.

Lightweight Equipment for Hiking, Camping and Mountaineering, Potomac Appalachian Trail Club, 1718 N St., NW,

Washington, D.C. 20036.

Mountaineering First Aid, A Guide to Accident Response and First Aid Care, by Dick Mitchell, The Mountaineers, Seattle, 1977.

Maps and Compasses, a User's Handbook, by Percy W. Blandford, TAB Books, Inc., Blue Ridge Summit, Pa., 1984.

First Aid along the Trail

by Robert Ohler, M.D.

Along the Appalachian Trail in New Hampshire and Vermont, hikers encounter a wide variety of terrain and climatic conditions. Prepare for the possibility of injuries. Some of the more common Trail-related medical problems are briefly discussed below.

Preparation is key to a safe trip. If possible, every hiker should take the free courses in advanced first aid and cardiopulmonary-resuscitation techniques offered in most communities by the American Red Cross.

Even without this training, you can be prepared for accidents. Emergency situations can develop. Analyses of serious accidents have shown that a substantial number originate at home, in the planning stage of the trip.

Think about communications. Have you informed your relatives and friends about your expedition: locations, schedule, and time of return? Has all of your equipment been carefully checked? Considering the season and altitude, have you provided for water, food, and shelter?

While hiking, set your own comfortable pace. If a hiker is injured or lost or a storm strikes, stop. Remember, your brain is your most important survival tool. Inattention can start a chain of events leading to disaster.

If an accident occurs, treat the injured first. If outside help is needed, at least one person should stay with the injured hiker. Two people should go for help and carry with them notes on the exact location of the accident, what has been done to aid the injured, and what help is needed.

The injured will need encouragement, assurances of help, and promotion of confidence by demonstrations of your competence. Treat him gently. Keep him lying down, warm, and quiet. Protect him from the weather with insulation below and above him. Examine him carefully, noting all possible injuries.

General Emergencies

Back or neck injuries: Immobilize the entire body where the victim lies. Protect head and neck from movement if the neck is injured. Treat as a fracture. Transportation must be on a rigid frame, such as a litter or a door. The spinal cord could be severed by inexpert handling. *This type of injury must be handled by a large group of experienced personnel. Outside help must be obtained.*

Bleeding: When bleeding is present, stop the flow of blood by using a method appropriate to the amount and type of bleeding. Exerting pressure over the wound with the fingers, with or without a dressing, may be sufficient. Minor arterial bleeding can be controlled with local pressure and bandaging. Major arterial bleeding might require compressing an artery against a bone to stop the flow of blood. Elevate the arm or legs above the heart. To stop bleeding from an artery in the leg, place a hand in the groin and press toward the inside of the leg. Arterial bleeding from an arm is stopped by placing a hand between the armpit and elbow and pressing toward the inside of the arm.

Apply a tourniquet only if you are unable to control severe bleeding by pressure and elevation. WARNING: this method should be used only when the limb will be lost anyway. Once applied, a tourniquet should only be removed by medical personnel equipped to stop the bleeding by other means and to restore lost blood. The tourniquet should be located between the wound and the heart. If there is a traumatic amputation (loss of hand, leg, or foot), place the tourniquet two inches above the amputation.

Blisters: Good boot fit, without points of irritation or pressure, should be proven before a hike. Always keep feet dry while hiking. Prevent blisters by responding early to any discomfort. Place adhesive tape or moleskin over areas of developing redness or soreness. If irritation can be relieved, allow blister fluid to be reabsorbed. If a blister forms and continued irritation makes draining it necessary, wash the area with soap and water and prick the edge of the blister with a needle that has been sterilized by the flame of a match. Bandage with a sterile gauze pad and moleskin.

Dislocation of a leg or arm joint is extremely painful. Do not try to put it back in place. With splints, immobilize the entire limb in the position it is found.

Exhaustion is caused by inadequate food consumption, dehydration and salt deficiency, overexertion, or all three. The victim may lose motivation, slow down, gasp for air, complain of weakness, dizziness, nausea, or headache. Treat by feeding, especially carbohydrates. Slowly replace lost water (normal fluid intake should be two to four quarts per day). Give salt dissolved in water (one teaspoon per cup). In the case of overexertion, rest is essential.

Fractures of legs, ankles, or arms must be splinted before moving the victim. After treating wounds, use any available material that will offer firm support, such as tree branches or boards. Pad each side of the arm or leg with soft material, supporting and immobilizing the joints above and below the injury. Bind the splints together with strips of cloth.

Shock should be expected after all injuries. It is a potentially fatal depression of body functions that is made more critical with improper handling, cold, fatigue, and anxiety. Relieve the pain as quickly as possible. Do not administer aspirin if severe bleeding is present; Tylenol or other non-aspirin pain relievers are generally more useful.

Look for nausea, paleness, trembling, sweating, or thirst. Lay the hiker flat on his back and raise his feet slightly or position him, if he can be safely moved, so his head is down the slope. Protect him from the wind and keep him as warm as possible. A campfire will help.

Sprains: Look or feel for soreness or swelling. Bandage and treat as a fracture. Cool and raise joint.

Wounds (except eye wounds) should be cleaned with soap and water. If possible, apply a clean dressing to protect the wound from further contamination.

Chilling and Freezing Emergencies

Every hiker should be familiar with the symptoms, treatment, and methods of preventing the common and sometimes fatal condition of hypothermia. Wind chill and/or body wetness, particularly aggravated by fatigue and hunger, can rapidly drain body heat to dangerously low levels. This often occurs at temperatures well above freezing. Shivering, lethargy, mental slowing, and confusion are early symptoms of hypothermia, which can begin without the victim's realizing it and, if untreated, can lead to death.

In New Hampshire and Vermont, temperatures can drop quickly at any time of the year, particularly at higher elevations. Hypothermia is a constant danger. Never start across a long, above-treeline stretch of Trail unless you are well fed and rested. Always keep dry, spare clothing and a water-repellent windbreaker in your pack, and wear a hat in chilling weather.

In adverse weather, take great care to wear warm, windproof, and water-repellent clothing. Wet clothing loses much of its insulating value, although wet wool is warmer than other wet fabrics.

It is of utmost importance to stay dry, beware of the chilling power of the wind, use spare clothing and raingear in poor weather, and, always, when in chilling conditions, suspect the onset of hypothermia.

To treat this potentially fatal condition, immediately seek shelter and warm the entire body, preferably by placing it in a sleeping bag and administering warm liquids. The body heat of another person may aid in warming.

The wind-chill chart on page 14 serves as a guide to the need of protection. It indicates the incredible cooling power of wind, which increases significantly in wet conditions.

A sign of *frostbite* is grayish or waxy, yellow-white spots on the skin. The frozen area will be numb. To thaw, warm the frozen part by direct contact with bare flesh. When first frozen, a cheek, nose, or chin can often be thawed by covering with a hand taken from a warm glove. Superficially frostbitten hands sometimes can be thawed by placing them under armpits, on the stomach, or between the thighs. With a partner, feet can be treated similarly. *Do not rub frozen flesh.*

Frozen, deeper layers of tissue beneath the skin are characterized by a solid, "woody" feeling and an inability to move the flesh over bony prominences. Tissue loss is minimized by rapid rewarming of the area in water slightly below 105 degrees Fahrenheit (measure accurately with a thermometer).

Thawing of a frozen foot should not be attempted until the patient has been evacuated to a place where rapid, controlled thawing can take place. Walking on a frozen foot is entirely possible and does not cause increased damage. Walking after thawing is impossible.

Never rewarm over a stove or fire. This "cooks" flesh and results in extensive loss of tissue.

Treatment of a deep freezing injury after rewarming must be done in a hospital.

Heat Emergencies

Exposure to extremely high temperatures, high humidity, and direct sunlight may cause various types of health problems associated with the temperature of the body.

Heat cramps are usually caused by strenuous activity in high heat and humidity, when sweating depletes salt levels in blood and tissues. Symptoms are intermittent cramps in legs and abdominal wall and painful spasms of muscles. Pupils of eyes may dilate with each spasm. The skin becomes cold and clammy. Treat with rest and salt dissolved in water (one teaspoon of salt per glass).

Heat exhaustion, caused by physical exercise during prolonged exposure to heat, is a breakdown of the body's heat-regulating system. The circulatory system is disrupted, reducing the supply of blood to vital organs such as the brain, heart, and lungs. The victim can have heat cramps and sweat heavily. Skin is moist and cold with face flushed, then pale. Pulse can be unsteady and blood pressure low. He may vomit and be delirious. Place the victim in shade, flat on his back, with feet 8-12 inches higher than head. Give him sips of salt water—half a glass every 15 minutes—for about an hour. Loosen his clothes. Apply cold cloths.

Heat stroke and sun stroke are caused by the failure of the heat-regulating system to cool the body by sweating. It is an emergency, life-threatening condition. Body temperature can rise to 106 degrees or higher. Symptoms include weakness, nausea, headache, heat cramps, exhaustion, body temperature rising rapidly, pounding pulse, and high blood pressure. The victim may be delirious or comatose. Sweating will stop before heat stroke becomes apparent. Armpits may be dry and skin flushed and pink, then turning ashen or purple in later stages. Move victim to cool place immediately. Cool the body in any way possible (*e.g*. sponging). Body temperature must be regulated artificially from outside of the body until the heat-regulating system can be rebalanced. Be careful not to overchill once temperature goes below 102 degrees.

Heat weakness: Symptoms are fatigue, headache, mental and physical inefficiency, heavy sweating, high pulse rate, and general weakness. Drink plenty of water, find as cool a spot as possible, keep quiet, and replenish salt loss.

Sunburn causes redness of the skin, discoloration, swelling, and pain. It occurs rapidly and can be severe at higher elevations. It can be prevented by applying a commerical sun screen; zinc oxide is the most effective. Treat by protecting from further exposure and covering the area with ointment and a dressing. Give the victim large amounts of fluids.

Artificial Respiration

Artificial respiration might be required when an obstruction constricts the air passages or after respiratory failure caused by air being depleted of oxygen, such as after electrocution, by drowning, or toxic gases in the air. Quick action is necessary if the victim's lips, fingernail beds, or tongue have become blue, if he is unconscious, or if the pupils of his eyes become enlarged. If food or a foreign body is lodged in the air passage, and coughing is ineffective, try to remove it with the fingers. If the foreign body is inaccessible, grasp the victim from behind, with one hand hold the opposite wrist, just below the breast-bone. Squeeze rapidly and firmly, expelling air forcibly from the lungs to expel the foreign body. Repeat this maneuver two to three times, if necessary.

If breathing stops, administer artificial respiration, as air may be forced around the obstruction into the lungs.

The mouth-to-mouth, or mouth-to-nose, method of forcing air into the victim's lungs should be used. The preferred method is:

1. Clear the victim's mouth of any obstructions.
2. Place one hand under the victim's neck and lift.
3. Place heel of other hand on the forehead and tilt head backwards. (Maintain this position during procedure). Use thumb and index finger to pinch nostrils.
4. Open your mouth and make a seal with it over victim's mouth. If the victim is a small child, cover both the nose and the mouth.
5. Breathe deeply and blow out about every five seconds, or 12 breaths a minute.
6. Watch victim's chest for expansion.
7. Listen for exhalation.

Lyme Disease

Lyme disease is contracted from bites of infected ticks. Hikers should be aware of the symptoms and monitor themselves and their partners for signs of the disease. When treated early, Lyme disease usually can be cured with antibiotics.

Hikers should inspect themselves for ticks and tick bites at the end of each day. The four types of ticks known to spread Lyme disease are smaller than the dog tick and not easily seen. They are often called "deer ticks" because they feed on deer, a host for the disease.

The early signs of a tick bite infected with Lyme disease are a red spot with a white center that enlarges and spreads, severe fatigue, chills, headaches, muscle aches, fever, malaise, and a stiff neck. However, one-quarter of all people with an infected tick bite show none of the early signs.

Later effects of the disease, which may not appear for months or years later, are severe fatigue, dizziness, shortness of breath, cardiac irregularities, memory and concentration problems, facial paralysis, meningitis, shooting pains in the arms and legs, and other symptoms resembling multiple sclerosis, brain tumors, stroke, alchoholism, mental depression, Alzheimer's disease, and anorexia nervosa.

Many doctors are not yet well-informed about the disease and can misdiagnose the symptoms. It may be necessary to contact a university medical center or other research center if you suspect you have been bitten by an infected tick. Unlike many other infectious diseases, it is not believed people can build a lasting immunity to Lyme disease. For that reason, a hiker who has contracted and been treated for the disease should still take precautions. *ATC*

First-Aid Kit

The following kit is suggested for those who have had no first-aid or other medical training. It costs about $15, weighs about a pound, and occupies about a 3" x 6" x 9" space.

Four 3" x 4" gauze pads
Five 2" bandages
Ten 1" bandages
Six alcohol prep pads
Ten large butterfly closures
One triangular bandage (40")
Two 3" rolls of gauze
Twenty tablets of aspirin-free pain killer
One 15' roll of 2" adhesive tape
One 3" Ace bandage
Twenty salt tablets
One 3" x 4" moleskin
Three safety pins
One small scissors
One tweezers
Personal medications as necessary

References

1. Red Cross first-aid manuals.

2. *Medicine for Mountaineering*, edited by James A. Wilkerson, M.D., published by The Mountaineers, Seattle (available from Eastern Mountain Sports or the Appalachian Mountain Club).

3. *Mountaineering First Aid : A Guide to Accident Response and First Aid*, by Dick Mitchell, published by the Mountaineers, Seattle, 1985.

4. *Emergency Survival Handbook*, by the American Safety League, 1985. A pocket-size book and survival kit with easy instructions.

Shelters and Campsites Along the Trail

The Appalachian Trail in New Hampshire and Vermont includes a chain of campsites a day's hike or less apart. Most campsites include a shelter or cabin. Shelters are generally three-sided with open fronts. They may have bunks or a wooden floor that serves as a sleeping platform. Water, a toilet, a fireplace, and, in some cases, tent platforms are usually available. Hikers must bring sleeping equipment, cooking utensils, and a stove.

The "Hiking and Camping Information" sections at the beginning of both the Vermont and New Hampshire chapters describe each state's shelter and campsite facilities in detail.

The chain of shelters and campsites is broken on parts of the Trail in the Presidential and Carter-Moriah ranges of New Hampshire. The few shelters available are a day's travel or more apart. Harsh weather in the Presidential Range makes shelters above timberline unfeasible. No shelters or campsites are located between Imp Campsite in the Carter-Moriah Range and Crag Camp (1.1 miles down a side trail) in the Presidential Range, a distance of 20.4 miles. In these areas, camping is often possible, or the hiker may choose to make use of the Appalachian Mountain Club's (AMC) huts. In the White Mountains, the AMC hut system extends along the Appalachian Trail for some 60 miles, from Carter Notch in the Carter-Moriah Range to Lonesome Lake just below (northeast of) Kinsman Ridge. The huts are closed structures with dormitories and blankets. Dinner and breakfast are served. Use of the huts permits crossing the White Mountains with minimum equipment. Complete information on the huts appears under "Hiking and Camping Information" in the New Hampshire chapter of this guide and in the indi-

in the New Hampshire chapter of this guide and in the individual sections where huts are located.

Shelter facilities along the Trail are provided primarily for the long-distance hiker who may have no other means of shelter. Persons planning short overnight hikes having access to the Trail from road crossings, are asked to carry tents. This is also good insurance, since the Trail is used heavily during the summer months and shelters are usually crowded. Camps and other organizations, such as Scouts, are asked to keep their groups small (eight to ten people, including leaders), carry tents, and not monopolize shelters. (See page 41.) Although shelter use is on a first-come, first-served basis, everyone is asked to cooperate and consider the needs of others. If the shelter has a register, please enter your name in it.

The shelters are provided for overnight stays only, and, except in cases of bad weather, injury, or other emergency, hikers are asked not to stay more than one or two nights. Hunters, fishermen, and other nonhikers are asked to not use the shelters as a base of operation.

Fires

Fires at campsites and shelters should be built in the fireplaces provided. Permits are not required, but be on the lookout for special bulletins about fire use. Details on fire regulations and permits are included under "Hiking and Camping Information."

No matter how many people use the fire at each campsite, all must share responsibility for it. Be especially alert for sparks blown from fires during high winds.

Increasing Trail use constantly decreases available firewood. In some areas, fuel is a serious problem. Use wood economically. If you use wood stored in a shelter or at a campsite, replenish the supply. Many campsites and shelter sites have suffered visible deterioration from hikers cutting wood from trees within the site. Use dead or downed wood only, even if this requires searching. No live trees should be cut.

Keep cooking fires small. Do not build bonfires. Hikers are encouraged to carry portable cooking stoves and use them instead of fires.

Upon leaving the campsite, even temporarily, ensure your fire is out *completely*. Douse with water and overturn the ashes until all underlying coals have been extinguished.

Water

The drinking water supply beside the campsite can be a lake, a stream, or a spring. Often, a hiker assumes that because of the natural and relatively uninhabited condition of the area the water is safe to drink. The purity of an unprotected water source cannot be guaranteed. Water should be boiled or chemically treated before use.

Avoid contaminating the water supply and the surrounding area. Dishes, clothes, and hands should never be washed in the water supply. Water should be drawn from the supply and washing done elsewhere.

Care and Use

Use facilities with care and respect. Do not carve initials or write on shelter walls. Do not use an axe on any part of the shelter or use benches or tables as chopping blocks. The roofing, especially corrugated aluminum, is easily damaged; do not climb on it. Avoid putting excess weight or strain on wire bunks; the breaking of one wire endangers air mattresses and sleeping bags.

Be considerate of the rights and needs of others around the shelters, especially during meal times. During the hours of 9 p.m. to 7 a.m., noise should be kept to a minimum for the sake of those attempting to sleep.

Take care to preserve the surroundings and the ecological integrity of the site. Vandalism and carelessness mar the site's pristine nature and cause maintenance problems.

Leave the shelter neat and in good condition. Do not leave any food in the shelter, as this may cause damage by animals. Remove unburned trash from the fireplace, including alumimum foil, and pack out excess food and refuse.

Animals

Many shelters, especially in the Green Mountains, have been damaged severely by porcupines. Carefully store food, equipment, and hiking boots to avoid damage.

Chipmunks, squirrels, and black bears may also visit campsites searching for food. Use extra care to maintain a clean camp and suspend food packs out of reach.

Beaver dams sometimes cause problems in low regions or along streams where they flood sections of the Trail. This can be confusing if encountered before the route is detoured. The traveller should carefully note where the Trail markings enter the flowage and then detour to one side, following the edge of the water until the Trail markings are seen again.

Transportation to the Trail

Road Access

Both the northern and southern ends of most sections in New Hampshire and Vermont are accessible by major highways, but these exceptions are noteworthy:

The northern end of Section 1 in New Hampshire (the southern Mahoosuc Range), the only section without road access, must be reached by trail. First follow the gravel Success Pond Road, beginning in Berlin, N.H., and ascend to the A.T. near the New Hampshire-Maine state line, the northern end of the section, via the Success or Carlo Col trails.

The Danby-Landgrove Road, the southern end of Section 5 and the northern end of Section 6 in Vermont, is paved from Danby on U.S. 7 east to the Trail crossing but is gravel-surfaced west to Landgrove. The Trail is best approached from Danby, but it can be reached from either direction. The road is not plowed in winter.

The Arlington-West Wardsboro Road, the southern end of Section 7 and the northern end of Section 8 in Vermont, is gravel-surfaced west of the Trail crossing to East Arlington but paved for much of the distance east of the Trail to West Wardsboro. In spring, the Trail is best approached from, but can be easily approached from either direction. The road is not plowed in winter between East Arlington and Stratton.

Except for the Success Pond Road,which is shown on Map No. 1, roads providing access to section ends are shown on most highway maps. Maps and other information concerning New Hampshire and Vermont are available from the New England Vacation Center, 1268 Avenue of the Americas, New York, N.Y. 10020, (212) 757-4455; the New Hampshire Division of Economic Development, P.O. Box 856, Concord, N.H. 03301; or the Agency of Development and Commercial Affairs, Vermont Travel Division, 61 Elm St., Montpelier, Vt. 05672 , (802) 828-3236.

In addition to the major roads at section ends, a number of other roads, often gravel or dirt, intersect the Trail in the middle of sections. These are shown on the guide maps.

Shuttle

AMC runs a hiker shuttle service in the White Mountains from June to September. For information on schedules and rates write to AMC Reservations (see "Important Addresses," page 301).

Bus Lines

In New Hampshire and Vermont, daily bus service is available directly to or within easy access of the A.T. By using connecting bus lines, transportation can be arranged from most of the U.S. Bus lines offering service to the Trail are:

Concord Trailways
Englander Coach Lines
Greyhound
Vermont Transit Lines

Railroads

Only one passenger train now operates in New Hampshire and Vermont. AMTRAK provides north-south rail service between Washington, D.C., and Montreal, Quebec, Canada via White River Junction, Vt. White River Junction is five miles south of the Trail crossing of the Connecticut River at Hanover, N.H., and Norwich, Vt. Only one daily round-trip is available on full service trains. For scheduling, call the toll-free (800) AMTRAK information number in your area.

Air Service

Commercial air service to cities in New Hampshire and

Vermont connects through New York, Albany, or Boston airports. Daily commercial service to the Rutland, Vt. airport (1.4 miles west of the A.T. on Vt. 103), and the Lebanon, N.H., airport (5 miles south of Hanover, N.H., adjacent to White River Junction, Vt.) have stops close to the A.T. Daily commercial service is available to a number of other airports in New Hampshire and Vermont more distant from the Trail.

The following airline companies serve New Hampshire and Vermont. For further information, call these airlines, or consult a travel agent:

Bar Harbor Airlines
Brockway Air
Command Airways
PBA (Provincetown-Boston Airlines)
Pilgrim Airlines
Precision Airlines
Ransome Airlines (Delta connection)

Taxis

Taxi service is available in or near the following cities along the Trail, with nearby sections listed in parentheses: White River Junction, Vt. (N.H. 9 and Vt. 1 to 3); Lebanon, N.H. (N.H. 9); Hanover, N.H. (N.H. 8 and 9); Woodstock, Vt. (Vt. 1-3); Rutland, Vt. (Vt. 3-5); Manchester Center, Vt. (Vt. 6 and 7); Bennington, Vt. (Vt. 8 and 9); and Williamstown, Mass. (Vt. 9).

Hitchhiking

Hitchhiking on interstate and limited-access highways is illegal in both New Hampshire and Vermont.

Suggested Trips

The A.T. and its extensive side-trail system in New Hampshire and Vermont provide innumerable possibilities for hiking and backpacking trips. The side trails of the White Mountains of New Hampshire and the Green Mountains of Vermont make loop trips possible. The segment of the A. T. between the White and Green mountains has fewer side trails, but offers excellent hiking. Trips in this area often require car shuttling to avoid retracing one's steps.

Below are suggested trips arranged according to the approximate number of days required to complete each. The state and A.T. sections are given before each listing. Remember that, in this guide, sections are numbered north to south.

One-day Trips

So many day trips are possible in these states, even just the best could not be listed here. The following are just a sample.

N.H. 1 Mt. Hayes via Centennial Trail (A.T.) from Hogan Road.
N.H. 1 Mt. Success via Success Trail from Success Pond Road.
N.H. 2 Carter Dome via Nineteen Mile Brook Trail, Carter Dome Trail, and A.T., beginning at N.H. 16. Return on A.T. and Nineteen Mile Brook Trail via Carter Notch (a loop hike).
N.H. 3 Mt. Clinton and Mt. Webster via Crawford Path and A.T. beginning on U.S. 302. Return via Webster-Jackson Trail (a loop hike).
N.H. 4 Ethan Pond and Thoreau Falls via A.T. from U.S. 302.

N.H. 4 Mt. Lafeyette, Mt. Lincoln, and Little Haystack Mountain via Old Bridle Path and A.T. Return on Falling Waters Trail (a loop hike).
N.H. 5 South Peak of Kinsman Mountain via A.T. from U.S. 3. Return on A.T. and Kinsman Pond Trail (a loop hike).
N.H. 6 Mt. Moosilauke via A.T. from N.H. 112 (the most scenic approach).
N.H. 7 Wachipauka Pond and Webster Slide Mountain via A.T. and side trail; begin on N.H. 25.
N.H. 8 Mt. Cube via A.T. from N.H. 25A or from dirt road into Quinttown.
N.H. 8 Smarts Mountain via A.T. from Lyme-Dorchester Road or from dirt road into Quinttown.
Vt. 3 The Lookout via A.T. from Vt. 12.
Vt. 4 Pico Peak and Killington Peak via A.T. from U.S. 4.
Vt. 5 White Rocks Mountain via A.T. from Vt. 140. Return via Keewaydin Trail and Vt. 140 (a loop hike).
Vt. 6 Baker Peak via Lake Trail and A.T. from U.S. 7. Return via Baker Peak Trail and Lake Trail (a loop hike).
Vt. 6 Styles Peak and Peru Peak via A.T. from USFS Road 21.
Vt. 6 Bromley Mountain via A.T. from Vt. 11 and 30.
Vt. 7 Spruce Peak and Prospect Rock via A.T. from Vt. 11 and 30.
Vt. 7 Stratton Mountain and Stratton Pond via Stratton Mountain Trail from Arlington-West Wardsboro Road. Return via A.T. (a long loop hike).
Vt. 9 East Mountain via Pine Cobble Trail (beginning from Mass. 2), A.T.; return on Broad Brook Trail. This is a long loop hike; it is also a good two-day trip.

Two- to Three-day Trips

Listed below are linear and loop trips. Hikers driving to the Trail and choosing a linear trip may have to arrange for a car at each end of their hike, or use AMC's shuttle service.

N.H. 1 Southern Mahoosuc Range: Mt. Success to Mt. Hayes to North Road via Success Trail from Success Pond Road and A.T.
N.H. 2 Carter-Moriah Range: U.S. 2 to Pinkham Notch (N.H. 16).
N.H. 3 Southern Presidential Range: U.S. 302 to Pinkham Notch (N.H. 16) via A.T. and Tuckerman Ravine Trail.
N.H. 4 Franconia Range via Greenleaf Trail from U.S. 3, and A.T. Trail passes over Mt. Lafayette, Mt. Lincoln, Little Haystack Mountain, and Mt. Liberty (side trail). This trip begins and ends on U.S. 3 and is almost a loop trip.
N.H. 5 Kinsman Ridge: Kinsman Notch (N.H. 112) to Franconia Notch (U.S. 3). Don't underestimate the time for this one.
N.H. 8 and 9 White Mountain Foothills: N.H. 25A to Hanover passing Mt. Cube, Smarts Mountain, and Holts Ledge (estimated time, 3 days).
Vt. 3 Green Mountain Foothills: Vt. 12 to U.S. 4, passing 'The Lookout" and through Gifford Woods State Park.
Vt. 4 The Coolidge Range: U.S. 4 to Vt. 103, passing Pico and Killington peaks.
Vt. 6 White Rocks Mountain to Bromley Mountain: Vt. 140 to Vt. 11 and 30 passing Little Rock Pond, Baker Peak, Styles Peak, and Peru Peak.
Vt. 7 The Ponds near Stratton: Arlington-West Wards-boro Road to Stratton and Bourn Pond via A.T. Return via Branch Pond Trail (a loop trip).

Vt. 7 Stratton Mountain via Stratton Mountain Trail, passing Stratton Pond. Return on A.T. (a loop trip).
Vt. 8 Glastenbury Mountain via A.T. from Vt. 9. Return on West Ridge Trail (a nice two-day loop trip).

Extended Trips

The few suggestions listed below are all linear, so the hiker with a car must make special plans for return transportation (see "Shuttles," page 34).

Maine 18 and N.H. 1 Mahoosuc Range: Grafton Notch (Maine Highway 26) to North Road (N.H.) passing over numerous open summits and through Mahoosuc Notch (estimated time three to five days).

N.H. 4 Crawfords and Franconias: U.S. 302 to U.S. 3, passing Ethan Pond, Mt. Guyot, Mt. Garfield, Mt. Lafayette, and a number of other peaks (three to five days).

Vt. 7 and 8 Southern Long Trail: Vt. 11 and 30 to Vt. 9 passing Prospect Rock, Stratton Pond, and Glastenbury Mountain (three to four days).

Trail Ethics

In New Hampshire and Vermont, the Appalachian Trail crosses private property, as well as public lands. In all cases, the land should be treated with care to preserve the beauty of the Trail environment and ensure the Trail's integrity.

Improper use can endanger the continuity of the Trail. Private landowners may order hikers off their property and close the route. Vandalism, camping, and fires where prohibited, and other abuse can result in Trail closure. Please follow a few basic guidelines.

Do not cut, deface, or destroy trees, flowers, or any other natural or constructed feature.

Do not damage fences or leave gates open.

Do not litter. Carry out all trash. Do not bury it for animals or others to uncover.

Do not carry firearms.

Be careful with fire. Extinguish all burning material; a forest fire can start more easily than many realize.

In short: take nothing but pictures, leave nothing but footprints, kill nothing but time.

Dogs are often a nuisance to other hikers and to property owners. Landowners complain of dogs running loose and soiling yards. The territorial instincts of dogs often result in fights with other dogs. Dogs also frighten some hikers and chase wildlife. If a pet cannot be controlled, it should be left at home; otherwise, it will generate ill will toward the Appalachian Trail and its users. Also, many at-home pets' muscles, foot pads, and sleeping habits are not adaptable to the rigors of A.T. hiking.

Hikers should ask for water and seek directions and information from homes along the Trail only when necessary. Some residents receive more hiker-visitors than they enjoy. Respect the privacy of people living near the Trail.

Hikers should keep to the defined Trail. Cutting across switchbacks, particularly on graded trails, disfigures the Trail, complicates route-finding, and causes erosion. The savings in time or distance is little; the damage is great. In areas where log walkways, steps, or rock treadway indicate special trail construction, hikers should take pains to use them. These have been installed to reduce Trail-widening and erosion. In areas above the treeline, it is of utmost importance to stay on the Trail. Plants and soil in these areas are extremely sensitive.

Group Hikes and Special Events

Special events, group hikes, or other group activities that could degrade the Appalachian Trail's natural or cultural resouces or social values should be avoided. Examples of such activities include publicized spectator events, commercial or competitive activities, or programs involving large groups.

The policy of the Appalachian Trail Conference is that groups planning to spend one or more nights on the Trail should not exceed 10 people, and day-use groups should not exceed 25 people, unless the local maintaining organization has made special arrangements to both accommodate the group and protect Trail values.

Natural History

Geology

by Dr. John Creasy
Assistant Professor of Geology
Bates College

Extending from Alabama to Newfoundland, the Appalachian Mountains originated from a complex series of geologic events culminating in a collision of the North American and European/African ("Eurafrican") continents. The crash of these two land masses forcefully closed the ocean separating them (the Proto-Atlantic) and folded, faulted, and uplifted the sediments that had accumulated at their shores. The Appalachian Mountains were pushed skyward. Subsequently, changing forces within the Earth caused the supercontinent formed by this violent union of North America and Eurafrica, known as Pangaea, to split.

The North Atlantic Ocean, at first a narrow rift, has since grown to its present size, and even now continues to widen a few centimeters each year. Meanwhile, erosion and uplift of the Appalachians exposed rocks that took part in this mountain building, which continues today.

The Appalachian Trail in Vermont and New Hampshire cuts across the results of these tumultuous billion years of earth history by traversing the northeasterly oriented geologic and topographic grain of the Appalachian Mountains.

Early Rumblings

The foundation of our continent, the so-called Precambrian "basement" rocks (exposed over large areas of Canada to the northeast of New England), was deformed several times during episodes of mountain building (orogenies) preceding the formation of the Appalachians.

When the North American continent split, creating an ocean basin, the east coastline of North America was hundreds of miles west of its present position. Shallow water covered what is now eastern New York and western Vermont, then part of the margin of the continent (the submerged continental shelf). Sediment deposited here formed sandstones and limestones.

Farther east, somewhere in central Vermont, the continental shelf abruptly ended at the edge of the continent. Here, where water depth dramatically increased, sediment was deposited in a great wedge, building eastward from the edge of the continent. This wedge formed siltstones, mudstones, and greywackes.

As forces within the earth changed, the continents reversed their motions, the Proto-Atlantic began closing, and the intervening ocean crust was pushed deep into the earth (a process termed subduction). An oceanic island arc developing above this zone of subduction began to approach the "quiet" margin of North America. Some 460 million years ago, the island arc and North America collided, strongly folding and faulting the wedge of sediment caught between them. Much of the formerly submerged continental margin, from eastern New York to the Connecticut River, rose above sea level. This completed the Taconic Orogeny, the first stage in the construction of the Appalachians.

From the south, the hiker enters Vermont in the old (Precambrian) basement that pokes through the core of the Green Mountains. With few exceptions, the Trail lies entirely within these billion-year old gneisses and schists as far north as Sherburne Pass. (The Green Mountains may have resulted from the Taconic Orogeny. The impact of the island arc may have "splintered" the brittle margin of the continent, driving these splinters of basement upward and westward to form them.)

The valley west of the A.T. (Bennington Valley in the south, Champlain Valley further north) is underlain by the limestones and quartzites of the former continental shelf, which were deposited before the continental collision, some 600 to 460 million years ago. Between Seth Warner Shelter and Vt. 103, a distance of 78 miles, the Trail is never far from the juncture (or unconformity) of the continental basement and these overlying "shelf" rocks. The upturned and very resistant white-colored shelf rock known as the Cheshire Quartzite forms much of the high ground (*e.g.* White Rock Mountain) traversed by the Trail near Manchester and again near South Wallingford. From Killington Peak, Vermont's second-highest mountain, vistas reveal the Champlain Valley, the Taconic Mountains, and the Adirondacks: more continental basement rising above surrounding shelf rocks.

When the Appalachian Trail turns eastward, leaving the Long Trail, it also leaves the continental basement. Between Sherburne Pass and the Lookout (13.9 miles east), the Trail crosses the rocks formed from sediment deposited in deeper water, beyond the continental shelf. High temperatures and pressures arising from the Taconic Orogeny altered the sedimentary character of these rocks. The hiker will see the resulting metamorphic rocks, mostly black and green schists.

The Collision

Even with all the splintering, folding, and faulting that occurred in the Taconic Orogeny, mountain building in New England still had quite a future—Eurafrica was coasting west toward America. At the end of the Taconic Orogeny, about 460 million years ago, the newly formed continental margin of New England lay near the present day Connecticut River as far north as Hanover, and then cut northeastward into Maine. The volcanic arc along the eastern edge of what was then New England, extinguished by the Taconic Orogeny, eroded and gradually subsided below sea level. Much of the area uplifted during the Taconic Orogeny was thus submerged and remained so for the next 100 million years.

During this time, a variety of rocks, including limestones and sandstones, formed on the submerged continental shelf across western Vermont. Deep-water rocks, forming from a thick wedge of sediment sifting into the deep sea, encroached westward upon the shelf rocks, and built eastward across submerged New Hampshire. To the east and northeast of the continent were active volcanic arcs.

Eurafrica continued westward. The Eurafrican continent collided with the sediment-bound margin of North America 360 million years ago. This, the Acadian Orogeny, united Eurafrica and New England as the continent of Pangaea.

The thick package of sediments caught between the two continents folded, faulted, metamorphosed, and locally melted to form granites. Much of New Hampshire and Maine were uplifted above sea level for the first time. The continental margin, which sank below sea level after the Taconic Orogeny, rose and remained above sea level.

From the Lookout, the A.T. goes east across the shelf rocks of the Acadian Orogeny and, at Norwich, Vt., reaches the old margin of the continent. The Trail does not cut directly east across the deep-water rocks of central New Hampshire, but swings northeast to Glencliff, following the fused margin of North America.

The rocks exposed between Hanover and Glencliff are mostly volcanics. These are rocks from the continental margin moved upward, flexing the overlying and younger shelf and deep-water rocks, analogous to the splintering of the continental basement to form the Green Mountains.

The high ground (*e.g.*, Mt. Cube, Holts Ledge, and Moose Mountain) is held up by one of these upturned shelf rocks—a white resistant quartzite (Clough quartzite). North of Glencliff, the A.T. strikes east, away from the continental margin, crossing the deep-water sediment, known as the Littleton Formation, which was caught between the colliding continents. These rocks are mostly mica-schists and gneisses; they are well exposed on Mt. Moosilauke. Granites generated during the collision are throughout New Hampshire and well exposed between Kinsman Notch and Lonesome Lake.

The Split

The "supercontinent" of Pangaea, formed in the Acadian Orogeny by the fusion of North America and Eurafrica, began to rift apart about 200 million years ago. The splitting did not follow the "suture" along which the older continents of North America and Eurafrica were joined. The continents were torn apart east of the suture, forming the present day edge of North America. Coastal Maine, eastern Massachusetts, and Connecticut are probably relics of the Eurafrican continent left behind.

As Pangaea split, volcanoes typical of continental terrains sprang up in a northerly line across northern New Hampshire, then extinguished. Little geologic activity has affected New England since this time, although continued rifting has made North America and Europe more distant neighbors.

Since its opening, the North Atlantic Ocean has received

much of the erosional products from the highlands of the Appalachians. The thick wedge of sediments now lying against the edge of our continent may in time form another chapter in the evolution of the Appalachians.

The White Mountains

Granites and related volcanic rocks underlie the many high peaks and ridges of the White Mountains traversed by the A.T. from Lonesome Lake to Webster Cliff. These rocks are the exposed subterranean roots of a volcanic field developed during the early rifting of Pangaea.

North of Webster Cliff, the Trail traverses the spectacular Presidential Range. Its alpine environment is held up by resistant rocks of the Littleton Formation. Much of the area has distorted layers (or folds) in the mica schists (metamorphosed mudstones) resulting from the forces of the continent to continent collision of the Acadian Orogeny.

The Present

The high mountains formed during the Acadian Orogeny have been eroded by water and wind and uplifted several times in the last 360 million years. The present topography is not just a result of that ancient mountain-building; it reflects the differential resistance to erosion of the rock types formed during those orogenic events. Running water is responsible for most of the erosion. The Presidential Range also exhibits evidence of recent glaciation, rivaled only by Katahdin.

Several continental glaciers, such as those presently developed in Greenland and Antarctica, covered northern New England in the last two million years. Evidence preserved in the Presidential Range reflects the most recent. Valley glaciers, like those in Alaska and Switzerland, once cut cirques and U-shaped valleys (such as Tuckerman Ravine, King Ravine, and the Great Gulf on the eastern side of the Presidential Range), perhaps as recently as 50,000 years ago.

A continental ice sheet, perhaps a mile or more in thickness, subsequently overrode northern New England, including Mt. Washington (6,288 feet). This ice sheet scoured and sculpted the mountains to their present forms. The many U-shaped "notches" or "gulfs" traversed by the A.T. in northern New England resulted.

The continental ice sheet retreated through the Presidential Range about 12,000 years ago, leaving a thick blanket of debris in the lowlands. On mountain peaks and flanks, bedrock pokes through, offering clues to the mountains' origins.

Debris is easily eroded by running water and by footsteps where the vegetation is cleared to form trails or roads. By man's measure, the mountain's ongoing history is timeless. It is the fragile environment of the mountains that is not.

References

The Evolution of North America, by P.B. King, third ed., Princeton, New Jersey, Princeton University Press, 1977 (includes many figures and maps).

Tectonics of the Appalachians, by John Rodgers, Wiley Interscience, New York, 1970.

Maps

Centennial Geologic Map of Vermont, 1961, scale 1:250,000. Geologic maps and reports are also available for each of the 15 minute quadrangles of Vermont.

Geologic Map of New Hampshire, 1955, scale 1:250,000. Geologic maps and accompanying reports, written for the layman, are also available (index upon request) from Vermont Development Department, 61 Elm Street, Montpelier, Vt. 05672; and from New Hampshire Department of Resources and Economic, P.O. Box 856, Concord, N.H. 03301

Plant Life

by Roger Stern, Appalachian Mountain Club, and Suzanne Crowley

The hiker passes a wide array of plant life while walking along the A.T. in New Hampshire and Vermont. The vegetation varies from field to forest and from valley to summit.

Trees

The trees throughout the lower elevations of the White Mountains in New Hampshire, as well as where the A.T. crosses the Green Mountains in Vermont, are predominately northern hardwoods. This forest, which extends up to 2,500 feet above sea level, is composed mainly of sugar maple, beech, birch trees, white pine, red oak, red maple, hemlock, white ash, and basswood.

In spring, the shrubby mountain ash and shadbush bloom. The mountain ash displays cream-white flowers after its large leaves unfold in early June. This small tree, seldom reaching 30 feet, is short-lived and prefers moist, sunny spots. In the fall, it decorates the woods with hanging clusters of bright orange-red berries. The mountain ash is not related to true ashes. The name comes from the similarity between its leaves and those of the ash trees. The mountain ash is actually a member of the rose family.

Thriving in the sun or shade, another understory tree, the serviceberry, or shadbush (maximum height of 50 feet), shows its white flowers before, or as, its leaves unfold. It buds in April and May when the shad ascend the New England rivers to spawn; hence its name. Its berry-like purplish fruit matures in late June.

Forest Flowers

Most of the herbaceous flowers in the hardwood forest are perennials that bloom for only a short time. The trout lily, or adder's tongue, which blooms in March, is most common in wet woods or meadows. From each stalk hangs a pendant yellow flower, resembling a miniature lily, with two mottled leaves at its base. Soon after blooming, the entire plant withers as its bulb begins to prepare for next spring's growth.

Trilliums also bloom in moist parts of hardwood forests. Their name is aptly derived from the Latin word for three. The trillium plant boasts a flower with three petals and three large, parallel-veined leaves, a sign of the lily family. Three varieties of trilliums, white, red, and painted, grow along the A.T. in New Hampshire and Vermont.

In clearings or areas that border an open field, day lilies and meadow rue grow. Day lilies are not true lilies, but the shape of their yellow or orange flowers resembles that of the lily family. The scientific name, *Hemerocallis*, originates from Greek words meaning "beautiful" and "day." The flowers, which bloom from May to July, are quite beautiful, but each bloom appears for only one day. The meadow rue exhibits graceful, lacy small leaves. It forms a bushy plant one to two feet tall. It, too, is an early bloomer, sporting a crown of numerous small white flowers. The plant's resemblance to the herb rue is the basis for its name.

Other common spring wildflowers are bluets, with small, delicate, pale-blue flowers forming large patches in sunny woods openings; hepatica, bearing small blooms of white, pink, lavender or blue on a low plant named for its liver-shaped, lobed leaves; and violets, a well-known flower that historically has provided medicinal functions ranging from preventing hangovers to helping "comfort and strengthen the heart."

Midsummer flowers bloom in July and August. Partridgeberry, orchids, and Indian pipes are a few. Partridgeberry has small pink or white, four-lobed flowers in pairs at each end of its creeping stem. The leaves, too, are small, paired, and rounded. The fruit, a single red berry, often develops by late July. The fragrance of the orchid's flowers is sometimes noticed before its showy blossoms come into view.

Lady's slipper usually grows in coniferous forests along edges of streams. The orchis is more common. It prefers coniferous swamps, bogs, spruce forests, and peaty soil. Growing to only four to ten inches in height, the Indian pipe is pipe shaped, as its name implies. The stem is a single, translucent, waxy tube ending with a nodding white or pink flower, which later turns black. Like mushrooms, this shade dweller is a saprophyte—receiving its energy from decaying organic matter rather than from the sun. Green chlorophyll, which produces carbohydrates (sugars) from sunlight, is absent, leaving the Indian pipe an unusual white color.

In late summer and fall, asters and goldenrods replace the summer flowers. The woods of New Hampshire and Vermont have several varieties of these members of the daisy family. Goldenrods are spikes two to five feet high. Many of the asters, which may have purplish, blue, pink, or white flowers, also bloom late.

Ferns

Ferns are a common ground covering of northern hardwood forests. In most wooded sections of the Northeast, 15 to 20 fern species can be found easily.

Wood fern and lady fern are similar in appearance and common in the hardwoods. Both form lacy plumes, and spores develop on the backs of the leaflets. A stem cut at the base and looked at in cross-section will show two small crescent shapes on the lady fern and five dots on the wood fern. They are the vascular bundles that transport water and nutrients through the fern.

Along hillsides or in meadows, hay-scented ferns often form great masses of feathery two- to three-foot foliage. This light-green fern looks more fragile than the lady fern. Standing separately, the fronds turn to follow the sun. The hay-scented fern smells sweet when crushed or dried.

The common polypody, one of the most abundant of the ferns, grows on shaded rocks. It is small, a few inches to a foot tall, but its dark, leathery leaflets are easily spotted.

Subalpine Plants

At elevations above the northern hardwood forest stands the spruce-fir or subalpine forest, beginning at about 2,500 feet above sea level. At this elevation, between the hardwood and alpine cover, black spruce, and balsam fir replace the hardwood species. The diversity of species declines as elevation increases. The subalpine forest occasionally includes mountain ash or striped maple but is mainly composed of spruce and fir, which are easily discerned. Spruce needles are sharp to the touch, and spruce cones hang as pendants. Fir needles are soft, and its cones stand on the branches.

Subalpine plants include mayflower, goldenthread, clintonia, bunchberry, starflower, woodsorrel, twinflower, and large-leaved aster. In boggy areas, sphagnum moss often grows with pale laurel, blueberry, and wild raisin.

At 4,000 feet, the spruce and fir become shrubby. This community of dwarfed trees is called *krummholz*. The dwarfing probably resulted from windborn ice destroying the growing tips. Repeated removal of vertically growing tips results in lateral growth. The *krummholz* reflects the depth of winter snow, as any tip above snowline for a winter probably will not survive. Because the *krummholz* is so dense, there is no ground cover, except in breaks of the canopy.

Alpine Plants

Above the twisted *krummholz*, at about 4,700 feet, lies the true alpine vegetation. Here, where the landscape is chiefly characterized by the absence of trees, grows a variety of fragile and often rare plants. Strong winds, which cause drifting snow, determine which plants will grow.

In snow-free areas, the dense, low-growing cushion plants such as Diapensia grow. Its dense mat of tiny overlapping leaves protects it from wind-blown ice. Its shape also deflects wind from the cushion.

Behind rocks and in depressions, protected from wind and abundant moisture, lie the snowbank communities. Mountain heath, dwarf willow, moss plant (not a true moss, but a flowering plant), and painted cup are some of the plants found here.

To maintain themselves through the harsh winters, most alpine plants have large storage sites for nutrients, many underground. Evergreen plants often have storage sites in their leaves. The round-leaved sundew, on the other hand, is insectivorous. A sticky substance on its leaves captures small insects. The leaves slowly close, and the plant digests the insect for its nutrients.

North of Mt. Washington and the Presidential Range, the A.T. traverses the Mahoosuc Range, which begins in New Hampshire and continues northeastward into Maine. On the peaks of this range, between the *krummholz* and the more alpine communities, are heath shrub communities with pockets of tundra bog. The heath is dominated by pale laurel and labrador tea. In bedrock depressions, under the sphagnum-moss cover, lie lenses of frozen peat. These often remain intact well into the growing season. In mid-July, the depth of these lenses is about 15 inches. They persist because of the insulating properties of dry sphagnum in warm, dry weather. The frozen peat cools the plant-root environment above it, creating a growing medium characteristic of higher elevations. In this way, tundra species grow although the elevations are much lower than the alpine zone in the Presidentials. Baked appleberry, black crowberry, and cotton grass are three such species.

All hikers should take pains to preserve the forest and flowers for others to enjoy. Many plants are rare or endangered. In alpine areas, stay on the established pathway. Plants here have adapted themselves to withstand the weather, but not crushing footsteps. Take home only pictures. Be a steward of the natural beauty along the Trail.

References

A Field Guide to Ferns, Peterson Field Guide Series by Boughton Cobb. Houghton Mifflin, Boston, 1956.

A Field Guide to Wildflowers, Peterson Field Guide Series by

Roger Peterson and Margaret McKenny. Houghton Mifflin, Boston, 1968.

Trees of Eastern and Central United States and Canada, by William Harlow. Dover Publications, New York, 1957.

Wildlife

by Dr. Rebecca Field
U.S. Fish and Wildlife Service

A variety of birds and animals lives along the Appalachian Trail in New Hampshire and Vermont. The leaf-strewn hardwood forest, shrubby abandoned pastures, spruce-covered knolls, bogs, marshes, and ponds are among the many different habitats, each providing a place for a wealth of animal species.

Some creatures ramble from one spot to another, but each demonstrates habitat preferences, adapting to its surroundings through evolution.

This section highlights some of the animals most likely to be seen while hiking the A.T. in New Hampshire and Vermont, arranged according to six easily identifiable habitats: the open water of lakes and ponds; bogs and marshes; the drier grasslands, open woodlands, thickets, and edges; deciduous forests; and coniferous or evergreen forests.

Lakes, Streams, Ponds, and Shores

During their spring and fall migrations, waterfowl use ponds and lakes as resting and feeding areas. Ducks (mallards, shovelers, black ducks, teal) prefer shallow water, where they feed on bottom vegetation. Other waterfowl (merganzers, goldeneyes, and rudy ducks) dive for their food. They eat both plants and underwater invertebrates. Since most waterfowl migrate through northern New England, the hiker will see them only during spring and fall.

Another bird, the loon, may be seen on a pond or lake and then suddenly plunge out of view. These birds, like diving waterfowl, find both protection and food beneath the surface. They have a yodeling, laugh-like call. Loons live in open water, except when they breed and nest, and will dive deeply in search of fish.

The kingfisher is a small bird often seen flying over open water. It usually hovers, searching for fish, and then dives, catching its prey with its long, sharp beak.

Many birds can be seen standing in shallow water along pond and lake shores, where they feed on small fish and invertebrates in the water and mud. Most conspicuous is the tall, long-necked great blue heron, which spears fish with its sharp beak. The smaller green heron also may be seen along the edge of ponds and streams. On the shore, the spotted sandpiper, a summer resident, walks along the edge of the water looking for food. As it looks, it constantly bobs its tail, giving it the nickname "teeter-tail."

Many mammals come to the edges of streams or ponds to drink or feed. Three small carnivores, the weasel, mink, and river otter, frequent wooded areas along streams and ponds. The river otter, which prefers open water, is the most aquatic of the three. Opossums and raccoons usually are not far from water. In shallow northern waters, as in the Mahoosuc Range of New Hampshire, you may see a moose. Since mammals are often nocturnal, you may be more successful at finding indirect signs of activity along a shore: pawprints in a muddy bank, scats along the shore, or chewed bark.

Beavers are the largest rodent in the area. These animals

build dams along streams and ponds in the midst of woodlands. They feed on hardwood trees at the water's edge and make shelter in lodges of mud and sticks. Ordinarily, beavers are not seen, but signs of their work—gnawed trees, dams, lodges, and ponds are common. Their ponds create a new aquatic habitat for many other creatures.

Amphibians and reptiles are most abundant in aquatic or moist habitats. Many species require water for laying their eggs. Turtles are found in still, shallow streams or creeks. Painted turtles are the most likely to be basking in the sun, though snapping turtles also may be seen. The stinkpot turtle sometimes climbs limbs that extend over the water. Newts and salamanders live in quiet, shallow water along the water's edge. Look carefully under small logs or rocks along the shore of creeks or streams and you may see a salamander. Several snakes also are found around quiet water or marshes, but the poisonous snakes of the wetlands in the southern United States are not found in northern New England.

Toads and frogs are more often heard than seen. On a spring evening, areas of still, shallow water can be alive with the choruses of several species. The high whistle of the spring peeper and the deep resonating tones of the bullfrog are most familiar. Also in the spring, look for egg masses or schools of tadpoles along the water's edge.

Bogs and Marshes

Freshwater bogs and marshes provide many of the habitat benefits of lakes, streams, and ponds: abundant moisture and some of the same food and shelter resources, but more vegetation, such as dense sphagnum, cattails, sedges, or reeds. Marshes may form a continuum of habitats in succession from open water to more wooded areas.

Wading birds, such as herons, bitterns, or rails, may be found in marshes. If you startle an American bittern, it points its bill straight up; this posture and the striped coloration make this bird hard to see. Rails are elusive birds but have distinctive voices of piping notes or metallic rattles.

The marsh hawk, as its name implies, frequents the marshy habitat. It often flies low over the ground, tilting from side to side, searching for prey, usually rodents. Sexes are easy to distinguish: the females are brown, and the males are grey. Barred owls and short-eared owls also may be seen over marshes. They are most active at dusk, flying silently, hunting for rodents and other small mammals.

The marsh wrens are also part of this community. Look for the short vertical tail, but you are more likely just to hear their rattling trill. A few of the warblers are summer residents of marshes, particularly the palm warbler and the northern waterthrush. The redwing and rusty blackbirds can also be seen in marshes.

Mammals of the marsh are similar to those species found near ponds and streams. In addition, you may find signs of bobcats (rare and solitary), black bears, and snowshoe hares. Most amphibians and reptiles seen along edges of open water also like marshy conditions. The eastern garter snake, northern water snake, and the smaller northern brown snake may be found in bogs or marshes. The four-toed salamander, a resident of sphagnum bogs, has a black-spotted white belly and a tail that breaks off when seized.

Grasslands

Grasslands in the eastern United States are open areas that usually are cleared and maintained. Unlike the West, the East lacks vast natural prairies, yet the many farmlands, pastures, and clearings along the Trail offer valuable habitats for a number of species.

Some birds of the open bogs, such as the marsh hawk, are also found in the open grasslands. In addition, the rough-legged and red-tailed hawks are typical of the open country. These large hawks generally soar high overhead and then dive upon their prey. The small sparrow hawk (or kestrel) perches on utility wires, watching for small animals, but primarily eats insects.

The killdeer, which calls its name, builds its nest on the ground in grasslands. If you should get too close, the adult will feign an injured wing, as it does to lure a predator from the nest area. The ruffed grouse also may be seen quietly crouching or strutting through woodsy clearings in the summer. The ring-necked pheasant may be flushed from farmlands; its loud, metallic honking is a frequent sound.

Songbirds of the grasslands include the fly-catching eastern kingbird, the eastern phoebe (with its raspy call of its name), and the white-rumped yellow-bellied sapsucker. Eastern bluebirds perch on utility wires. Watch for the swooping flight of the barn swallow, cliff swallow, and purple martin. Eastern meadowlarks and bobolinks can be spotted on fence posts or on the ground. The melodious call of the meadowlark is a familiar sound of a pasture. The savannah, vesper, chipping, and field sparrows are all summer residents of the grasslands. In the winter, you may see another sparrow, the snow bunting.

Open grasslands provide little cover for most mammals. Some small mice, voles, and moles live in this habitat. They are usually too quick to be seen by the passing hiker. Most other mammals of the grasslands stay near shelter, in thickets or brushpiles, although rabbits hop across open fields between spots of better cover.

The dryness of grasslands makes these areas unattractive for most amphibians and reptiles. The animals in this group that can endure drier conditions are more likely found in woodlands or in rocky, mountainous areas. However, you may come across an occasional wood turtle or leopard frog in the summer.

Woodlands, Edges, and Thickets

Woodlands are open, often second-growth, forests that may be in transition between fields and dense woods. Low shrubs and brushy thickets may be found here. Where a forest is directly adjacent to an open area, it is called an edge habitat. These edges provide abundant cover for a great diversity of animals.

Many birds are found in woodlands and the edges of forests. If water is nearby, you may see a colorful wood duck or hear its whistle call. Those ducks nest in tree holes. The Cooper's hawk, sharp-shinned hawk, broad-winged hawk, and red-shouldered hawk are a few of this group of birds in Vermont or New Hampshire woodlands. Another common group, the owls, are represented by the screech owl or long-eared owl. During the day, you may be lucky to spot an owl sitting close to a tree trunk. They spit up pellets of the indigestible hair and bones of their prey to the woodland floor.

Many songbirds like the woodland and edge habitat. Yellow-bellied sapsuckers are a common woodpecker. Several flycatchers, such as the least flycatcher, the olive-sided flycatcher, and the eastern wood pewee, feed on the many insects in thickets. Chickadees can be found all year long. The grey catbird is a good mimic and may fool you with its imitations of other birds' calls. Several warblers, such as the yellow warbler, chestnut-sided warbler, mourning warbler, and common yellowthroat frequent the thicket. The indigo bunting is a small blue bird of edge habitats. The common rufous-sided towhee sings "drink your tea" or calls with a loud "chat." Several sparrows (tree sparrow, white-throated sparrow, and song sparrow) are also common along forest edges.

A brushy area provides plenty of cover for small mammals. Mice, voles, squirrels, chipmunks, and rabbits escape predators in the dense thicket. The spine-covered porcupine curls up in woodland trees in the day and prowls for food at night, often gnawing on woody plants. Foxes, either the red or grey, can be spotted in sparsely wooded areas. White-tailed deer feed on the vegetation of woodlands or nearby meadows. Watch for them especially at dusk; as they bound away, they flip their white tails in the air.

Wherever there is moist soil, you may find some amphibians and reptiles. Wood turtles may stray some distance from open water. The garter snake, ringneck snake, and milk snake live in woodlands. The red-backed salamander is one of the most terrestrial salamanders, usually hiding under rocks or logs. Few frogs leave wetland areas for drier habitats, although the spring peeper, pickerel frog, and wood frog wander into moist woodlots.

Deciduous Forests

Deciduous forests are made up of broad-leafed trees that usually lose their leaves in the fall. Mature forests in northern New England may include beech, birch, maple, oak, and elm.

Several types of birds are common in deciduous forests. Where the forest is moist, you may see a red-shouldered hawk or flush the elusive woodcock, ordinarily hard to spot with its effective camouflage. The peregrine falcon and golden eagle, now endangered species, can still be seen in higher country. Open deciduous forest is a favorite habitat for the screech owl and the broad-winged hawk.

Woodpeckers are common in these woods and often are heard hammering for insects on dead or dying trees. The downy woodpecker, the similar but larger hairy woodpecker, the northern flicker, and the yellow-bellied sapsucker all frequent these forests. The pileated woodpecker, a large New England woodpecker, breeds throughout the area.

Many kinds of songbirds frequent deciduous woods. The eastern wood pewee and the great crested flycatcher feed on flying insects. The blue jay, American robin, American crow, and black-capped chickadee are year-round residents.

The small nuthatches can be spotted climbing along the tree bark. The brown creeper is well camouflaged but also may be seen climbing the tree bark. Where the forest has a thick understory, you may hear the long, flutelike song of the wood thrush. The veery also has a flutelike call, consisting of descending notes.

As a group, warblers prefer deciduous or coniferous woods. A common one, the ovenbird, calls "teacher, teacher." Another group common in deciduous forests is the insect-eating vireos.

The male scarlet tanager is easily spotted by its bright red body and contrasting black tail and wings. The rose-breasted grosbeak has a distinctive red bib.

Deciduous forests are home to several types of mammals. Where the soil is moist and soft, shrews and moles burrow extensive tunnel networks. Weasels, martens, fishers, and raccoons also prefer moist habitats and seldom are far from water. Bats spend the days in caves in wooded areas, coming out in the early evening to feed on insects. When the forested area is open and near meadows, you may see white-tailed deer, especially in the evening or morning. Unlike most mammals, squirrels, chipmunks, and woodchucks are active during the day in the forest. The terrestrial amphibians and reptiles mentioned in the last section are also found in deciduous forests.

Coniferous Forests

Coniferous trees, commonly known as evergreens, do not shed their leaves seasonally. Their leaves are shaped like needles, and the surrounding soil tends to be acidic.

Hawks are common in coniferous forests. The goshawk prefers mature forests while the sharp-shinned hawk and merlin are found in open forest. Grouse are found in coniferous woods year long. In the spring, you can hear their deep, muffled drumming, part of their courtship ritual. The long-eared owl and the great-horned owl are active at night in this habitat. In thickets of evergreen forests, the tiny saw-whet owl can be found year long.

Ravens are seen soaring at high elevations in coniferous habitats. They are distinguished from crows by their larger size, wedge-shaped (rather than rounded) tail, and distinctive croaking call. The boreal chickadee of higher elevations has a brown cap, rather than the black cap of its relative, the black-capped chickadee, of lower country. You may hear the winter wren singing; look for its short, stiff tail. Dark-eyed juncos and white-throated sparrows also may be seen in this habitat. These birds migrate vertically, ascending into the mountains during the summer to nest and raise young and descending to lower country in fall to pass the winter.

Among mammals, black bears are active at night in coniferous forest. Near swamps, the bobcat is a rare sight, but it is worth watching for tracks. Porcupines can be spotted in the daytime as a ball of spines curled up on a tree branch.

Few amphibians and reptiles are specific to coniferous habitats. Those previously listed as terrestrial species also can be found in evergreen forests. The timber rattlesnake, a rare sight in New England, can be found in mountainous regions. In winter, several rattlers congregate in dens, often with other snakes. Most often, rattlers are found in second-growth forests where rodents are plentiful.

Despite the large number of animals mentioned, this description has been only a brief overview of the fauna along the A.T. in New Hampshire and Vermont. Only the most common habitats have been covered, and the hiker will undoubtedly come across other species. The hiker should take time to watch, listen, and explore each habitat to increase the chances of seeing wildlife. Hikers wishing to have complete information about identification, distribution, and characteristics of animals along the Trail should obtain one of the field guides mentioned below. In addition to these references, it is wise to contact authorities of national or state forests and parks in the area for information on specific flora and fauna.

References

The *Peterson Field Guide Series* from Houghton Mifflin Company gives information on a wide variety of fauna. There are guides available on amphibians and reptiles, mammals, birds, butterflies, animal tracks, insects, and birds' nests.

Birds of North America, by C. S. Robbins et al. Golden Press, New York, 1966.

The Audubon Society Field Guide to North America's Birds (Eastern Region), by J. Bull and J. Farrand. Alfred A. Knopf, New York, 1977.

The Appalachian Trail in New Hampshire

Through the northern part of New Hampshire, the Appalachian Trail follows the lofty ridgecrests of the White Mountains. In the southern part, it traces a route through the hardwood country of the eastern slope of the Connecticut River Valley. Through the White Mountains, the A.T. is rugged, often steep, and sometimes wet, but passes through a variety of habitats. The route ascends high, rocky, and barren ridges divided by deep notches or valleys, often also cut by sharp cols between high peaks. It follows footpaths and woods roads through dense hardwood and coniferous forests and crosses rushing mountain streams. Along the Connecticut River Valley, in the southern part of the state, the Trail passes through a succession of pastures, cleared hills, patches of timber, ravines, and peaks as it traverses the broken ridgecrest of the White Mountain foothills. The rough terrain makes hiking in New Hampshire strenuous yet rewarding. In the New Hampshire part of this guide, each section generally describes one range.

The Maine-New Hampshire state line crosses the Trail through the middle of the Mahoosuc Range of northern New Hampshire and northwestern Maine, which has no easy road access. For this reason and because the range is most often hiked as a unit, this guide begins at Grafton Notch in Maine and covers the last (southern) section of the Trail described in the *Appalachian Trail Guide to Maine.*

The Trail ascends from Grafton Notch and traverses the remote and rugged Mahoosuc Range, with many open summits. Along the way, the hiker must wind, crawl, and jump through the boulder-clogged and cave-ridden Mahoosuc

Notch. The Trail descends from the range and crosses the Androscoggin River Valley and then climbs to the crest of the Carter-Moriah Range, which it follows to the open Carter Dome before dropping into Carter Notch at Carter Lakes. From Carter Notch, the Trail rises sharply to Wildcat Mountain, then descends steeply over exposed ledges into Pinkham Notch, where the Pinkham Notch Camp and the North Country headquarters of the Appalachian Mountain Club are located.

From Pinkham Notch, the Trail ascends and then drops through the Great Gulf Wilderness, climbing to the rocky summit of Mt. Madison, which marks the northern end of the alpine Presidential Range, a rocky, tundra-covered ridge. The Trail passes close to the summits of Mt. Adams, Mt. Jefferson, and Mt. Clay and then ascends to Mt. Washington (6,288 feet), the highest peak in the northeastern United States. From the summit of Mt. Washington, the Trail descends south, skirting Mt. Monroe, passing over Mt. Franklin, skirting Mt. Eisenhower, passing over Mt. Pierce (Mt. Clinton), and reentering woods. It continues on the ridge, passing over Mt. Jackson and Mt. Webster, before dropping into Crawford Notch State Park.

From Crawford Notch, the Trail climbs to cross the lower flank of the Willey Range, passes through Zealand Notch, and then ascends to cross the Zealand Ridge, the Garfield Ridge, and the alpine Franconia Range, where it passes over Mt. Lafayette (5,249 feet), the highest peak in the area. The Trail drops from the Franconia Ridge into Franconia Notch and Franconia Notch State Park.

From Franconia Notch, the Trail once again ascends. It follows the crest of the wooded Kinsman Ridge to Kinsman Notch, which has evidence of intensive glacial activity preserved in the Lost River Reservation. From Kinsman Notch the Trail makes a spectacular ascent to the summit of the massive, bald Mt. Moosilauke (4,802 feet), the southwest edge of the White Mountains. From the summit, the Trail descends to Glencliff.

Between Glencliff and the Connecticut River, the physical and cultural features characteristic of upland northern New England become strikingly evident. Many of the low ridges and rolling hills have reverted to woodland. The many large fields and clearings, cellar holes, stone fences, lilac and apple trees, cemeteries, and abandoned roads are evidence of a time, less than a century ago, when this was a prosperous area of farms and small hamlets. No traveler exploring New England on foot should neglect this section of the Trail.

Beginning at Glencliff, the Trail climbs Wyatt Hill, passing by scenic Wachipauka Pond and over the low summit of Mt. Mist, before descending to cross N.H. 25C. The Trail follows Atwell Hill Road with Mt. Piermont looming large to the west. It then turns into the woods and, with little change in elevation, follows a succession of trails and woods roads past the northwest shore of Baker Pond (901 feet) to N.H. 25A.

From the highway, the A.T. climbs Mt. Cube (2,911 feet), drops to Quinttown, and then climbs to the firetower on Smarts Mountain (3,240 feet). The Trail descends steeply from the firetower to the Dartmouth Skiway and then climbs Holts Ledge. Continuing on trails and woods roads through hardwood forest, pastures, and fields, the Trail passes over the North and South Peaks of Moose Mountain and over Velvet Rocks to the small town of Hanover, where Dartmouth College is located. At Hanover, the Trail descends to the Connecticut River (400 feet), the border between New Hampshire and Vermont.

The Appalachian Mountain Club is responsible for maintaining the Trail from Grafton Notch (Maine 26) to Kinsman

Notch (N.H. 112), although parts are also maintained by the United States Forest Service (USFS). The Gulfside Trail, in the Northern Presidential Range, is marked with yellow paint. For further information on these sections of Trail, contact the AMC, Pinkham Notch Camp, Box 298, Gorham, N.H. 03581, (603) 466-2721.

The Dartmouth Outing Club (DOC) maintains the Trail from the Connecticut River to Kinsman Notch (N.H. 112). This part is blazed with standard white A.T. blazes and the orange and black DOC blazes. For further information on this section, contact the Dartmouth Outing Club, Robinson Hall, Box 9, Hanover, N.H. 03755, (603) 646-2428.

Hiking and Camping Information

White Mountain National Forest

For two-thirds of its length in New Hampshire, the A.T. crosses the White Mountain National Forest (WMNF). The WMNF covers 730,000 acres in Maine and New Hampshire, accommodating timber and wildlife management, watershed protection, and recreation. Most of the land in the White Mountains in northern New Hampshire is a part of the WMNF. Instructions for using the forest in each section area are listed under "Regulations."

In recent years, use of backcountry trails and facilities in the White Mountains has increased dramatically. Soil erosion, loss of vegetation, water pollution, and disposal of human waste have become major problems. In certain areas, scarred trees, eroded trails, and hardened campsites indicate use is causing steady deterioration. Some areas of the forest may never recover. An example is Franconia Ridge, where compaction and erosion from hikers' footsteps has left a broad, gutted footway. In other places, campers have cut trees, trampled vegetation, and polluted water. These problems have necessitated regulations to lessen the impact camping and hiking have on plant life, soils, and water.

Restricted Use Areas (RUA)

To prevent harming the forest's fragile ecosystems, and to allow damaged areas to rehabilitate, the USFS has designated parts of the A.T. as Restricted Use Areas (RUA). RUA information can be found under "Regulations."

When in a RUA, and not staying at a hut or shelter, you must camp off the Trail. In RUAs, off-trail camping and wood fires are limited to areas below timberline (where trees are at least eight feet tall); at least 200 feet off the Trail; and one-quarter mile from any road, hut, shelter, lake, or stream. Federal citations are issued for violations.

Full information on RUAs is posted at trailheads. In the summer, USFS ridge-runners patrol the RUAs daily, offering assistance and information. For further information on RUA policy, contact:

Supervisor's Office
White Mountain National Forest
P.O. Box 638, 719 Main St.
Laconia, N.H. 03246
(603) 524-6450

Appalachian Mountain Club
Pinkham Notch Camp
P.O. Box 298
Gorham, N.H. 03581
(603) 466-2721

Wildernesses

The Trail passes briefly through the Great Gulf Wilderness. No facilities exist in this area, but off-Trail camping is allowed. The Trail also skirts the northern boundary of the Presidential Range-Dry River Wilderness and closely parallels the northern and western borders of the Pemigawassett Wilderness. These lands were set aside by Congress to preserve distinctive natural qualities.

Caretakers

Full-time AMC summer caretakers maintain and supervise several backcountry shelters and campsites in the White Mountains. At these areas, described in the shelter part of each section, a fee is charged to partially defray costs. Hikers are asked to cooperate with caretakers to use trails and shelters in an ecologically sound manner.

Carry In/Carry Out

Help keep the mountains clean of litter by carrying out all trash and cans. Most AMC campsites have facilities for composting food waste, but, in areas where these facilities do not exist, carry out all garbage.

State Parks

The A.T. passes through three state parks within the WMNF: Franconia Notch State Park (see Section 4), Crawford Notch State Park (see Section 3), and the summit of Mt. Washington (see Section 3). These parks were established by the state of New Hampshire to ensure these scenic areas would always be public domain. In state parks, camping is permitted only in designated campgrounds, huts, or shelters. Camping is not permitted on Mt. Washington's summit.

Private Lands

Between the Connecticut River and Glencliff (Sections 7 to 9), much of the Trail passes across private land. In these sections, camping and fires are not permitted except at designated sites.

Campsites

A campsite generally refers to a site with a shelter, water, toilet facilities, fireplace, and tent platforms. Platforms allow tenting in rugged or steep terrain. They also concentrate, or at least localize, soil compaction. Some campsites have a caretaker, and a fee is charged (usually $3.00).

Tentsites

These have only tent platforms or tent pads, fireplace, toilet, and water. Some have a caretaker and a fee.

Shelters

A number of Adirondack (three walls, open front) shelters, which accommodate 5 to 14 people, are along the Trail. Shelters are located near water and have fireplaces and toilet facilities. Many sites have shelters as well as tent platforms. At some sites, a caretaker is in residence, and a fee is charged.

Cabins

A cabin is a closed shelter with water, fireplace, and toilet, and some have more elaborate facilities, such as bunks and stoves. Some sites have a caretaker, and a fee will be charged. Complete details are available from the Appalachian Mountain Club (see "Important Addresses," page 301).

AMC Huts

The AMC hut system is a chain of mountain hostels providing meals, lodging, and trail and weather information. The system has ten huts, all located on or close to the A.T. They are the only facilities of their kind along the Trail.

All AMC huts, but particularly those on the Presidential Range, serve a specific management purpose. The WMNF's close proximity to the large population areas of southern New England and Canada attracts large numbers of hikers. This heavy use is a potential threat to mountain ecosystems, particularly the fragile alpine zone. The huts, located in areas of heavy use, alleviate pressure on the environment by centering activity in durable man-made buildings. On the Presidential Range, where both weather and regulations prohibit tenting or open shelters, the huts are the only available shelter.

Reservations for overnight lodging are strongly recommended. The huts are open from early June to early September. In 1987, lodging, supper, and breakfast cost $34.50 for adults, $17.50 for children. Lodging and breakfast only cost $25.50 for adults, $13.00 for children; and lodging and supper cost $28.50 for adults, $14.50 for children. Some huts open in mid-May and remain open through mid-October on a caretaker basis (lodging only). Two huts, Carter and Zealand, are open in winter. For reservations and further information, write or call the Reservations Secretary, AMC, Pinkham Notch Camp, Gorham, N.H. 03581, (603) 466-2727. AMC members receive a $3.00-a-night discount.

Public Accommodations

In addition to the huts, a wide range of commercial accommodations is available along the public roads the Trail crosses. These are described in each section.

Grafton Notch (Maine 26) to Maine-New Hampshire State Line

The Mahoosuc Range in Maine

14.4 Miles

The Mahoosuc Range

The Mahoosuc Range is a long northeast-to-southeast mountain chain, which extends from Grafton Notch, Maine, to Androscoggin Valley, New Hampshire. Its many summits and open ledges provide splendid views of this wild area of northeast New Hampshire and northwest Maine.

The Trail crosses six major mountain peaks in this section: Old Speck, Mahoosuc Arm, Fulling Mill Mountain, North Peak of Goose Eye, and Mt. Carlo. Because the range (which also includes Mt. Success and Cascade Mountain, traversed in the next section) is accessible by road only at its ends, it is usually hiked in its entirety (two sections, 31.1 miles). The total climb in either direction is approximately 8,000 feet.

This section is very wild and rugged. Be prepared for frequent climbs and descents, and a rough, wet footway. Do not underestimate the time necessary to traverse the range (three to five days). This section has no major stream crossings, and water may be scarce.

The Trail crosses wet, boggy areas along the range, both high on the ridge and in sags between peaks. Although these bogs appear stable, even limited trampling breaks down the vegetation and soil structure, leading to unpleasant, muddy areas. To keep hikers from widening the footway, extensive log walkways or bog bridges have been installed. Hikers should use the walkways to prevent further damage and to allow regeneration of the parts of the bogs already damaged.

The A.T. follows the Mahoosuc Trail, a rugged crestline footpath for its entire distance along the ridge. At the northern end of the range, from Grafton Notch to Old Speck, the Trail follows the Old Speck Trail. At the southern end, from the Androscoggin Valley to Mt. Hayes, the Trail follows the Centennial Trail. East of the Maine-New Hampshire state line, the Trail passes through Grafton Notch State Park. West of the state line, the A.T. is on National Park Service land, except for the lower mile of the Centennial Trail, which is on New Hampshire's Leadmine State Forest. Most of the side trails are on private land.

Brief Description of Section

The Trail in this section crosses rugged, mountainous terrain. It passes Speck Pond, a scenic tarn. At its northern end, in Grafton Notch, it skirts the cliffs of the Eyebrow. The major peaks the A.T. traverses in this section, from north to south, are:

Old Speck, 4,180 feet (0.3 mile on side trail)
Mahoosuc Arm, 3,777 feet
South Peak, Fulling Mill Mountain, approximately 3,400 feet
North Peak, Goose Eye Mountain, 3,680 feet
West Peak, Goose Eye Mountain, 3,860 feet
Mt. Carlo, 3,565 feet

The Trail also passes through Mahoosuc Notch, a deep cleft between Mahoosuc Arm and Fulling Mill Mountain. Giant boulders from the notch's sheer walls have clogged the floor, necessitating a climb around the huge obstructions. Ice is found in caves here as late as July. In some places, hikers must remove their packs to climb under boulders and through caves. Although the notch is only about one mile long, considerable time should be set aside for its traverse.

The A.T. in this section is intersected by four side trails from north of the range, all maintained by the AMC. They all end on the Success Pond Road, reached from Berlin, N.H. (directions on page 78). From north to south, they are:

Speck Pond Trail (junction with A.T. 4.8 mi. from north end of section).
Mahoosuc Notch Trail (junction with A.T. 8.1 mile from north end of section).
Goose Eye Trail (junction with A.T. 12.2 mile from north end of section).
Carlo Col Trail (junction with A.T. 13.9 miles from north end of section).

For a description of all trails on the range, refer to the AMC's *White Mountain Guide* or *Maine Mountain Guide*, available from AMC (see "Important Addresses," page 301).

This guide begins in Grafton Notch, Maine. The Trail north in Maine is covered on *Appalachian Trail Guide to Maine Maps* available from the Appalachian Trail Conference or Maine Appalachian Trail Club (see "Important Addresses," page 301).

Road Approaches

Only the northern end of this section is accessible by car on Maine 26. Parking is available where Maine 26 intersects the A.T. in Grafton Notch. It is 12 miles from U.S. 2, north on

Maine 26, to the Trail crossing. It is 18 miles from the town of Bethel, Maine, to the Trail via U.S. 2 and Maine 26. The small village of Upton, near Umbagog Lake, is seven miles north on Maine 26.

The Trail may be approached from the gravel Success Pond Road, which parallels the Mahoosuc Range to the north. This road, a private James River Company road open to public use, begins in Berlin, N.H. (see "Road Approaches," Section 1). From this road, the hiker may ascend any of four AMC side trails to intersect the A.T. at various points along the Mahoosuc Range.

Maps

Map No. 1 (this guide)
MATC Map No. 8, Maine 17 to Maine-N.H. Line
AMC Carter-Mahoosuc Map
USGS 15 minute topographic quadrangles:
  Old Speck, Maine
  Bethel, Maine
  Milan, N.H.
  Gorham, N.H.
USGS 7 1/2 minute topographic quadrangle:
  Shelburne, N.H.

Shelters and Campsites

This section has two shelters and a campsite with shelter. Because of heavy use at the Speck Pond site, the AMC stations a caretaker there during summer to supervise use of the shelter and tentsites and charges a fee.

Speck Pond Campsite: Built and maintained by AMC 4.8

miles from north end of section; accommodates 10; also 4 tent platforms; caretaker in residence; water from small spring or from pond, a scenic mountain tarn; fee $3.00.

Next shelter or campsite: north 5.3 miles (Grafton Notch Lean-to); south 5.1 miles.

Full Goose Shelter: Rebuilt 1970 and maintained by AMC 9.9 miles from north end of section; accommodates 12; on short side trail; water from small spring down side trail.

Next shelter or campsite: north 5.1 miles; south 4.3 miles.

Carlo Col Shelter: Rebuilt 1976 and maintained by AMC 0.5 mile from south end of section; down Carlo Col Trail 0.3 miles from A.T.; accommodates 14; water from small stream; Carlo Col Trail continues past shelter to Success Pond Road.

Next shelter or campsite: north 4.3 miles; south 5.4 miles (Gentian Pond Campsite).

Regulations

Throughout this section, camping should be limited to the shelter sites. Off-Trail camping is limited. Do not camp in the fragile alpine bogs. State fire laws require wood and charcoal fires be built only at designated shelter sites. At other places along the Trail, only gas stoves are permitted.

Supplies and Services

The supply point nearest to this section is Gorham, N.H. (P.O. 03581, phone, supermarket, laundromat, restaurants, equipment, bus stop), about 14 miles from the southern end of the section, reached by continuing on the A.T. to U.S. 2 and from there 3.5 miles west into Gorham.

From the northern end of the section in Grafton Notch, it is 18 miles south on Maine 26 and U.S. 2 to the town of Bethel (P.O. 04217, phone, groceries, bus stop).

Public Accommodations

This section has no public accommodations near the Trail.

Trail Description, North to South

Miles	Data
0.0	Just N of Grafton Notch State Park trails parking area, leave road on W side. Hikers should leave cars in parking area. A.T. (Old Speck Trail) skirts N side of parking area. Pass prominent directional signs near parking area.
0.1	Bear left on A.T. at trail junction. Trail to right is **Eyebrow Trail,** which ascends the N side of the prominent cliffs on side of notch. This trail again intersects A.T. near top of cliffs.
0.3	Cross brook. Beyond, Trail parallels this brook up S side of Eyebrow over several wide switchbacks. Ascend steadily.
1.1	In small box canyon, turn right and cross brook. This is last sure water source until Speck Pond.
1.2	Reach upper junction of Eyebrow Trail. A.T. turns left and ascends toward the North Ridge. It is 0.1 mi. to right on Eyebrow Trail to top of Eyebrow Cliffs, with sheer 800-ft. drop to the floor of the notch.
1.5	Reach crest of North Ridge. The Trail swings S on ridge, climbing steadily toward Old Speck.

3.0 Cross wooded knob and descend into small col on ridge.

3.1 Reach junction with **Link Trail** to the left, which descends for 0.3 mi. to a brook and start of **East Spur Trail**. A.T. continues ahead along ridge.

3.4 Begin steep ascent up side of E-W summit ridge.

3.5 After passing an open meadow area, reach junction with **Mahoosuc Trail**. A.T. turns right (W) along this trail and descends gradually. To left, it is a gentle climb of 0.3 mi. to the summit of **Old Speck Mountain** (4,180 ft.). East Spur Trail descends the mountain from the summit.

3.8 Trail descends steeply along open, scrubby boulder slope, the result of an old slide.

4.1 Intermittent spring 20 yds. to left in small sag. Trail ascends gradually beyond.

4.4 At top of knob, descend steeply toward Speck Pond.

4.8 At junction of trails, reach **Speck Pond Campsite**. To right is the **Speck Pond Trail**, leading 3.3 mi. W to the Success Pond Road. A.T. (Mahoosuc Trail) turns sharp left and skirts E side of Speck Pond.

5.0 Cross outlet of Speck Pond and bear right. Ascend steadily.

5.6 Reach summit of **Mahoosuc Arm** (3,777 ft.). **May Cut-off** to Speck Pond Trail goes to right. Descend over ledges, gradually at first, then steeply.

6.7 Cross brook. Mahoosuc Notch Two (a smaller version of the main notch) is to right, upstream. Beyond, slab S slope of sheer-walled Mahoosuc Mountain.

7.2 At E end of **Mahoosuc Notch**, turn right and follow Bull Branch of Sunday River upstream. Route through notch is difficult and dangerous. Great care should be taken to avoid slipping on damp moss. Follow blazes over and under boulders.

8.1 At W end of notch, reach trail junction. A.T. (Mahoosuc Trail) turns sharp left and ascends steeply uphill. Ahead, the **Mahoosuc Notch Trail** leads W off range 2.8 mi. to the Success Pond Road.

9.0 Emerge from woods and cross ridge top with sparse growth.

9.1 Reach bare crest of **South Peak of Fulling Mill Mountain** (approximately 3,400 ft.). Bear right and descend through open growth.

9.9 Just past bottom of sag, pass **Full Goose Shelter**. A side trail leads SE 250 yds. to water. A.T. beyond ascends steeply for 0.2 mi., then less steeply.

10.1 Emerge from woods into scrub growth.

10.6 Reach open **North Peak of Goose Eye Mountain** (3,680 ft.) and turn left along line of cairns into sag ahead.

11.8 Reach summit of **East Peak of Goose Eye Mountain** (3,794). Turn right, descend into a col.

12.1 Reach trail junction. A.T. turns left and bypasses West Peak of Goose Eye, descending steeply into sag. Ahead, **Goose Eye Trail** ascends 0.1 mi. to summit of **West Peak of Goose Eye Mountain** (3,860 ft.), then descends W off the range 3 mi. to the Success Pond Road.

12.9 Reach bottom of sag. Begin ascent of Mt. Carlo.

13.5 Reach open summit of **Mt. Carlo** (3,565 ft.). Bear right and descend toward col ahead.

13.9 At junction of trails, at floor of Carlo Col, A.T. (Mahoosuc Trail), continues ahead. To right is **Carlo**

Col Trail, leading NW off the range 2.6 mi. to the Success Pond Road. Down this side trail 0.3 mi. is the **Carlo Col Shelter**. Ahead, A.T. ascends steeply over ledges, then levels out.

14.4 Reach **Maine-N.H. state line**, at cut-out strip, with the boundary line marked by yellow blazes. This is end of section; the elevation here is 2,972 ft. To continue ahead, cross cut-out strip and descend.

Trail Description, South to North

Miles **Data**

0.0 The **Maine-N.H. state line** is marked by yellow blazes along a cut-out strip. At this point, the A.T. follows the **Mahoosuc Trail** and is 2.0 mi. E of Mt. Success and 16.5 mi. NE of U.S. 2. The elevation is 2,972 ft. A.T. ascends gradually from state line, then descends steeply into Carlo Col, a small box canyon.

0.5 At junction of trails, at floor of Carlo Col, A.T. continues ahead. To left is **Carlo Col Trail,** leading NW off the range 2.6 mi. to the Success Pond Road. (This road is reached from Berlin, N.H., and parallels the range.) Down this side trail 0.3 mi. is **Carlo Col Shelter**. A.T. beyond ascends steeply out of col.

0.9 Reach open summit of **Mt. Carlo** (3,565 ft.). Bear left, enter woods, descending into sag ahead.

1.5 Cross bottom of sag and begin ascent toward Goose Eye Mountain.

2.0 Emerge from woods and continue to ascend, crossing heath and scrub.

2.3 At trail junction, turn right and descend gradually. To left is **Goose Eye Trail,** which ascends 0.1 mi. to the summit of **West Peak of Goose Eye Mountain** (3,860 ft.), then descends W off the range 3 mi. to the Success Pond Road.

2.6 After crossing low sag, reach **East Peak of Goose Eye Mountain.** Bear left toward North Peak of Goose Eye Mountain, descending into sag between the two peaks on open, alpine ridge.

2.9 Reach floor of sag in small box canyon. Continue descent.

3.2 Reach floor of second wooded canyon, then ascend steadily beyond.

3.8 Reach **North Peak of Goose Eye Mountain** (3,680 ft.). Turn right and descend.

4.8 At bottom of sag, pass **Full Goose Shelter**. A side trail leads SE 250 yds. to water. Beyond, A.T. ascends steeply toward Fulling Mill Mountain.

5.3 Reach crest of **South Peak of Fulling Mill Mountain** (approximately 3,400 ft.). Descend gradually at first, through scrub growth, then very steeply 0.5 mi. toward Mahoosuc Notch.

6.3 At bottom of descent, at W end of notch, reach junction of trails. The A.T. turns sharp right and proceeds easterly into notch. To left is the **Mahoosuc Notch Trail**, leading W off the range 2.8 mi. to the Success Pond Road. The route through the notch is difficult and dangerous. Take great care to avoid slipping on damp moss. Follow blazes over and under boulders.

7.3 At E end of notch, turn left and away from Bull Branch of Sunday River.

7.6 With huge boulder on right, bear left across S

slope of sheer-walled Mahoosuc Mountain. Cross brook. Mahoosuc Notch Two (a smaller version of the main notch) is to left upstream. Ascend very steeply beyond for 0.9 mi.

8.8 Reach open summit of **Mahoosuc Arm** (3,777 ft.). Descend steadily through woods. **May Cut-off** to Speck Pond Trail off to left.

9.4 Cross outlet of Speck Pond and skirt E side of Pond. At junction of trails, reach **Speck Pond Campsite**. To left is the **Speck Pond Trail**, leading 3.3 mi. W off the range to the Success Pond Road. A.T. bears right and ascends steeply away from pond.

10.3 In small sag at base of Old Speck, an intermittent spring is 20 yds. to right. Ascend steeply along old, open, scrubby slide. Beyond, Trail gradually ascends along a ridge leading easterly toward the summit of Old Speck.

10.9 Turn sharp left, leaving the Mahoosuc Trail. Trail ahead continues 0.3 mi. to the summit of **Old Speck** (4,180 ft.). From the summit, the **East Spur Trail** leads down the mountain along the open East Spur, then swings back to meet the **Link Trail**. The A.T. skirts a meadow then descends steeply N along a long ridge.

11.3 In a small col on the ridge, reach upper junction with Link Trail, to right, which descends 0.3 mi. to a brook and the lower end of the East Spur Trail. Ahead, ascend over wooded knob then descend gradually along the North Ridge.

12.9 Bear right and leave North Ridge. The trail swings SE and descends to a lower ridge.

13.2 In level area, reach upper junction of **Eyebrow**

Trail. To left, it is 0.1 mi. to the top of the Eyebrow Cliffs, with a sheer 800-ft. drop to the floor of Grafton Notch below. The Eyebrow Trail continues beyond the top of the cliffs around the N end and descends to rejoin the A.T. near the floor of the notch. Ahead, the A.T. continues to descend into a small box canyon.

13.3 Cross small brook, then descend paralleling brook to S over a series of switchbacks.

14.1 Cross mountain brook at bottom of main descent.

14.3 Reach lower junction with Eyebrow Trail coming in on left. A short distance beyond, pass prominent directional sign for the Grafton Notch State Park trail system. The Trail then skirts to the N of the trails parking area, where all hikers using the notch's trail system park their cars.

14.4 Reach Maine 26, end of section. To continue on Trail, cross road. The description of the A.T. continues on *Appalachian Trail Guide to Maine Maps.* North from this point it is:

0.4 mile to Grafton Notch Lean-to
0.9 mile to Table Reck
2.9 miles to West Peak of Baldpate
3.8 miles to East Peak of Baldpate
7.2 miles to Frye Brook Lean-to
7.5 miles to Andover B-Hill Road

Maine-New Hampshire State Line to AndroscogginValley (U.S. 2)

Section 1 New Hampshire

16.7 Miles

Brief Description of Section

Refer to the description of the Mahoosuc Range in the previous section. The Trail in this section passes four scenic mountain tarns: Gentian Pond, Moss Pond, Dream Lake, and Page Pond. The major peaks from north to south are:

Mt. Success, 3,565 feet
Cascade Mountain, 2,631 feet
Mt. Hayes, 2,555 feet (0.2 mile on side trail)

The A.T. in this section is intersected by four side trails, all maintained by the AMC. From north to south, they are:

Success Trail (junction with A.T. 1.3 miles from north end of section)
Austin Brook Trail (junction with A.T. 4.8 miles from north end of section)
Peabody Brook Trail (junction with A.T. 6.8 miles from north end of section)
Mahoosuc Trail (junction with A.T. 3.9 miles from south end of section)

Four more feeder trails from where Success Pond Road intersects the A.T. north of the Maine-N.H. line. The Carlo Col Trail junction is the closest, at a half-mile.

For a comprehensive description of all trails on the range, refer to the *AMC White Mountain Guide*. For current Trail information, contact the Appalachian Mountain Club (see "Important Addresses," page 301).

Road Approaches

The Trail is not directly accessible by road at the north end. It can be reached 1.3 miles south of the Maine-N.H. border via the Success Trail. The Success Trail begins on the gravel Success Pond Road, 8.7 miles from Berlin, N.H. The road is a James River Company road open to public use but accessible only from Berlin and sometimes difficult to find. In Berlin, cross to the east side of the Androscoggin River by the 12th Street Bridge at the northern end of town (not in the center). After crossing, turn right onto Hutchins Street and proceed 0.4 mile. Turn left at stop sign, cross railroad tracks, and immediately turn right by Liberty Market. Continue south 0.4 mile and turn left onto second dirt road (sometimes obscure) between the piles of pulpwood (not always there) in the James River Company mill yard. Cross the yard and continue ahead on the Success Pond Road. Be alert for fast-moving, large pulpwood trucks.

At the southern end of the section, the Trail crosses U.S. 2 3.6 miles east of Gorham, N.H., but cars are normally left 0.8 miles north of U.S. 2 on the Hogan Road (ample parking), where the Trail turns right into the woods on the Centennial Trail, or at the junction of Hogan Road and North Roads.

Maps

Map No. 1 (this guide)

AMC Carter-Mahoosuc Map
USGS 7 1/2 minute topographic quadrangles:
Shelburne, N.H.
Berlin, N.H.

Shelters and Campsites

The section has one campsite and one tentsite.

Gentian Pond Campsite: Rebuilt 1974 and maintained by AMC, 4.8 miles from north end of section; accommodates 14; 4 tent platforms; water from brook 150 yards north of shelter.

Next shelter or campsite: north 5.4 miles (Carlo Col Shelter); south 5.0 miles.

Trident Col Tentsite: Primitive site rebuilt 1978 and maintained by AMC 9.8 miles from north end of section on short side trail; accommodates 8; tentpads only; water from stream 100 yards northwest of shelter.

Next shelter or campsite: north 5.0 miles; south 8.5 miles (Rattle River Shelter).

In addition to these sites, Carlo Col Shelter is located a half-mile north of the Maine-New Hampshire border, 0.3 miles down the Carlo Col Trail.

Regulations

Throughout this section, camping is limited to designated sites. Off-Trail camping opportunities are limited. Do not camp in fragile alpine bogs. State fire laws require wood and charcoal fires be built only at designated sites. Use dead and downed wood only. At some sites, only camping stoves are permitted.

Supplies and Services

The supply point nearest this section is Gorham, N.H. (P.O. 03581, phone, supermarket, laundromat, restaurants, bus stop, equipment), 3.6 miles west of the southern end of the section. Supplies can also be obtained in Berlin, at the end of Success Pond Road.

From the Trail crossing of U.S. 2, it is one mile east to a store (phone, limited supplies) and two miles west to a restaurant.

In an emergency, call the New Hampshire State Police (603) 846-5500 or (800) 852-3411; or AMC Pinkham Notch Camp (603) 466-2727.

Public Accommodations

Gorham, 3.6 miles west on U.S. 2 from the southern end of the section, has a number of motels, a guesthouse (inexpensive), and camping, as does Berlin, at the end of the Success Pond Road. On U.S. 2, two miles west of the Trail crossing, tourist cabins and a camping area are available.

Trail Description, North to South

Miles	Data
0.0	Section begins at **Maine-N.H. state line** (2,972 ft.). The boundary is marked by yellow blazes along a cleared strip. Descend SW to rough col and ascend along flank of unnamed 3,335 ft. peak N of Mt. Success.
1.2	**Success Trail** descends right 3.0 mi. to the Success Pond Road. Ascend N ridge of Mt. Success.
1.8	Reach summit of **Mt. Success** (3,565 ft.). Descend SW to ledges of lower peak of Mt. Success.
2.1	Enter woods. Descend steeply W and SW.
3.2	Cross brook in col. Climb SW over two humps and then to ridgetop. Drop generally S down ridge and through spruce grove.
4.8	Reach **Gentian Pond Campsite** (2,166 ft.). **Austin Brook Trail** descends left 3.3 mi. to the North Road in Shelburne, N.H. Water can be obtained from a small inlet brook at the NE side of the pond by following a path 300 yds. N from shelter. Beyond the shelter, the Trail crosses the outlet brook of Gentian Pond, passes around the SW (left) side of the pond, and climbs steeply.
5.1	Pass along NW shore of **Moss Pond.** Ascend NW and W, then descend through swampy woodland. Cross the inlet brook of Dream Lake, briefly follow a lumber road.
6.9	**Peabody Brook Trail** leads left, passes the Dryad Fall Trail in 100 yds., and descends 3.1 mi.

to the North Road. The **Dryad Fall Trail** descends past a series of cascades and also leads to the North Road. Just beyond junction, recross inlet brook of **Dream Lake** and continue around the lake's N end. Climb around the end of a small ridge, descend to cross the upper (left) branch of Peabody Brook, and then climb W.

8.0 Reach **Wocket Ledge,** a spur of Bald Cap. A side trail leads NW 50 ft. to ledges. Descend steeply SW, then gradually W.

8.8 Pass to the S of **Page Pond** (cross on beaver dam). Descend W over S flank of peak W of Page Pond. Continue traversing the side of two more similar peaks. These three peaks form the Trident. Climb briefly NW.

9.8 Reach Trident Col. **Trident Col Tentsite** is 175 yds. right on a side trail. Water from a brook 100 ft. NW of the campsite. The A.T. climbs steeply SW beside ledges to E peak of Cascade Mountain It continues W and SW, rising gradually.

10.9 Reach summit of **Cascade Mountain.** (2,631 ft.). The Trail veers sharply NW back into the woods and then descends the SW ridge of Cascade Mountain Pass through col between Cascade Mountain and Mt. Hayes. Water is just E of the Trail. Climb N ridge of Mt. Hayes.

12.8 A.T. diverges left from Mahoosuc Trail following the **Centennial Trail** (constructed in 1976, the centennial year of the AMC). The Mahoosuc Trail continues straight ahead 0.2 mi. to the summit of **Mt. Hayes** (2,555 ft.). Descend SE on Centennial Trail over a series of open ledges, and then climb slightly.

13.2 Reach an easterly summit of Mt. Hayes on open ledges. Descend SE to small valley, then climb briefly.
14.9 Turn sharp left where ledge ahead provides excellent views of Mt. Washington and the Moriahs. Cross logging road.
15.3 Cross brook (reliable water). Continue on woods road. Trail soon turns right off woods road. Descend gradually, then more steeply.
15.8 Descend stone steps. Head SE to woods road and follow right.
15.9 Turn left onto graveled **Hogan Road** at lower end of Centennial Trail.
16.2 Turn right onto paved **North Road.**
16.4 Cross **Androscoggin River** by Leadmine Bridge with small dam and power plant on right.
16.5 Cross Canadian National (Grand Trunk) Railroad tracks.
16.7 Reach section end at U.S. 2, 3.6 mi. E of Gorham (760 ft.). To continue on Trail, turn left, cross Rattle River on highway bridge, and then turn right onto Rattle River Trail.

Trail Description, South to North

Miles **Data**
0.0 From U.S. 2, 3.6 mi. E of Gorham (760 ft.), take **North Road** N.
0.2 Cross Canadian National (Grand Trunk) Railroad tracks.
0.3 Cross **Androscoggin River** on Leadmine Bridge with a small dam and power plant on left.
0.5 Turn left from North Road onto graveled **Hogan**

Road.

0.8 Turn right onto woods road, the beginning of the **Centennial Trail**, opposite clearing and parking area. (The trail was constructed in 1976, the centennial year of the AMC.) Trail turns left off woods road in 50 yds., heading NW.

0.9 Trail ascends steeply over stone steps, then more gradually, with views of the Androscoggin River Valley. Beyond, Trail turns left onto woods road.

1.4 Cross small brook. Cross logging road.

1.8 Turn sharply right. Ascend moderately to open ledges.

3.5 Reach easterly summit of Mt. Hayes with views of Carter-Moriah Range and Northern Presidentials. Continue across open ledges.

3.9 Reach junction with **Mahoosuc Trail** (to left). **Mt. Hayes** (2,555 ft.) is 0.2 mi. left on this trail. Bear right and descend N to col between Mt. Hayes and Cascade Mountain. Water may be found in col just E (right) of Trail. Beyond col, climb Cascade Mountain by SW ridge.

5.8 Reach summit of **Cascade Mountain** (2,631 ft.). Trail veers sharply left back into woods, heads NW and W, crosses the east peak of Cascade Mountain, and then descends steeply to the NE and E.

6.9 Reach Trident Col. **Trident Col Tentsite** is 175 yds. left on side trail with water from brook 100 ft. NW. About 0.3 mi. beyond the col, the A.T. briefly follows an old logging road, turns left (SE), and descends, traversing the ridge past this peak (E of the col) and two others, which form the Trident. Beyond the Trident, the Trail continues E, crosses three gullies (possible water), and begins ascent.

7.9 Pass to S of **Page Pond** and cross outlet on beaver dam. Climb gradually E, then steeply NE.

8.7 Reach **Wocket Ledge**, a spur of Bald Cap. The Trail descends E, crosses the upper (left) branch of Peabody Brook, climbs around the end of a small ridge, and then gradually descends to **Dream Lake**. The Trail bears left, continuing around the N end of the lake.

9.8 Cross inlet brook of Dream Lake. Just beyond, reach junction where **Peabody Brook Trail** descends right, passing Dryad Fall Trail in 100 yds. and descending 3.1 mi. to the North Road. The **Dryad Fall Trail** descends past a series of scenic cascades and also leads to the North Road. From Dream Lake, the A.T. recrosses the inlet brook and continues NE through sometimes swampy woodland, ascending at first, then descending.

11.5 Reach **Moss Pond** and follow NW shore. About 0.3 mi. past the pond, the A.T. turns abruptly right and descends to Gentian Pond. It passes along the SW shore of the pond and crosses the outlet brook.

11.9 Reach **Gentian Pond Campsite** (2,166 ft.). From here, the **Austin Brook Trail** descends right 3.3 mi. to the North Road in Shelburne. Water from a small brook at the NE side of the pond, reached by a path leading 300 yds. N from the shelter. Beyond the shelter, the A.T. ascends through a spruce grove to the ridge, crosses a small col, and then climbs over two steep humps.

13.5 Cross small brook in col after second hump. Ascend steeply NE.

14.6 Leave woods onto open ledges of lower peak of

Mt. Success.

14.9 Reach summit of **Mt. Success** (3,565 ft.) and then descend N to col.

15.5 Reach junction where **Success Trail** descends left 3.0 mi. to the Success Pond Road. Climb NW along the flank of unnamed 3,335-ft. peak N of Mt. Success, pass through col, and continue NW.

16.7 Reach **Maine-N.H. state line** (2,972 ft.), where the section ends. The border is marked by yellow blazes along a cleared strip. From this point, the A.T. continues N on the **Mahoosuc Trail**.

Androscoggin Valley (U.S. 2) to Pinkham Notch (N.H. 16)

Section 2 New Hampshire

20.0 Miles

Brief Description of Section

The Carter-Moriah Range offers rugged walking on an uninterrupted footpath. The Trail drops precipitously into Carter Notch and passes the Carter Lakes but traces a high ridgecrest route for the rest of its length. For most of its length, the Trail in this section passes through White Mountain National Forest (WMNF), and hikers should take care to follow WMNF regulations (see "Regulations"). From the Androscoggin Valley (approximately 800 feet above sea level) in the north, the Trail follows the Rattle River Trail up the ridge, the Kenduskeag Trail, Carter-Moriah Trail, and Wildcat Ridge Trail along the ridge, and descends across the "Wild Kittens" (small peaks) and the Lost Pond Trail to Pinkham Notch (approximately 2,000 feet). The major peaks the Trail traverses in this section are, from north to south:

Mt. Moriah, 4,049 feet
North Carter Mountain, approximately 4,530 feet
Mt. Lethe, 4,584 feet
Middle Carter Mountain, approximately 4,600 feet
South Carter Mountain 4,458 feet
Mt. Hight, 4,675 feet
Carter Dome, 4,832 feet
Wildcat Mountain, 4,422 feet

Allow three days to traverse this section. Water may be scarce on the ridge.

This section has a number of side trails, described briefly in the trail data, which provide interesting side or loop hikes. Four trails provide access to the A.T. from N.H. 16 on the west side of the range, and five trails on the east side lead to different parts of the WMNF. Hikers may ride the Wildcat Gondola, when it is in operation, from Pinkham Notch to Peak E of Wildcat Mountain. For complete information, see the *AMC White Mountain Guide.* For current trail conditions and answers to questions concerning material not in this guide, contact the information desk at AMC Pinkham Notch Camp (see "Important Addresses," page 301).

Road Approaches

Both the north and south ends of this section are accessible from major highways. At the north end, the Trail crosses U.S. 2, a major east-west thoroughfare, 3.6 miles east of Gorham, N.H. (parking). At the south end, the Trail crosses N.H. 16 at Pinkham Notch (parking), 8 miles north of Jackson, N.H., and 12.0 miles south of Gorham.

Theft and vandalism have been reported at both parking areas. Do not leave valuables in cars.

Maps

Map No. 2 (this guide)
AMC Carter-Mahoosuc Map
White Mountain National Forest Map (1:250,000)
AMC Mt. Washington Range Map
USGS 15 minute topographic quadrangles:
North Conway, N.H.

Crawford Notch, N.H.
Mt. Washington, N.H.
USGS 7 1/2 minute topographic quadrangles:
Wild River, N.H.
Carter Dome, N.H.

Shelters and Campsites

This section has two shelters.

Rattle River Shelter: Built and maintained by USFS 1.6 miles from section's north end; accommodates 8; water from river.

Next shelter or campsite: north 8.5 miles (Trident Col Tentsite); south 6.0 miles.

Imp Campsite: Built and maintained by AMC 7.6 miles from section's north end; 0.1 mile down side trail; accommodates 10; 5 tent platforms; water from brook by shelter.

Next shelter or campsite: north 6.0 miles; south 16.7 miles (Osgood Tentsite).

Carter Notch Hut, is located 7.9 miles south of Imp Campsite and 5.4 miles north of Pinkham Notch at the section's southern end (see "Public Accommodations").

Regulations

Except for its northern 0.8 mile (private land where camping is not advised), this entire section is located within WMNF, where varying regulations apply.

Camping and wood or charcoal fires are prohibited in the following areas *except at designated sites*: above treeline (defined as areas where trees are less than eight feet tall), within one-quarter mile of Imp Campsite and Carter Notch Hut, within one-quarter mile of intersection of the Carter-Moriah Trail (A.T.) and the Carter Dome Trail (Zeta Pass), in Cutler River Drainage, and within one-quarter mile of N.H. 16 in Pinkham Notch.

Campfire permits are required for open fires *outside* WMNF lands. They can be obtained from AMC at Pinkham Notch (see "Important Addresses," page 301).

Supplies and Services

The supply point nearest this section is Gorham, N.H., 3.6 miles west of the northern end of the section (P.O. 03581, phone, supermarket, laundromat, restaurants, bus stop, and equipment).

Limited supplies and services (candy, fruit, phone, meals, bus stop) are available at Pinkham Notch Camp at the southern end of the section.

In an emergency, call the Imp Campsite, Carter Notch Hut, Pinkham Notch Camp (603) 466-2721, or New Hampshire State Police (603) 846-5500 or (800) 852-3410.

Public Accommodations

Gorham, 3.6 miles west on U.S. 2 from the northern end of the section, has motels, a guesthouse, and camping areas. On U.S. 2, two miles west of the Trail crossing, cabins and a camping area are available.

AMC built and maintains two huts where lodging and family-style meals are available. Reservations may be made by calling or writing the Reservations Secretary, Pinkham Notch Camp (see "Important Addresses," page 301).

Carter Notch Hut: Oldest hut still in use, erected 1914, 5.4 miles from southern end of section on short side trail; reservations strongly recommended; accommodates 40; ample water.

Pinkham Notch Camp: Extensive mountain facility located on N.H. 16 at south end of section; reservations required; meals served; information desk; hot drinks and snacks; packup room; phone; showers; accommodates 107.

Trail Description, North to South

Miles	Data
0.0	From junction of U.S. 2 and North Road, 3.6 mi. E of Gorham, the Trail proceeds E on U.S. 2, crossing Rattle River on highway bridge.
0.2	Turn right through parking lot onto **Rattle River Trail** and ascend gradually on woods road.
1.0	Pass lumber-camp site.
1.6	Pass **Rattle River Shelter;** water available from river.
2.2	Take right fork and cross brook. Ascend steeply.
3.3	Cross Rattle River and climb steeply.
4.3	Reach junction where A.T. turns right onto **Kenduskeag Trail** and continues over wooded summit of **Middle Moriah Mountain**. (The Kenduskeag Trail also leads left to Shelburne Trail, which leads N to U.S. 2 and S to Wild River.

5.0 Pass through marshy sag, and ascend steeply through woods.

5.7 Reach junction where Kenduskeag Trail ends. The A.T. turns left onto Carter-Moriah Trail and descends S, swingingW, along the wooded ridge. At junction, the **Carter-Moriah Trail** also leads right (N) reaching the rocky sum(4,049 ft.). (From the summit, the Carter-Moriah Trail continues N, descending 4.5 mi. to U.S. 2 in Gorham.)

6.9 Reach junction in col. **Stony Brook Trail** descends right 3.5 mi. to N.H. 16, and **Moriah Brook Trail** descends left to Wild River. The A.T. ascends ahead on Carter-Moriah Trail.

7.2 Trail bears left, climbing S.

7.5 Pass across open knob, then descend SW.

7.6 Reach junction where side trail descends right 0.1 mi. to **Imp Campsite**. The Trail continues across stream.

7.7 Turn sharp left and climb S.

8.7 Ascend past spring.

8.9 Pass over wooded summit of **North Carter Mountain** (4,530 ft.).

9.1 **North Carter Trail** descends right (W) 1.2 mi. to Imp Trail, which descends 2.3 mi. more to N.H. 16. Cross boggy area and ascend.

9.9 Reach open ledges of **Mt. Lethe** (4,584 ft.).

10.1 Cross wooded summit of **Middle Carter Mountain** (4,600 ft.).

11.2 Pass over wooded summit of **South Carter Mountain** (4,458 ft.) and descend.

12.0 Reach **Zeta Pass** (3,990 ft.), where **Carter Dome Trail** descends right 1.9 mi. to Nineteen Mile Brook Trail, which leads 1.9 mi. to N.H. 16. Water is generally found near path in Zeta Pass. In other direction, Carter Dome Trail coincides with the Carter-Moriah Trail for 150 ft., then diverges right and ascends, bypassing Mt. Hight. The A.T. bears left and ascends steeply toward Mt. Hight.

12.5 Reach open summit of **Mt. Hight** (4,675 ft.). The Trail descends slightly and continues SW through scrub growth.

12.9 Carter Dome Trail enters from right and rejoins the A.T. One hundred ft. beyond, the **Black Angel Trail** descends left (E) to Wild River. The A.T. continues ahead, climbing an open slope.

13.3 Reach open summit of **Carter Dome** (4,832 ft.). The Rainbow Trail descends left (E) to Perkins Notch and Wild River. The A.T. descends SW.

13.3 Side trail leads 50 yds. right to spring. From here, the Trail drops very steeply.

14.5 Reach junction in Carter Notch where Carter-Moriah Trail ends and the A.T. turns right onto **Nineteen Mile Brook Trail**, skirts shore of pond, and ascends. Left of the junction, the Nineteen Mile Brook Trail passes between the two small Carter Lakes and reaches **AMC Carter Notch Hut** in 0.1 mi. From the hut, Wildcat River Trail descends S toward Jackson.

14.6 Reach height of land (3,388 ft.) and junction where the Trail turns left onto **Wildcat Ridge Trail** and ascends steeply on switchbacks. The Nineteen Mile Brook Trail continues ahead, descending in 3.5 mi. to N.H. 16.

15.2 Reach summit of **Wildcat Mountain** (4,422 ft.). Continue S through woods along ridge.

15.5 Cross **Peak B** (4,320 ft.).

16.0 Cross **Peak C** (4,298 ft.). Descend along ridge.

16.5 Pass through Wildcat Col.

16.7 Pass spring.

17.0 Swing around N end of **Peak D** (4,000 ft.), passing wooden observation platform with views of Tuckerman (left) and Huntington (right) ravines on Mt. Washington, as well as the Northern Presidential Range. Wildcat Mountain Gondola terminal building is here (light refreshments). When in operation, the gondola descends NW to N.H. 16. Also, any number of ski trails may be descended to N.H. 16. The A.T. continues SW on ridge.

17.3 Cross summit of **Peak E** (4,041 ft.).

17.5 Pass over lower Peak E and continue to upper ledges. The descent from here is exceptionally steep; use extra care.

18.1 Pass trail on right leading 25 yds. to spring and continue steep descent. Pass middle ledges.

18.6 Pass lower ledges and continue descent. Moderate grade.

19.1 Reach junction where Trail turns right onto **Lost Pond Trail**. Ahead, the Wildcat Ridge Trail descends 0.1 mi. to N.H. 16 at Glen Ellis Falls.

19.3 Pass around E edge of **Lost Pond** and descend gradually to Ellis River, following E bank upstream. Where Square Ledge Trail bears right, A.T. turns left across a small marsh on wooden bridge.

20.0 Reach N.H. 16 at **Pinkham Notch Camp**. To continue on A.T., cross highway and follow Tuckerman Ravine Trail for 250 ft., where A.T. branches right.

Description, South to North

Miles	Data
0.0	From **Pinkham Notch Camp**, cross N.H. 16 and follow **Lost Pond Trail**. Cross small bog by means of wooden bridge. Where Square Ledge Trail leads left, the Trail turns right (S) along the E bank of Ellis River. Ascend slightly from river.
0.7	Pass around E edge of **Lost Pond** and continue along outlet stream.
0.9	Reach junction where A.T. turns left onto **Wildcat Ridge Trail**. To the right, the Wildcat Ridge Trail leads 0.1 mi. to N.H. 16 at Glen Ellis Falls.
1.1	Begin exceptionally steep ascent. Use extra care.
1.4	Reach lower ledges. Ascend past middle ledges.
1.9	Pass trail on left leading 25 yds. to spring and continue ascent.
2.3	Reach upper ledges.
2.5	Pass over lower Peak E of Wildcat Mountain.
2.7	Cross summit of **Peak E** (4,041 ft.), swing N, descend slightly, and pass near Wildcat Mountain Gondola terminal building (light refreshments). Any number of ski trails may be descended W to N.H. 16. When in operation, the gondola descends NW to N.H. 16. Ascend NE from terminal building to **Peak D** (4,000 ft.), passing a wooden observation platform with views of Tuckerman (left) and Huntington (right) ravines on Mt. Washington, as well as the Northern Presidential Range.
3.5	Pass through Wildcat Col and ascend along ridge.
4.0	Reach **PeakC** (4,298 ft.). Pass along ridge, through next col, and over the wooded summit of **Peak B** (4,320 ft.). Swing N and ascend gradually.

4.8 Reach summit of **Wildcat Mountain** (4,422 ft.). Descend on switchbacks into Carter Notch.

5.4 Reach junction in **Carter Notch** (3,388 ft.) where **Nineteen Mile Brook Trail** descends left 3.5 mi. to N.H. 16. The A.T. turns right here, descending to lake on Nineteen Mile Brook Trail.

5.5 Reach junction where A.T. turns left and follows **Carter-Moriah Trail**, ascending very steeply E. From this junction, Nineteen Mile Brook Trail continues ahead, passes between the two small Carter Lakes, and reaches **Carter Notch Hut** in 0.1 mi. (From hut, Wildcat River Trail descends S toward Jackson.)

6.2 Side trail leads 50 yds. left to spring. The A.T. ascends less steeply.

6.7 Reach open summit of **Carter Dome** (4,832 ft.). Rainbow Trail descends right to Perkins Notch and Wild River. A.T. continues N on the Carter-Moriah Trail, descending.

7.1 Reach junction where **Black Angel Trail** descends right (E) to Wild River. One hundred ft. farther, where Carter Dome Trail leads left, bypassing the summit of Mt. Hight, the A.T. ascends right through scrub growth.

7.5 Reach open summit of **Mt. Hight** (4,675 ft.). Beyond, descend steeply.

8.0 Carter Dome Trail enters from left. Beyond, in low point of **Zeta Pass** (3,990 ft.), reach junction where **Carter Dome Trail** descends left 1.9 mi. to Nineteen Mile Brook Trail, which descends 1.9 mi. to N.H. 16. Water is generally found near path in Zeta Pass. From pass, A.T. ascends N steadily.

8.8 Reach summit of **South Carter Mountain** (4,458

ft.) and continue N through woods along ridge.

10.0 Pass over **Middle Carter Mountain** (4,600 ft.) to open ledges on **Mt. Lethe** (4,584 ft.). From this viewpoint, descend and cross boggy area.

10.9 **North Carter Trail** descends left (W) 1.2 mi. to Imp Trail which descends 2.3 mi. more to N.H. 16. The A.T. ascends NE.

11.1 Reach summit of **North Carter Mountain** (4,530 ft.). Descend steeply.

11.3 Pass spring.

12.3 Turn sharp right (E) and continue on level.

12.4 Cross stream and reach junction. Side trail descends left 0.1 mi. to **Imp Campsite**. The A.T. climbs steeply NE.

12.5 Pass across open knob, and descend N.

12.8 Trail bears right and proceeds NE.

13.1 Reach junction in col. **Stony Brook Trail** descends left 3.5 mi. to N.H. 16 and **Moriah Brook Trail** descends right to Wild River. The A.T. continues on Carter-Moriah Trail, ascending NE along ridge through woods and gradually N.

14.3 Reach junction where A.T. turns right onto Kenduskeag Trail and descends steeply NE, and Carter-Moriah Trail, continues ahead reaching, just beyond, the summit of **Mt. Moriah** (4,049 ft.). (From summit, Carter Moriah Trail continues N, descending 4.5 mi. to U.S. 2 in Gorham.)

15.0 Pass through marshy sag and continue over wooded **Middle Moriah Mountain**.

15.7 Reach junction where A.T. turns left onto Rattle River Trail and descends steeply. The Kenduskeag Trail continues to Shelburne Trail, which leads N to U.S. 2 and S to Wild River.

16.7 Cross Rattle River and descend less steeply.
17.8 Cross brook.
18.4 Pass **Rattle River Shelter** with water from river. From shelter, Trail follows an old logging road N.
19.8 Reach U.S. 2 and turn left (W).
20.0 Reach **North Road**, the end of the section, 3.6 mi. E of Gorham on U.S. 2. To continue on Trail, turn right onto North Road.

Pinkham Notch (N.H. 16) to Crawford Notch (U.S. 302)

Section 3 New Hampshire

24.9 Miles

Brief Description of Section

The Presidential Range is the highest mountain group traversed by the A.T. north of Clingmans Dome in North Carolina. For most of the nearly 13-mile distance between Mt. Madison to Mt. Pierce (Mt. Clinton), the Trail is above treeline. From Pinkham Notch (approximately 2,000 feet above sea level) in the north, the Trail gradually ascends on the Old Jackson Road to the Mt. Washington Auto Road. It crosses the Auto Road into the Great Gulf Wilderness, descends gradually on the Madison Gulf Trail, follows the Osgood Cut-off, and then ascends steeply on the Osgood Trail to the ridge above treeline. From Madison Hut, it continues to follow the ridgecrest on the Gulfside Trail to the summit of Mt. Washington, where P.T. Barnum declared the view was "the second-greatest show on earth!"

The Trail gradually descends on the Crawford Path, past Lakes of the Clouds, to Mt. Pierce (Clinton). It reenters the woods and follows Webster Cliff Trail across a sometimes open ridge and the Webster Cliffs to Crawford Notch (1,277 feet) and the southern end of the section. Most of the section is within the White Mountain National Forest (WMNF). The southern end lies within Crawford Notch State Park.

The elevation change in this section is enormous, but it is covered as the hiker ascends to the ridge at one end and descends at the other. Many less significant climbs are along the ridgecrest. The A.T. passes over the highest Presidential summits but bypasses many others that can be reached by short loop trails, scarcely increasing the total distance traveled. The major peaks traversed in the section, from north to south, are:

Mt. Madison, 5,363 feet
Mt. Washington, 6,288 feet
Mt. Franklin, 5,004 feet
Mt. Eisenhower, 4,761 feet
Mt. Pierce (Mt. Clinton), 4,310 feet
Mt. Jackson, 4,052 feet
Mt. Webster, 3,910 feet

The alpine ridge of the Presidential Range is exposed to the storms that rise rapidly and are often violent, with hurricane-force winds and freezing conditions, even in summer. Carry ample extra clothing and if weather becomes threatening, promptly descend to shelter by the shortest route. If severe weather is predicted (forecasts available at Pinkham Notch Camp, Madison Hut, Lakes of the Clouds Hut, and Mizpah Hut), take the shortcut between Lakes of the Clouds and Pinkham Notch via Tuckerman Ravine and Hermit Lakes (shelter), which eliminates crossing the Northern Presidential Range. Even this route can be forbidding in bad weather and should be approached cautiously.

Treeline in the Presidential Range is at about 4,200 feet. Above this altitude, only stunted *krummholz* (spruce) and alpine plants survive the severe weather. The vegetation is extremely vulnerable to damage by foot traffic, evident in many places where the obliteration of the alpine tundra has given way to erosion, visibly scarring the mountainside. To prevent trampling vegetation and erosion, and allow successful regeneration of damaged areas, rock steps and borders have been installed in several parts of the section. Hikers are urged to closely follow the established treadway to keep the impact of their passage to a minimum.

The system of side trails on this section is comprehensive and offers the hiker many choices for exploring the Presidential Range. Many of these trails are briefly noted in the trail description. For complete information, refer to the *AMC White Mountain Guide or AMC Guide to Mt. Washington and the Presidential Range;* both describe the region in detail. For information on these books, current trail conditions and answers to questions concerning material not in this guide, contact the information desk at AMC Pinkham Notch Camp (see "Important Addresses," page 301).

Mt. Washington Summit

Mt. Washington (6,288 feet) is the highest U.S. peak north of the Carolinas and east of the Mississippi and part of the N.H. State Park System. The Mt. Washington Cog Railway, the world's first mountain-climbing railway, ascends from Marshfield Station three miles up the steep western ridge of the mountain to the summit. The Mt. Washington Auto Road (toll road), beginning on N.H. 16, winds eight miles up the east side of the mountain to the summit. The Summit House, owned by the state and located just north of the highest point on the mountain, has a snack bar, souvenir shop, toilets, telephone, and post office. The Mount Washington Observatory is in the north end of the building. South of the summit is the old Tip-Top House, with two broadcasting towers, housing a radio and television station.

Mt. Washington has long been a center of attention. The first path to the summit was cut in 1819 by a father-and-son team, Abel and Ethan Allen Crawford, who later established the first tourist hostelries in the notch now bearing their name. In 1839, Thomas, a younger son of Abel, converted the Crawford Path into a bridle path, the first of its kind to the summit. The first bridle path from the east was constructed between 1851 and 1861 and started at the Glen House, where the Auto Road begins.

The summit stands well above treeline and, with the 20-mile ridge of the Presidential Range, forms an arctic island in New England, with permafrost, arctic flora resembling that of northern Labrador, and some of the worst weather in the world. The severity of weather is due to high winds and frequent sharp temperature changes, influenced by air masses flowing from the south, west, and the St. Lawrence River Valley in the north.

The first weather observatory was established on the summit in 1870 and was staffed by the U.S. Signal Corps year until 1892. The present observatory was initiated in 1932 by Joe Dodge, former AMC hut system manager, and Bob Monahan, Dartmouth College weather buff. The observatory was quartered during winter in the summit stage office, donated by the Mt. Washington Auto Road officials. In 1934, the observatory measured a wind velocity of 231 miles per hour, the strongest wind ever recorded in the world. The observatory is manned throughout the year, carrying out scientific experiments and recoriings, including a morning report on the summit weather conditions. The observatory is not open to the public, but a museum located on the lower floor of the Sherman Adams Building contains summit artifacts and exhibits of unusual flora and fauna. An admission fee supports the observatory.

Because of the violent weather, the Crawfords provided crude stone huts for shelter. The first summit house was built in 1852, and the Tip-Top House in 1853. These small structures became inadequate, and the first large summit house was opened in 1874. It was destroyed by a fire that swept the summit in 1908.

Construction of the Carriage Road began in 1851 and it opened in 1861. Today, thousands of cars ascend the eight miles to the summit, at grades up to 12 percent.

The cog railway began operating in 1869. Its trestle over Jacob's Ladder, at a 37.4-percent grade, is the steepest in the world. Sylvester Marsh built the 3.5-mile railroad and powered it by a coal-fired steam engine, which is still used by the present owner, Ellen Teague. The railway was honored at its 100th birthday by designation as a national historical mechanical and civil-engineering landmark.

In 1937-38, a radio tower was installed. FM radio broadcasted from the summit as early as 1941. In 1954, the current television transmitter was added. Small buildings for these operations have been built and maintained under the most trying weather conditions. A snow vehicle is used for the weekly change of personnel in the winter.

Until recently, the summit has been privately owned. From early grants and purchases, it passed to to Colonel Henry Teague of the cog railway, who left it to Dartmouth College; and it is now owned by the state of New Hampshire.

Crawford Notch State Park

Crawford Notch was discovered in 1777 by Timothy Nash while he was hunting moose on Cherry Mountain. He spied a defile in what was then considered an impassable wall of mountains.

Soon after Nash's discovery, a road was built through the notch. It was rough, crossing the Saco River 32 times. In some places, horses had to be lifted or lowered by ropes. As poor as it was, the route was far preferable to traveling around the White Mountains. The first shipment from the coast made through the notch was a barrel of rum, which was sampled freely during the venture and arrived a great deal lighter than when it began its voyage.

In 1825, Samuel Willey and his family moved into the notch and opened a hostel. The next year, the calamitous "Willey Slide" shook the notch, taking the lives of the entire family. Tons of debris suddenly and violently slid and fell from the valley walls, partly determining the shape of the notch today. Despite the devastation of the slide, activity in the notch did not slow down; it was an important commercial route and a prime spot for summer tourists.

Today, the notch is preserved in Crawford Notch State Park. The Willey House Site and Willey Slide are still visible one mile north of the Trail crossing. A snack bar and souvenir shop are nearby. The Crawford House, although not the original, burned to the ground in 1976. In 1979, the Appalachian Mountain Club bought the Crawford House site, 3.7 miles north of the Trail crossing on Rt. 302. Here, the club maintains a hostel for lodging and the old depot as an information center.

Road Approaches

Both ends of this section are accessible by major highways. At the northern end, the Trail crosses N.H. 16 at Pinkham Notch (parking), 8 miles north of Jackson, N.H., and 12 miles south of Gorham, N.H. At the southern end, the Trail crosses U.S. 302 in Crawford Notch opposite the road to the former Willey House Station(parking), 8 miles north of Bartlett, N.H., and ten miles south of Twin Mountain, N.H. Both ends of the section have experienced theft and vandalism. Do not leave any valuables in vehicles.

Maps

Map No. 2 (this guide)
AMC Mt. Washington Range Map
White Mountain National Forest Map (1:250,000)
USGS 15 minute topographic quadrangles:
  Mt. Washington, N.H.
  Crawford Notch, N.H.

Shelters and Campsites

Because of the alpine nature of this section, few overnight facilities are available, except for AMC huts, Randolph Mountain Club (RMC) facilities off the Trail (Perch, Crag Camp, Gray Knob), and USFS tentsites (Osgood and Valley Way). Anticipate long hiking days.

Three shelters, all some distance off the Trail, one campsite, and one public campground (on U.S. 302) are located in the section. AMC's Lakes of the Clouds Hut, in addition to its regular services (see "Public Accommodations"), offers lodging for backpackers.

Osgood Tentsite: (USFS) Four tent platforms, spring; near junction of Osgood Trail and Osgood Cut-off.

Next shelter or campsite: north 16.7 miles (Imp Campsite); south 3.4 miles.

Valley Way Tentsite: (USFS) Four tent platforms, spring; 0.6 mile down Valley Way side trail.

Next shelter or campsite: north 3.4 miles; south 2.6 miles.

Crag Camp: Closed cabin, maintained by Randolph Mountain Club (RMC) 8.0 miles from north end of section; 1.1 miles down side trail; blankets, cooking utensils, gas stove; accommodates 12; $3.00 fee charged; ample water.

Next shelter or campsite: north 2.6 miles , south 0.5 mile.

Gray Knob: Closed cabin, maintained by RMC and Town of Randolph, 8.0 miles from north end of section; 1.2 miles down side trail; blankets, cooking utensils, gas stove; accommodates 14; $3.00 fee charged; ample water.

Next shelter or campsite: north 2.6 miles; 0.5 mile.

The Perch Shelter: Built and maintained by RMC 8.6 miles from north end of section; 0.9 mile down side trail; accommodates 8; $2.00 fee charged; ample water.

Next shelter or campsite: north 0.5 mile; south 5.0 miles.

Lakes of the Clouds Hut: AMC mountain hut refuge room 14.4 miles from north end of section; reservations recommended; accommodates 8; hut meal not required; cooking room; fee charged; ample water.

Next shelter or campsite: north 5.0 miles; south 4.6 miles.

Nauman Tentsite: Built and maintained by AMC adjacent to Mizpah Spring Hut, 5.9 miles from south end of section; 6 tent platforms; accommodates 20; $3.00 fee charged; ample water. Caretaker in attendance.

Next shelter or campsite: north 4.6 miles; south 5.9 miles.

Dry River Campground: Operated and maintained by New Hampshire Division of Parks in Crawford Notch State Park; on U.S. 302 1.5 miles south of Trail crossing; 24 tentsites; ample water.

Next shelter or campsite: north 5.9 miles; south 3.5 miles (Ethan Pond Campsite).

This section has four AMC mountain huts, which are described under "Public Accommodations."

Regulations

The southern part of this section lie in Crawford Notch State Park, where camping and fires are not permitted except at Dry River Campground. The rest of the Trail passes through WMNF, where special regulations apply.

Camping or wood or charcoal fires are prohibited within one-quarter mile of Madison Hut, the Perch Shelter, Gray Knob Cabin, Crag Camp Shelter, Lakes of the Clouds Hut, and Mizpah Spring Hut, except at designated areas.

Camping or wood or charcoal fires are prohibited above treeline. The A.T. from Mt. Madison to Mt. Pierce (Clinton), a distance of nearly 13 miles, is mostly above treeline. (Treeline is an area where trees are less than eight feet tall.)

Camping or fires are prohibited in the Cutler River Drainage (this includes the 1.7-mile section of Trail between Pinkham Notch Camp and the Auto Road) or within one-quarter mile of N.H. 16 in Pinkham Notch. In the Great Gulf Wilderness (between the Auto Road and Osgood Tentsite), only off-Trail camping, at least 200 feet from the Trail, is allowed.

Campfire permits are required for open fires inside WMNF lands. Permits can be obtained at Pinkham Notch Camp, in Crawford Notch State Park at the Willey House, and from other cooperators (inquire locally).

The A.T. passes along the border but does not enter the Presidential Range-Dry River Wilderness in the southern part of the section.

Supplies and Services

Gorham is 12 miles north of Pinkham Notch on N.H. 16 (P.O. 03581, phone, supermarket, laundromat, restaurants, bus stop, equipment). Nine miles south is Jackson (P.O. 03846, phone, basic supplies, restaurants, bus stop). Eight miles south of Jackson is North Conway, a large business center (supermarkets, specialty hiking equipment, hospital, cobbler, bus stop).

From the Trail crossing at U.S. 302, it is one mile north to the Willey House (phone, snacks), 3.7 miles north to Crawford Notch (information, lodging, hostel), and 10 miles north to Twin Mountain (P.O. 03595, phone, groceries, restaurants, bus stop). Bartlett is 13 miles south (P.O. 03812, phone, basic groceries, meals, bus stop). North Conway, via U.S. 302, is 12 miles south of Bartlett.

In an emergency, contact the New Hampshire State Police (603) 846-550) or (800) 852-3411, or AMC Pinkham Notch Camp (603) 466-2721.

Public Accommodations

The AMC maintains four huts in this section where lodging and family-style meals are available. The huts may be the only conveniently located shelter on the ridge. Reservations are usually necessary and may be made at any hut or by calling or writing the Reservations Secretary, Pinkham Notch Camp, (see "Important Addresses," page 301).

Pinkham Notch Camp: Extensive mountain facility located on N.H. 16 at north end of section; reservations required; meals served; information desk; hot drinks and snacks; packup room; phone; showers; accommodates 107.

Madison Springs Hut: At treeline, built on site of first AMC refuge, 7.1 miles from north end of section; reservations recommended; accommodates 50; ample water.

Lakes of the Clouds Hut: Above treeline 14.4 miles from north end of section; backpacker rates in refuge room; reservations strongly recommended; accommodates 90; water.

Mizpah Spring Hut: Built and maintained by AMC 5.9 miles from south end of section; reservations strongly recommended; accommodates 60; ample water.

Lodgings are also available in Gorham, Jackson, Bartlett, and at inns south of the Trail crossings at both U.S. 302 and N.H. 16.

Trail Description, North to South

Miles	Data
0.0	From N.H. 16, pass AMC Pinkham Notch Camp and follow Tuckerman Ravine Trail W for 250 ft. Turn right onto **Old Jackson Road** (trail) and ascend. The **Tuckerman Ravine Trail** continues ahead, ascending gradually 2.4 mi. to Hermit Lake Shelter and steeply through the ravine 4.8 mi. to Tuckerman Junction. From here, it is 0.5 mi. farther to the summit of Mt. Washington, where the trail meets the A.T., or 0.8 mi. across Bigelow Lawn on the Tuckerman Crossover to Lakes of the Clouds, where it also meets the A.T. The route to Lakes of the Clouds, eliminating the Northern Presidential Range, is recommended in bad weather but should be approached with caution.
1.4	In about 1 mi., near a brook, turn sharply left away from roadbed and climb steeply. The **Raymond Path** soon leads left, climbing SW across the mountainside to the Tuckerman Ravine Trail. After the A.T. crosses a brook, the **Nelson Crag Trail** leads left, ascending past Nelson Crag and continuing to the Mt. Washington Auto Road near the summit.
1.7	Cross **Auto Road** near its 2 mi. post, and follow **Madison Gulf Trail** with little elevational change, into Great Gulf Wilderness.
1.8	Side trail leads right 200 yds. to **Lowe's Bald Spot** (2,860 ft.).
2.2	Cross twin brooks.
3.7	The A.T. (Madison Gulf Trail) intersects the **Great Gulf Trail** and the A.T., Madison Gulf, and Great

Gulf trails coincide for a distance. They cross the West Branch of the Peabody River via a suspension bridge, go up a ridge, then down across Parapet Brook foot bridge (native log).

3.8 Cross **Parapet Brook.** One hundred ft. farther, Madison Trail (A.T.) turns left and the Great Gulf Trail goes to the right downstream and descends 2.6 miles to the Great Gulf trailhead on Rt. 16.

3.9 A.T. turns sharp left at intersection along the Madison Gulf Trail for 0.2 mile to its intersection with the **Osgood Cut-off.** From this junction, the Madison Gulf Trail climbs 2 mi. to Starlake Trail, which 0.2 miles farther rejoins the A.T. at Madison Hut. This route avoids ascending Mt. Madison by Osgood Ridge. The A.T. follows the Osgood Cutoff to its intersection with the Osgood Trail.

4.3 Reach the intersection of Osgood Cutoff with the **Osgood Trail**, where **Osgood Tentsite** is located. Spring on right is last sure water. Turn left onto Osgood Trail and ascend steeply.

5.5 Reach treeline on crest of Osgood Ridge. *For the next 12.7 mi., the Trail is almost entirely above treeline and should be attempted only in favorable weather.*

6.0 Cross first peak on Osgood Ridge.

6.2 Reach **Osgood Junction**. Here, the **Daniel Webster (Scout) Trail** descends right 3.5 mi. to Dolly Copp Campground. The **Parapet Trail** leads left and contours the S side of Mt. Madison. It is sheltered from winds, avoids the ascent of Mt. Madison, and leads to Madison Hut in 1.0 mi. The A.T. continues up the ridge on the Osgood Trail, passing over the second peak.

6.5 **Howker Ridge Trail** descends right (N) 4.4 mi. to Dolly Copp Road near Randolph.

6.7 Reach summit of **Mt. Madison** (5,363 ft.). The **Watson Path** descends right (N) via Valley Way 3.4 mi. to Appalachia parking lot on U.S. 2. The A.T. descends SW ridge of Mt. Madison.

7.1 Reach **AMC Madison Springs Hut**. Star Lake is 0.2 mi. S. Among the trails descending N, **Valley Way** reaches the **Valley Way Tentsite** and spring 0.6 mi. from hut, and the Appalachia parking lot on U.S. 2 in 3.5 mi. The **Air Line**, more scenic, descends in 3.8 mi. to Appalachia. From hut, A.T. follows the Gulfside Trail, crossing nearby Snyder Brook and ascending SW.

7.4 Air Line descends right 75 yds. and continues 3.3 mi. more to Appalachia parking lot. Two hundred ft. farther on the A.T. (Gulfside Trail), Air Line climbs left 0.8 mi. to the summit of Mt. Adams (5,798 ft.). The A.T. ascends gradually SW.

8.0 Reach **Thunderstorm Junction,** marked by a massive rock cairn more than 10 ft. high. From here, **Lowe's Path** ascends left 0.3 mi. to the summit of Mt. Adams and descends right 1.2 mi. to **Gray Knob** (cabin) and 4.5 mi. to U.S. 2 at Lowe's Service Station. Also from this junction, the **Spur Trail** descends N 1.1 mi. to **Crag Camp** (cabin) and the **Great Gully Trail** descends N into King Ravine. The A.T. continues on the Gulfside Trail, passing a grassy area in saddle between Mt. Adams on left and Mt. Sam Adams on right.

8.2 **Israel Ridge Path** leads left 0.4 mi. to summit of Mt. Adams.

8.4 Pass **Peabody Spring** (unreliable) in swampy

grass area on right. A few yards beyond, pass more reliable water at base of conspicuous boulder to right of Trail.

8.6 **Israel Ridge Path** descends right 0.9 mi. to **The Perch Shelter** and 4.4 mi. to Bowman on U.S. 2. The A.T. follows the narrow ridge between Castle Ravine on the right and Jefferson Ravine on the left with fine view of the latter.

9.4 In **Edmands Col,** the **Randolph Path** leads right 0.2 mi. to **Spaulding Spring** and descends 1.1 mi. to The Perch Shelter. To left, the **Edmands Col Cut-off** in 30 yds. passes **Gulfside Spring,** which seldom fails. The Trail continues across the E side of Mt. Jefferson.

9.5 **Jefferson Loop** diverges right from A.T., leading 0.3 mi. to the summit of Mt. Jefferson (5,715 ft.). From the summit, the **Caps Ridge Trail** descends W 2.4 mi. to Jefferson Notch Road. The A.T. continues along the E flank of the summit.

9.8 Reach junction where the **Six Husbands Trail** descends very steeply left (E) into Jefferson Ravine and Great Gulf Wilderness. A spring 100 yds. down this trail. The Six Husbands Trail also climbs right to the summit of Mt. Jefferson. The A.T. continues ahead.

10.0 On smooth, grassy plateau known as Monticello Lawn, Jefferson Loop enters from right, 0.3 mi. from the summit.

10.2 Pass the **Cornice Trail,** decending right. This trail and Caps Ridge Trail descend in 2.4 mi. to Jefferson Notch Road.

10.6 **Sphinx Trail** descends steeply left into Great Gulf Wilderness Area.

10.8 In the Clay-Jefferson Col, the **Mt. Clay Loop** leads left and passes over the summits of Mt. Clay (5,532 ft.). The graded Gulfside Trail (A.T.) avoids the summits and continues across the W side of the ridge.

10.9 Loop trail on right passes unreliable **Greenough Spring**.

11.4 Pass junction where **Jewell Trail** descends right 2.9 mi. to Marshfield Station. The A.T. descends slightly.

11.7 In the Clay-Washington Col, the Mt. Clay Loop comes in from left. Trail continues around the headwall, ascending gradually.

11.8 The **Westside Trail** diverges right, contouring around the summit of Mt. Washington and rejoining the A.T. (shortcut to Lakes of the Clouds). The A.T. ascends between the edge of the gulf and the Mt. Washington Cog Railway.

12.3 Reach junction where **Great Gulf Trail** descends steeply left into Great Gulf. A.T. turns right, crosses railway, and continues across side of Mt. Washington to junction with Trinity Heights Connector, which climbs left to summit (0.1 mi.).

12.9 Reach summit of **Mt. Washington** (6,288 ft.), the highest point on the A.T. N of Tennessee (the actual summit is S of the Summit House). From the summit, the Mt. Washington Auto Road descends E 8 mi. to the Glen House site on N.H. 16. The **Tuckerman Ravine Trail** descends E 4.1 mi. to Pinkham Notch Camp. From the summit, the A.T. descends on the **Crawford Path**, passing a stone horse corral and Gulfside Trail, then steeply down the SW side of Mt. Washington.

13.5 **Westside Trail** enters from right. Just beyond, the **Davis Path** leads left and follows the Montalban Ridge 14.4 mi. S to U.S. 302. The A.T. descends more gradually, passing between the two Lakes of the Clouds. Here, the **Camel Trail** to Boott Spur and the **Tuckerman Crossover** enter from left. (Both may be followed to Pinkham Notch Camp.)

14.4 Reach AMC **Lakes of the Clouds Hut.** From the hut, the **Ammonoosuc Ravine Trail** descends right 2.5 mi. to Marshfield Station, the base station of the Mt. Washington Cog Railway. The A.T. continues on the Crawford Path.

14.5 **Monroe Loop** diverges right and climbs the two sharp peaks of Mt. Monroe (5,385 ft.). The A.T. contours around the E side of the peak, passing the **Dry River Trail,** which descends left down the headwall of Oakes Gulf and into the Presidential-Dry River Wilderness.

15.1 Monroe Loop enters from right. The A.T. continues on the Crawford Path.

15.9 Pass just W of summit of Mt. Franklin (5,004 ft.), and descend quite steeply.

16.2 Pass spring.

16.4 Reach junction where the **Mt. Eisenhower Trail** descends left into Oakes Gulf and the Presidential-Dry River Wilderness. One hundred ft. farther, the **Edmands Path** descends right 2.9 mi. to Mt. Clinton Road. Beyond, the Mt. Eisenhower Loop diverges right. In pleasant weather, this loop is recommended for the views from the summit of **Mt. Eisenhower** (4,761 ft.) The A.T. skirts the E side of the summit through scrub growth (a better route in foul weather).

17.0 **Mt. Eisenhower Loop** enters from right.

17.5 Pass spring.

18.2 Reach junction where the A.T. turns left onto **Webster Cliff Trail**. The Crawford Path continues straight, descending 2.9 mi. to U.S. 302 at Crawford House. As an alternative to the A.T., follow the Crawford Path to U.S. 302, continue from Crawford House site, climbing W 1.4 mi. on Avalon Trail to A-Z Trail, which may be followed 3.7 mi. to Zealand Trail. Here, the alternate route turns left and rejoins the A.T. in 0.3 more mi. at Zealand Pond, just below Zealand Falls Hut.

18.3 Reach summit of **Mt. Pierce** (Mt. Clinton, 4,310 ft.). Descend through scrub and enter woods. Cross meadow-like summit of south peak of Mt. Pierce, and descend steeply through woods.

19.0 Reach AMC **Mizpah Spring Hut** and **Nauman Tentsite**. To left, **Mt. Clinton Trail** descends into Oakes Gulf and the Presidential Range-Dry River Wilderness Area (entry permit required). To right, **Mizpah Cut-off** descends 0.8 mi. to the Crawford Path and 1.8 mi. farther to U.S. 302 at the Crawford House site. The A.T. continues along wooded summit of the divide.

20.1 In open area, turn right where path ahead leads to outlook. The Trail passes through several scenic open meadows and then ascends through scrub and over ledges.

20.6 Reach summit of **Mt. Jackson** (4,052 ft.). The Jackson fork of the **Webster-Jackson Trail** descends right 2.7 mi. to U.S. 302 at the maintenance buildings of the N.H. Department of Highways, 0.4 mi. S of the Crawford House site. From the summit, the A.T. crosses three small humps and descends steeply. It then follows ridge and ascends gradually.

21.8 The Webster fork of the **Webster-Jackson Trail** descends right, joins the Jackson fork, and continues down to U.S. 302 in a total of 2.3 mi. The A.T. ascends slightly.

21.9 Reach summit of **Mt. Webster** (3,910 ft.). The Trail follows edge of **Webster Cliffs.**

23.1 Pass last viewpoint and begin steep and winding descent through hardwood forest.

24.8 Cross Saco River on bridge.

24.9 Reach U.S. 302 and end of section, 1 mi. S of the Willey House site in Crawford Notch State Park. **Dry River Campground** is 1.5 mi. left (S). To continue on Trail, cross highway and ascend on road to former Willey House Station.

Trail Description, South to North

Miles **Data**

0.0 Opposite road to former Willey House Station on U.S. 302 (1,277 ft.), 1 mi. S of the Willey House site in Crawford Notch State Park and 1.5 mi. N of Dry River Campground, A.T. follows the **Webster Cliff Trail** E. In 150 yds., cross Saco River on bridge. Ascend through hardwood forest and begin steep, winding climb.

1.8 Reach first viewpoint from **Webster Cliffs**. For the next 1.5 mi., route follows the edge of the cliffs.

3.0 Reach summit of **Mt. Webster** (3,910 ft.), and descend slightly.

3.1 The Webster fork of the **Webster-Jackson Trail**

descends left 2.3 mi. to U.S. 302 at the maintenance building of the N.H. Highway Department, 0.4 mi. S of the Crawford House site. The A.T. follows the ridge to a sharp ascent, crosses three small humps, and then ascends NE.

4.3 Reach summit of **Mt. Jackson** (4,052 ft.). The Jackson fork of the **Webster-Jackson Trail** descends left, joins the Webster fork, and continues down to U.S. 302 in a total of 2.7 mi. The A.T. descends over ledges and through woods and then passes through several meadows.

4.8 Where side trail to a nearby outlook diverges right, the A.T. turns left and continues along wooded ridge.

5.9 Reach AMC **Mizpah Spring Hut** and **Nauman Tentsite**. To right, **Mt. Clinton Trail** descends into Oakes Gulf and the Presidential Range-Dry River Wilderness. To left, **Mizpah Cut-off** descends 0.8 mi. to the Crawford Path and 1.8 mi. more to U.S. 302 at the Crawford House site. The A.T. continues on the Webster Cliff Trail, climbing steeply through woods beyond hut to the alpine summit of the south peak of Mt. Pierce. The Trail then reenters woods and ascends through scrub.

6.6 Reach summit of **Mt. Pierce** (Mt. Clinton, 4,310 ft.). From the summit, the route is mostly above treeline for the next 12.7 mi. and should be attempted only in favorable weather. Continue straight ahead.

6.7 Reach junction where the Webster Cliff Trail ends and the A.T. continues NE along the ridge on the **Crawford Path**. It is 2.9 mi. W via the Crawford Path to U.S. 302 at the Crawford House site.

7.4 Pass spring.

7.8 **Mt. Eisenhower Loop** diverges left. In pleasant weather, this loop is recommended for the fine views from the summit of **Mt. Eisenhower** (4,761 ft.). The A.T., on the Crawford Path, skirts the summit through scrub growth (a better route in foul weather).

8.4 Reach junction where northern end of the Mt. Eisenhower Loop enters from left. Beyond, the **Edmands Path** descends left 2.9 mi. to Mt. Clinton Road. One hundred ft. farther, the **Mt. Eisenhower Trail** descends right into Oakes Gulf and the Presidential Range-Dry River Wilderness Area. The A.T. continues along the ridge.

8.7 Pass good spring and climb quite steeply.

9.0 Pass just W of summit of **Mt. Franklin** (5,004 ft.) and continue on Crawford Path with views on right into Oakes Gulf.

9.8 The **Monroe Loop** diverges left and climbs the two sharp peaks of Mt. Monroe (5,385 ft.). The A.T. contours around the E side of the peak, passing the **Dry River Trail**, which descends right down the headwall of Oakes Gulf and into the Presidential Range-Dry River Wilderness.

10.4 Monroe Loop enters from left.

10.5 Reach AMC **Lakes of the Clouds Hut**. From the hut, the **Ammonoosuc Ravine Trail** descends left 2.5 mi. to Marshfield Station, the base station of the Mt. Washington Cog Railway. The A.T. continues NE on the Crawford Path between the two Lakes of the Clouds, passing the junction where the **Camel Trail** to Boott Spur and the **Tuckerman Crossover** diverge right. The Tuckerman

Crossover leads 0.8 mi. E across Bigelow Lawn, the flat area S of the cone of Mt. Washington, to Tuckerman Junction. From Tuckerman Junction, the Tuckerman Ravine Trail descends E, (steep and treacherous) 1.2 mi. to Hermit Lake Shelter and 2.4 mi. farther to AMC Pinkham Notch Camp, to rejoin the A.T. This route, eliminating the the northern Presidential Range, is recommended in bad weather but should be approached with caution. From Lakes of the Clouds, the A.T. continues N, crossing the W side of Bigelow Lawn.

11.4 Reach junction where the **Davis Path** leads right and follows the Montalban Ridge 14.4 mi. S to U.S. 302. Just beyond, the **Westside Trail** contours left 0.9 mi. around the W side of the cone of Mt. Washington and rejoins the A.T. N of the summit. The A.T. climbs the steep cone of Mt. Washington, passing the old stone horse corral and Gulfside Trail (leading left).

12.0 Reach summit of **Mt. Washington** (6,288 ft.), the highest point on the Appalachian Trail N of Tennessee (the actual summit is just S of the Summit House). From the summit, the Mt. Washington Auto Road descends E 8 mi. to the Glen House site on N.H. 16. Also, the Tuckerman Ravine Trail descends E 4.1 mi. to Pinkham Notch Camp on N.H. 16 and there rejoins the A.T. From the summit, descend via the Trinity Heights Connector (0.1 mi.) to the Gulfside Trail, which A.T. then follows N.

12.6 Just after crossing the cog railway, reach junction where the A.T. turns sharp left to continue on the Gulfside Trail. Ahead, the **Great Gulf Trail** descends steeply into the Great Gulf Wilderness.

13.1 The Westside Trail enters from left. The A.T. descends into Clay-Washington Col.

13.2 **Mt. Clay Loop** diverges right, passing over the summits of Mt. Clay (5,532 ft.). The A.T. continues along the ridge on the W side of the summits.

13.5 Pass junction where **Jewell Trail** descends left 2.9 mi. to Marshfield Station.

14.0 Loop trail leads left to unreliable **Greenough Spring.**

14.2 In the Clay-Jefferson Col, the **Mt. Clay Loop** comes in from the right. A.T. ascends N gradually.

14.3 The **Sphinx Trail** descends steeply right into Great Gulf Wilderness.

14.8 The **Cornice Trail** descends left, crossing the Caps Ridge Trail (the Caps Ridge Trail may be descended to Jefferson Notch Road) and then contours N to the Castellated Ridge. The A.T. continues along the ridge.

14.9 On smooth, grassy plateau known as Monticello Lawn, **Jefferson Loop** leads left over the summit of Mt. Jefferson (5,715 ft.). From the summit, the **Caps Ridge Trail** descends W 2.4 mi. to the Jefferson Notch Road. The A.T. goes around the E side of Mt. Jefferson, passing the **Six Husbands Trail**, which descends steeply E into Great Gulf Wilderness (100 yds. down this trail is a spring), and ascends W to the summit of Mt. Jefferson.

15.5 Descend past N end of Jefferson Loop. Beyond, reach **Edmands Col,** which has a bronze memorial tablet to J. Reynor Edmands, who made most of the graded paths in the northem Presidentials. The **Randolph Path** leads left 0.2 mi. to **Spaulding Spring** and descends 1.1 mi. to **The Perch Shel-**

ter. To right, the **Edmands Col Cut-off** in 30 yds. passes Gulfside Spring, which seldom fails. From the col, the A.T. ascends on narrow ridge between Castle Ravine on left and Jefferson Ravine on right, with fine views of the latter.

16.4 **Israel Ridge Path** descends left 0.9 mi. to **The Perch Shelter** and 4.4 mi. to Rowman on U.S. 2.

16.5 Water is usually found at the base of a conspicuous boulder to left of Trail. A few yards beyond, the less reliable **Peabody Spring** is on left, in a swampy, grassy area.

16.8 Israel Ridge Path diverges on right, leading 0.4 mi. to summit of Mt. Adams (5,798 ft.). The A.T. passes a grassy area in the saddle between Mt. Sam Adams on left and Mt. Adams on right.

16.9 Reach **Thunderstorm Junction,** marked by a massive rock cairn more than 10 ft. high. From here, **Lowe's Path** ascends right 0.3 mi. to the summit of Mt. Adams and descends left 1.2 mi. to **Gray Knob** (cabin) and 4.5 mi. to U.S. 2 at Lowe's Service Station. Also from this junction, the **Spur Trail** descends N 1.1 mi. to **Crag Camp** (cabin), and the **Great Gully Trail** descends N into King Ravine. The A.T. continues on the Gulfside Trail, descending gradually NE.

17.5 The **Air Line** (trail) climbs right 0.8 mi. to the summit of Mt. Adams. Beyond, the Air Line descends left 3.3 mi. to Appalachia parking lot on U.S. 2.

17.8 Cross Snyder Brook and reach AMC **Madison Springs Hut**. Among the numerous trails descending N, the **Valley Way** reaches the **Valley Way Tentsite** and spring 0.6 mi. from hut and the

Appalachia parking lot on U.S. 2 in 3.5 mi. Ascending S, the **Parapet Trail** passes by Star Lake, contours around the S side of Mt. Madison, and rejoins the A.T. in 1.0 mi. This trail is sheltered from NW winds and avoids the ascent of Mt. Madison (a better choice in foul weather). Starting at Star Lake, the **Madison Gulf Trail** descends into Great Gulf Wilderness and rejoins the A.T. in approximately 2 mi., a route avoiding Osgood Ridge. From Madison Hut, the A.T. climbs the steep SW ridge of Mt. Madison.

18.2 Reach summit of **Mt. Madison** (5,363 ft.). The **Watson Path** descends left (N) 1 mi. to the Valley Way, which leads 2.1 mi. to Appalachia parking lot. The A.T. descends along the crest of the E ridge on the Osgood Trail.

18.5 **Howker Ridge Trail** descends left 4.4 mi. N to Dolly Copp Road near Randolph. The A.T. continues on the ridgecrest on the Osgood Trail, SE.

18.7 Reach **Osgood Junction.** Here, the Parapet Trail comes in on the right from Madison Hut, and the **Daniel Webster (Scout) Trail** descends 3.5 mi. left (E) to Dolly Copp Campground. Descend on Osgood Ridge on **Osgood Trail** crossing small peak.

19.4 Enter woods, and continue steep descent.

20.6 At the junction of the **Osgood Trail** and **Osgood Cut-off** is the Osgood Tentsite and spring. Turn right onto Osgood Cut-off and descend to Great Gulf Wilderness. A spring is on left at boulder. Ahead, the Osgood Trail continues approximately 0.8 mi. to the Great Gulf Trail, which continues 1.8 miles to the Great Gulf trailhead on Rt. 16.

21.0 **Madison Gulf Trail** enters from right. A.T. continues left on Madison Gulf Trail and descends ridge.

21.1 Great Gulf Trail enters from left and coincides with Madison Gulf Trail. Descend ridge and cross the Parapet Brook foot bridge (native log), then over a ridge. Cross over the West Branch of Peabody River via a suspension bridge. After bridge, the A.T. turns left on Madison Gulf Trail and the Great Gulf Trail turns right upstream.

22.7 Cross twin brooks.

23.1 A short side trail leads left 200 yd. to **Lowe's Bald Spot** (2,860 ft.), a rocky knob with view of the Northern Presidentials and the Carter-Moriah Range. A.T. continues S with little elevational change, leaving Great Gulf Wilderness.

23.2 Cross **Mt. Washington Auto Road**. A.T. now follows the **Old Jackson Road** (trail). Pass through an old gravel pit, and enter woods.

23.4 **Nelson Crag Trail** leads right, ascends past Nelson Crag, and continues to the Auto Road. Beyond, after the A.T. crosses a brook, the **Raymond Path** leads right, climbing SW across the mountainside to the Tuckerman Ravine Trail. The A.T. drops steeply and then turns sharp right onto the roadbed of the abandoned Jackson Road. It follows this road, descending gradually, passing several old roads.

24.9 Turn left onto the Tuckerman Ravine Trail, and reach AMC **Pinkham Notch Camp** on N.H. 16.To continue on the Trail, cross the highway and follow the Lost Pond Trail.

Crawford Notch (U.S. 302) to Franconia Notch (U.S. 3)

Section 4 New Hampshire

27.3 Miles

Brief Description of Section

Crossing the Willey Range, and Zealand, Garfield, and Franconia ridges, this is the longest section of uninterrupted footpath on the A.T. in New Hampshire or Vermont. The A.T. traces a route partly through dense hardwood and coniferous forests and partly across high ridges and summits.

Most of the Trail lies along the edges of the Pemigewasset Wilderness. Beginning on the Ethan Pond Trail, the A.T. climbs steeply from the floor of Crawford Notch (1,277 feet), crosses a low point in the Willey Range (2,907 feet), passes Ethan Pond and Thoreau Falls, and follows an old logging railroad bed through Zealand Notch. Ascending Zealand Ridge, north of the Pemigewasset Wilderness on the Twinway (trail), it continues, always high on the ridge on the north, then west, sides of the Pemigewasset area, on Garfield Ridge Trail and Franconia Ridge Trail. For two miles on the sometimes narrow and precipitous Franconia Ridge, the Trail passes above treeline, providing a vista from the summit of Mt. Lafayette (5,249 feet), the highest peak in this section. The Trail descends from Franconia Ridge on Liberty Spring Trail into Franconia Notch State Park to U.S. 3 (1,450 feet). Water is scarce on the ridgecrests.

Franconia Ridge is exposed to the full force of storms, which rise rapidly and violently, producing winds of hurricane-force and freezing conditions, even in summer. Carry extra clothing, and if weather becomes threatening promptly descend to shelter by the shortest route.

This section is within White Mountain National Forest (WMNF) except the southern end, which lies within Franconia Notch State Park, and the northern end, which lies in Crawford Notch State Park.

This section has numerous steep ascents and descents at the section ends and on a number of peaks. The Trail passes over major peaks, which are, from north to south:

Mt. Guyot, 4,560 feet
South Twin Mountain, 4,902 feet
Mt. Garfield, 4,488 feet
Mt. Lafayette, 5,249 feet
Mt. Lincoln, 5,089 feet
Little Haystack Mountain, approximately 4,760 feet
Mt. Liberty, 4,459 feet (on short side trail)

Treeline on Franconia Ridge occurs at approximately 4,200 feet. Above this altitude, only stunted *krummholz* (spruce) and a wealth of alpine species prevail against the severe weather. This vegetation is extremely vulnerable to damage by foot traffic. In many places the obliteration of the alpine tundra has given way to erosion, visibly scarring the mountainside. To prevent trampling vegetation, and to allow successful regeneration of damaged areas, rock steps and low stone walls have been installed in many places. Hikers are urged to closely follow the established treadway in order to keep the impact of their passage to a minimum.

The extensive system of side trails in this section gives the hiker a variety of possibilities for loop hikes, side trips, and alternate routes to the A.T. Most side trails are briefly noted in the trail description, but, for complete information, consult the *AMC White Mountain Guide*. This guide and current Trail information are available from the AMC, Pinkham Notch Camp (see "Important Addresses," page 301).

The Pemigewasset Wilderness

In this section, the A.T. passes through the valley and along the ridges making up the western and northern edges of the Pemigewasset Wilderness, an 18,560-acre tract of undeveloped mountain land where the forests were once extensively logged. Although much of the timber was clear-cut around the turn of the century, the tract is now completely reforested. In 1969, the USFS established much of this tract as the Lincoln Woods Scenic Area. It became a congressionally approved wilderness area in 1986.

Logging began before 1900 and continued until just after World War II. On a clear day, hikers can see south from Zealand, Garfield, and Franconia ridges into a densely forested landscape that was once a clear-cut area. The most striking evidence of the logging past is the striated appearance of the forest where logging roads once cut across the mountainside. In Zealand Notch, the hiker walks along the bed of the former Zealand Valley Railroad, which was used to transport timber out of the notch before 1900. This was the first part of the wilderness to be cut.

Most of the timber logged in the White Mountains, including Zealand Notch and the "Pemi", was removed by one of 17 railroads. The Lincoln and East Branch Railroad (now the Kancamagus Highway), leading from Lincoln northeast into the wilderness, was the largest, composed of more than 60 miles of track. The Zealand branch was known as the steepest and most crooked in New England. Like the A.T. in Zealand Notch, many trails in the wilderness follow former railroad rights-of-way. Relics of the logging and railroad history are still found in the the forest.

During the logging years, forest fires swept the "Pemi" and left marks visible today. In 1903, the Zealand Notch area burned. In 1907, a fire ravaged much of the "Pemi," burning the Zealand and Garfield ridges on which the A.T. now passes. Mt. Guyot and Mt. Garfield, now open summits, were both wooded until fire burned their forest cover. The forest is still in the succession stage of regrowth.

Franconia Notch State Park

This park was established to protect the area's spectacular natural features and geologic curiosities. The Basin, located one mile north of the Trail crossing at the bottom of Basin-Cascades Trail, is a glacial pothole, 20 feet in diameter, carved in granite at the base of a waterfall some 25,000 years ago. The Old Man of the Mountains, a 40-foot stone profile of a man's face formed by five separate ledges of Cannon Cliff, stands 1,200 feet above Profile Lake. It can be viewed best from Profile Clearing, 4.9 miles north of the Trail crossing on U.S. 3. Just north of the clearing is the aerial tramway to the summit of Cannon Mountain.

The Flume, 0.9 mile south of the Trail crossing, is a natural chasm 800 feet long, with granite walls 6,070 feet high and 12 to 20 feet wide, viewed from boardwalks within the gorge itself (fee charged).

Road Approaches

Both the north and south ends of this section are accessible from major highways. At the north end, the Trail crosses U.S. 302 in Crawford Notch opposite Willey House Station

Road, eight miles north of Bartlett and nine miles south of Bretton Woods. Southbound hikers should leave their cars at the end of the Willey House Station Road (ample parking) 0.3 miles west of U.S. 302.

At the south end of the section, the Trail crosses U.S. 3 at Whitehouse Bridge, 5.8 miles north of North Woodstock and 10.2 miles south of Franconia. A parking lot is just north of the New Hampshire State Park Flume Complex, with access to the A.T. via the one-mile long Whitehouse Trail.

Theft and vandalism have occurred at these locations. Do not leave valuables in cars.

Maps

Map No. 3 (this guide)
AMC Franconia Map
White Mountain National Forest Map (1:250,000)
Franconia Notch State Park Map
USGS 15 minute topographic quadrangle:
Crawford Notch, N.H.
USGS 7 1/2 minute topographic quadrangles:
South Twin Mountain, N.H.
Franconia, N.H.
Lincoln, N.H.

Shelters and Campsites

Three campsites, one shelter, and two tentsite are located in this section, and two public campgrounds.

Dry River Campground: In Crawford Notch State Park on U.S. 302 1.5 miles south of Trail crossing; 24 tentsites; ample water.

Next shelter or campsite: north 5.9 miles (Nauman Tentsite); south 3.5 miles.

Ethan Pond Campsite: Built and maintained by AMC at Ethan Pond 3.5 miles from north end of section, on short side trail; accommodates 10; also 5 tent platforms, accommodates 28; caretaker, $3.00 fee; water from brook by site.

Next shelter or campsite: north 3.5 miles; south 8.1 miles.

Guyot Campsite: Shelter rebuilt 1977 and maintained by AMC 11.6 miles from north end of section, on side trail approx. 0.7 mile from A.T.; accommodates 12; also 6 tent plafforms, accommodates 24; caretaker in residence; $3.00 fee charged; water from spring at site.

Next shelter or campsite: north 8.1 miles; south 5.1 miles.

13 Falls Tentsite: Maintained by AMC. 10.6 miles from south end of section, on 1.2 side trail; caretaker; fee charged; water on site.

Next shelter or campsite: north 5.1 miles; south 0.5 mile.

Garfield Ridge Campsite: Shelter rebuilt 1970 and maintained by AMC 10.1 miles from south end of section, 0.1 mile up side trail; accommodates 12; also 6 tent platforms, accommodates 24; caretaker in residence; $3.00 fee charged; water from spring on A.T.

Next shelter or campsite: north 0.5 mile; south 7.4 miles.

Liberty Spring Tentsite: Built and maintained by AMC (no shelter) 2.5 miles from south end of section; 11 tent platforms; accommodates 42; caretaker in residence; $3.00 fee charged; water from spring at site.

Next shelter or campsite: north 7.4 miles; south 2.4 miles.

Lafayette Campground: Operated and maintained by New Hampshire Division of Parks in Franconia Notch State Park approximately 2.5 miles north of Trail crossing on U.S. 3; 98 tentsites; fee charged; limited provisions, showers, phone; ample water.

Next shelter or campsite: north 2.4 miles; south 4.6 miles (Kinsman Campsite).

The three AMC mountain huts in this section are described under "Public Accommodation."

Regulations

The northern 2.5 miles of this section lie in Crawford Notch State Park; the last southern mile, in Franconia Notch State Park. Camping and fires are prohibited in these parks except at the two campgrounds.

The rest of the Trail in this section lies within the WMNF. Camping and wood or charcoal fires are prohibited above treeline because of the fragility of this area. Treeline is defined as an area where trees are less than eight feet tall. This includes parts of the Franconia Range.

Camping and wood or charcoal fires are prohibited within one-quarter mile of Zealand Falls Hut, Mt. Guyot Campsite, Galehead Hut, Garfield Ridge Campsite, or Liberty Springs Campsite, except at designated areas. Camping and wood or charcoal fires are prohibited within 200 feet of the A.T. from Galehead Hut to Liberty Springs Tentsite or on Liberty Springs Trail to state park lands.

Supplies and Services

From the Trail crossing at U.S. 302, at the northern end of

the section, it is one mile north to the Willey House (phone, snacks), 3.7 miles north to Crawford Notch (information, lodging, hostel), and ten miles north to Twin Mountain (P.O. 03595, phone, groceries, restaurants, bus stop). Bartlett is 13 miles south (P.O. 03812, phone, basic groceries, meals, bus stop). Twelve miles south of Bartlett is North Conway (full services, specialty hiking stores, cobbler, hospital).

From the Trail crossing at U.S. 3, at the southern end of the section, it is approximately 2.5 miles north to Lafayette Campground (limited provisions, showers, phone), 4.9 miles to Franconia Notch State Park headquarters (aerial tramway, phone, snacks, souvenirs, bus stop), 10.2 miles to Franconia (P.O. 03580, restaurants, supermarket, laundromat, phone, equipment, bus stop), and 20 miles to Littleton (full services, hospital, cobbler, bus stop). Also from the Trail crossing on U.S. 3, it is 0.8 miles south to Flume Store (snacks, phone, souvenirs, bus stop), 5.8 miles to North Woodstock (P.O. 03262, phone, supermarket, restaurants, specialty backpacking store, laundromat, bus stop), and 6.8 miles to Lincoln (P.O. 03251, groceries, laundromat, phone, Linwood Medical Center).

In an emergency, contact any AMC hut or shelter caretaker or the New Hampshire State Police, (603) 846-5500 or (800) 852-3411.

Public Accommodations

At the three AMC huts located in this section, lodging and family-style meals are available. Reservations are necessary and may be made at any AMC hut or by calling or writing the Reservations Secretary, Pinkham Notch Camp (see "Important Addresses," page 301).

Zealand Falls Hut: Built and maintained by AMC 7.6 miles from north end of section; reservations strongly recommended; accommodates 36; ample water.

Galehead Hut: Built and maintained by AMC in center of section; reservations strongly recommended; accommodates 38; ample water.

Greenleaf Hut: Built and maintained by AMC at treeline 6.3 mi. from S end of section; 1.1 miles down side trail; reservations strongly recommended; accommodates 36; ample water.

From the Trail crossing at U.S. 3, it is 10.2 miles north to Franconia (motels, cabins), 1.6 miles south to a roadway lined with motels and cabins, and 5.8 miiles south to North Woodstock (motels, guest house). Lodging is also available south of the Trail crossing on U.S. 302 and Bartlett.

Trail Description, North to South

Miles	Data
0.0	From U.S. 302 in Crawford Notch, proceed uphill on Willey House Station Road. **Dry River Campground** is 1.5 mi. S on U.S. 302 in Crawford Notch State Park. Ascend path at right of parking area for 50 yds., cross railroad tracks, and follow **Ethan Pond Trail,** ascending steeply through woods.
0.5	Pass **Arethusa-Ripley Falls Trail,** leading left 0.4 mi. to Ripley Falls, 2.5 mi. to Arethusa Falls, and 3.8 mi. back to U.S. 302. For the next half-mile the Trail ascends steeply and then more gradually.
1.6	Pass **Kedron Flume Trail,** which descends very steeply right (NE) to Willey House on U.S. 302.
1.9	Reach junction. A.T. turns left onto the **Ethan Pond Trail** and ascends. Ahead, the **Willey Range Trail** leads across Kedron Brook and ascends 1.0 mi. to Mt. Willey and 2.3 mi. to Mt. Field, where it may be followed to the A-Z Trail or Avalon Trail.
2.2	Reach height of land and descend, entering old logging road.
3.5	Side trail leads right 200 yds., past Ethan Pond, to **Ethan Pond Campsite**. The A.T. continues on level terrain.
4.3	Cross brook.
4.4	Reach junction where E fork of **Shoal Pond Trail** goes left; in 0.4 mi., the W fork goes left. This trail leads S 0.8 mi. to Shoal Pond and continues to Stillwater Junction in the Pemigewasset Wilderness.
5.1	Bear right, cross North Fork on wood-span bridge, and turn left downstream.

5.3 Reach junction where **Thoreau Falls Trail** leads left, passing the falls (camping prohibited) and continuing 5.1 mi. to Wilderness Trail, which leads in 6.5 mi. to the Kancamagus Highway. The A.T. follows an old railroad grade on gradual curve N into Zealand Notch, and then along the side of Whitewall Mountain.

6.1 Pass **Zeacliff Trail,** left across brook and climbing in 1.5 mi., to rejoin the A.T. at the top of Zeacliff. The A.T. continues along the side of Whitewall Mountain.

6.9 Cross brook.

7.4 Reach junction where Ethan Pond Trail ends and the A.T. turns left onto the Twinway, passing left of Zealand Pond, and ascends. To the right, **Zealand Trail** descends gradually 0.3 mi. to A-Z Trail (an alternate to the A.T. starting N on Mt. Pierce) and 2.5 mi. to Zealand Road (passable by car) 6.3 mi. from U.S. 302 at Zealand Campground.

7.6 Pass AMC **Zealand Falls Hut** and ascend.

7.7 The **Lend-a-Hand Trail** diverges right, ascending to Mt. Hale in 2.5 mi. From there, Hale Brook Trail descends 2.4 mi. to the Zealand Road leading to U.S. 302. Beyond the Lend-a-Hand junction, the A.T. crosses Whitewall Brook, ascends SW moderately through woods, and crosses another brook.

8.7 A 100-yd. side loop to the A.T. swings left to an E lookout at the edge of Zeacliff. The Trail turns W and follows ridge on level.

8.9 **Zeacliff Trail** enters from left.

9.2 Side trail descends left 0.1 mi. to **Zeacliff Pond**.

9.5 Pass view with Zeacliff Pond below and continue along Zealand Ridge.

10.4 Cross knob (an obscure side trail leads right to Zealand Mountain), descend into minor col, and ascend SW.

11.6 Reach open summit of **Mt. Guyot** (4,560 ft.). Beyond, the **Bondcliff Trail** leads left approximately 0.5 mi. to side trail descending left 0.2 mi. to **Guyot Campsite** (spring). From the shelter side trail, the Bondcliff Trail continues S 1.3 mi. to Mt. Bond, 2.8 mi. to Bondcliff, 6.0 mi. to the Wilderness Trail at Camp 16, and by this trail 5.0 mi. more to the Kancamagus Highway. At the junction with Bondcliff Trail, the A.T. follows the ridge NW.

13.7 Reach summit of **South Twin Mountain** (4,902 ft.). Just below the summit, turn left. The **North Twin Spur** leads right (N) 1.3 mi. to summit of North Twin. From there the **North Twin Trail** descends 7.5 mi. to U.S. 3, 2.3 mi. W of Twin Mountain. From South Twin Mountain the A.T. descends steeply W over rocky slope.

14.5 Reach junction where the Twinway ends and the A.T. continues ahead, descending through forest on the Garfield Ridge Trail. Fifty ft. to the left of this junction is AMC **Galehead Hut**.

15.1 **Gale River Trail** descends right 5.8 mi. to U.S. 3 at "Five Corners," opposite Trudeau Road. The A.T. follows wooded ridge.

15.4 Pass outlook on knob (3,590 ft.), descend into col, and continue along ridge.

16.7 Reach junction where **Franconia Brook Trail** descends left (S) 1.2 mi. to **13 Falls Tentsite**, 5.0 mi. to the Wilderness Trail, which leads 2.8 mi. more through the Pemigewasset Wilderness to the Kancamagus Highway. The A.T. descends to col and then ascends steeply.

17.2 Reach junction where side trail leads right 0.1 mi. to **Garfield Ridge Campsite** (shelter) with water from spring at this junction. A.T. ascends steeply.

17.4 **Garfield Trail** descends right 5.6 mi. to U.S. 3 at Gale River. The A.T. continues to ascend steeply.

17.5 Pass point 150 ft. N of the summit of **Mt. Garfield** (4,488 ft.). Descend steeply W on the cone of Mt. Garfield, pass to left of Garfield Pond, and continue along Garfield Ridge.

18.4 Pass through swampy col.

19.4 In col, water may be found in woods to right. Begin climb of Mt. Lafayette.

20.1 Pass treeline and continue ascent. The next 2 mi. are narrow, above treeline, and should be hiked only in favorable weather.

20.3 **Skookumchuck Trail** descends right (W) 3.6 mi. to junction of U.S. 3 and Interstate 93. The A.T. continues up rocky ridge.

20.6 Pass over **North Peak of Mt. Lafayette.**

21.0 Reach summit of **Mt. Lafayette** (5,249 ft.). Remains of the summit-house foundation are just below summit. The **Greenleaf Trail** descends right (W) 300 yds. to a spring, 1.1 mi. to AMC **Greenleaf Hut**, and 3.3 mi. to U.S. 3 at Profile Clearing. From Greenleaf Hut, one can descend on the bridle path to **Lafayette Campground** on U.S. 3. From the Lafayette summit, A.T. descends S, passing over a minor summit in a half-mile.

22.0 Pass over the summit of **Mt. Lincoln** (5,089 ft.). Beyond, the drop on each side of the ridge is precipitous, and the Trail passes many rocky points.

22.7 Pass over the summit of **Little Haystack Moun-**

tain (approximately 4,760 ft.). From here, **Falling Waters Trail** descends right 2.8 mi. to **Lafayette Campground** on U.S. 3. Enter woods and descend steeply over rough ledges.

24.5 Reach junction where the A.T. turns right onto the **Liberty Spring Trail** and descends steeply. Ahead, the **Franconia Ridge Trail** continues S 0.3 mi. to the summit of Mt. Liberty (4,459 ft.), 1.4 mi. to the summit of Mt. Flume, and 1.5 mi. to Flume Slide Trail. Here, the Osseo Trail begins and descends S along the ridge, via Osseo Peak, 5.3 mi. to the Kancamagus Highway E of Lincoln.

24.8 Pass **Liberty Spring Campsite** with spring just off Trail to left. Descend steeply through evergreens and then hardwoods.

26.3 Cross brook and, within 0.3 mi., two more brooks.

26.6 At trail junction, Flume Slide Trail leads left 3.8 mi. to the summit of Mt. Flume. The A.T. continues its descent.

27.3 Cross two small brooks. Section ends where paved bike trail intersects Liberty Spring Trail. To continue on A.T., turn left onto bike trail, cross creek on steel bridge, turn right under U.S. 3 and onto Cascade Brook Trail. To reach Flume Complex, follow bike path in other direction to Whitehouse Trail.

Trail Description, South to North

Miles **Data**

0.0 From intersection of paved bike path and **Liberty Spring Trail**, near U.S. 3, enter woods on Liberty

Spring Trail. Cross two small brooks. Trail soon follows an old logging road.

0.4 At trail junction, **Flume Slide Trail** leads right 3.8 mi. to the summit of Mt. Flume. The A.T. ascends steadily straight ahead.

0.7 Cross brook and, within the next 0.3 mi., two more brooks. Trail climbs with increasing steepness.

2.4 Pass **Liberty Spring Campsite** with spring just off Trail to right. Ascend steeply.

2.7 Reach **Franconia Ridge**. The A.T. turns N (left) onto **Franconia Ridge Trail** and ascends gradually, then steeply, over rough ledges. South (right) on this trail, it is 0.3 mi. to the summit of Mt. Liberty, 1.4 mi. to Mt. Flume, and 1.5 mi. to the upper end of Flume Slide Trail. Here, the Osseo Trail begins and descends S on the ridge, via Osseo Peak, 5.3 mi. to the Kancamagus Highway E of Lincoln.

4.6 Reach **Little Haystack Mountain** (approximately 4,760 ft.). **Falling Waters Trail** descends left 2.8 mi. to **Lafayette Campground** on U.S. 3. A.T. continues ahead. For the next 2 mi., the ridge is narrow and above treeline and should be traversed only in favorable weather.

5.3 Pass over the summit of **Mt. Lincoln** (5,089 ft.) and another minor peak in 0.4 mi., and steeply ascend the rocky cone of Mt. Lafayette.

6.3 Reach summit of **Mt. Lafayette** (5,249 ft.). Remains of the summit-house foundation are just below summit. The **Greenleaf Trail** descends left (W) 300 yds. to a spring, 1.1 mi. to AMC **Greenleaf Hut** and U.S. 3 at Profile Clearing. From Greenleaf Hut one may descend on the bridle path 2.5 mi. to **Lafayette Campground** on U.S. 3.

From the summit, the A.T. descends N on **Garfield Ridge Trail.**

6.7 Pass over **North Peak of Mt. Lafayette** and descend steeply.

7.0 **Skookumchuck Trail** descends left (W) 3.6 mi. to the junction of U.S. 3 and I-93. A.T. descends NE.

7.2 The A.T. passes treeline and descends along ridge.

7.9 In col, water may be found under moss in stream bed about 150 yds. to left. The A.T. continues NE along Garfield Ridge.

8.8 Cross swampy col. Pass to right of Garfield Pond and ascend steeply E.

9.7 Pass 150 ft. N of the summit of **Mt. Garfield** (4,488 ft.), to foundation remains of firetower. Descend NE side of the cone of Mt. Garfield.

10.0 Reach junction where the **Garfield Trail** descends left 5.6 mi. to U.S. 3 at Gale River. The A.T. descends steeply E.

10.1 Reach junction where side trail leads left 0.1 mi. to **Garfield Ridge Campsite** (shelter) with water from spring at this junction. The Trail descends into col.

10.6 Reach junction where **Franconia Brook Trail** descends S (right) 1.2 mi. to **13 Falls Tentsite,** 5.0 mi. to the Wilderness Trail, which leads 2.8 mi. through the Pemigewasset Wilderness to Kancamagus Highway. A.T. continues straight, ascending along ridge.

11.6 Pass through col marking the end of Garfield Ridge. Continue along wooded ridge, passing outlook on knob (3,590 ft.).

12.2 **Gale River Trail** descends left 5.8 mi. to U.S. 3 at "Five Corners," opposite Trudeau Road to Bethlehem Junction. A.T. ascends SE through forest.

12.8 **Garfield Ridge Trail** ends, and the A.T. continues ahead, climbing steeply E on the Twinway. Fifty ft. to the right of this junction is the AMC **Galehead Hut.**

13.6 Just short of **South Twin Mountain** summit (4,902 ft.), the **North Twin Spur** leads left (N) 1.3 mi. to North Twin summit. From here, the**North Twin Trail** descends 7.5 mi. to U.S. 3, 2.3 mi. W of Twin Mountain. A.T. continues on the Twinway, descending SE from South Twin Mountain following the ridge.

15.6 Reach junction where **Bondcliff Trail** leads right approximately 0.5 mi. to side trail descending left approximately 0.2 mi. to **Guyot Shelter** (spring). From the shelter side trail, the Bondcliff Trail continues S 1.3 mi. to Mt. Bond, 2.8 mi. to Bondcliff, 6.0 mi. to Wilderness Trail at Camp 16, which leads 5.0 mi. to Kancamagus Highway. At the junction with Bondcliff Trail, the A.T. turns left, crosses the open summit of **Mt. Guyot** (4,560 ft.), and descends its NE ridge.

16.6 Pass through minor col, ascend to knob (an obscure side trail leads left to Zealand Mountain), and continue along Zealand Ridge.

17.8 Pass viewpoint with nearby Zeacliff Pond below.

18.1 Side trail descends right 0.1 mi. to **Zeacliff Pond**, and A.T. continues E on ridge.

18.4 Reach junction where **Zeacliff Trail** descends right very steeply 1.5 mi. and rejoins the A.T. on the Ethan Pond Trail.

18.6 A 100-yd. side loop to the A.T. leads right to E lookout at the edge of **Zeacliff**. The Trail turns NW, descends steeply through woods, crosses a brook, and continues through woods.

19.5 Cross Whitewall Brook. Two hundred ft. beyond, the **Lend-a-Hand Trail** leaves left, ascending to Mt. Hale in 2.5 mi. From there, Hale Brook Trail descends 2.4 mi. to the Zealand Road, to U.S. 302.

19.7 Pass AMC **Zealand Falls Hut** and descend E, passing to right of **Zealand Pond.**

19.9 Reach junction where Twinway ends and the A.T. turns right onto **Ethan Pond Trail**. The **Zealand Trail** continues left 0.3 mi. to A-Z Trail and 2.5 mi. to Zealand Road (passable by automobile), 6.3 mi. from U.S. 302 at Zealand Campground. An alternate to the A.T., the A-Z Trail may be followed right (E) from the Zealand Trail 3.7 mi. to the Avalon Trail, which may be followed 1.4 mi. to U.S. 302. From here, the Crawford Path may be ascended 2.9 mi. to Mt. Pierce to rejoin the A.T. on the Presidential Range. From the end of the Twinway, continue on the Ethan Pond Trail along old railroad grade on side of Whitewall Mountain.

20.4 Cross brook.

21.2 Lower end of the **Zeacliff Trail** enters from right. The A.T. makes a gradual curve eastward around the end of Whitewall Mountain.

22.0 Reach junction where **Thoreau Falls Trail** leads right, pass falls (camping prohibited) and continuing 5.1 mi. to **Wilderness Trail**, which leads 6.5 mi. to Kancamagus Highway.

22.2 Cross the North Fork on wood-span bridge and bear left on old logging road.

22.5 Reach junction where W fork of **Shoal Pond Trail** turns right; in 0.4 mi., E fork turns right. This trail leads S 0.8 mi. to Shoal Pond and to Stillwater Junction in the **Pemigewasset Wilderness.**

23.0 Cross brook.

23.8 Side trail leads left 200 yds., past Ethan Pond, to **Ethan Pond Campsite**. The A.T. ascends gradually.

25.1 Reach height of land and descend.

25.4 Reach junction where **Willey Range Trail** leads briefly left across Kedron Brook and then ascends 1.0 mi. to Mt. Willey and 2.3 mi. to Mt. Field, from which it may be followed to the A-Z Trail or Avalon Trail. The A.T. bears right, descending on the Ethan Pond Trail.

25.7 **Kedron Flume Trail** descends steeply L (NE) 1.3 mi. to Willey House (food, drink, phone, bus) on U.S. 302. A.T. descends SE less steeply.

26.7 Pass **Arethusa-Ripley Falls Trail** leading right 0.4 mi. to Ripley Falls, 2.5 mi. to Arethusa Falls, and 3.8 mi. to U.S. 302. The A.T. crosses railroad tracks and descends.

27.0 Reach parking area and hard-surfaced **Willey House Station Road**. Descend on road.

27.3 Reach U.S. 302, 1.0 mi. S of the Willey House site. To continue on Trail, cross road and ascend on Webster Cliff Trail. Dry River Campground is 1.5 mi. S on U.S. 302.

Franconia Notch (U.S. 3) to Kinsman Notch (N.H. 112)

Section 5 New Hampshire

15.5 Miles

Brief Description of Section

Most of the Trail in this section lies along the northeast-to southwest-running Kinsman Ridge, passing through heavily wooded country and past several mountain tarns (ponds) and cascades.

From its northern end on U.S. 3 (1,450 feet) in Franconia Notch State Park (see description in Section 4), the Trail climbs northwest on Cascade Brook Trail. At Lonesome Lake, a high mountain tarn on the shoulder of Cannon Mountain, the Trail ascends on the wet and sometimes steep Fishin' Jimmy Trail. Reaching Kinsman Pond, another high tarn, the Trail ascends on the Kinsman Ridge Trail to the north (4,293 feet) and south (4,358 feet) peaks of Kinsman Mountain. The Trail descends past Harrington Pond and the cascades along Eliza Brook. Between Eliza Brook and Kinsman Notch (1,870 feet), the Trail follows a wooded ridge.

The elevation change from Franconia Notch to Kinsman Mountain is considerable, but gradual. The Trail rises and falls, and the footway is often wet and rugged. Water is scarce on the southern part of the ridge.

Many waterfalls and cascades are located in this section, some on short side trips. The Upper (0.1-mile round trip), Middle (0.7-mile round trip), and Lower (1.2 miles round trip) Kinsman Falls are on the Basin-Cascades Trail near the northern end. At the south end, in Kinsman Notch, Lost River (which can be reached on a half-mile side trail leaving the A.T. 0.1 mile north of the Notch) flows into an underground gorge and through a series of cascades and caves.

Side trails in this section offer many possibilities for loop hikes, side trips, and alternate A.T. routes. Side trails are noted in the trail data, but, for complete information, consult the *AMC White Mountain Guide*. The guide and current trail information are available from the AMC, Pinkham Notch Camp, (see "Important Addresses," page 301).

Lost River

The brook draining the southern part of Kinsman Notch was aptly named Lost River. It disappears below the surface in a narrow, steep-walled glacial gorge. This geologic curiosity and the surrounding area have been preserved by the Society for Protection of New Hampshire Forests as the Lost River Reservation (phone, cafeteria, souvenirs, no accommodations), a half-mile east of the Trail crossing on N.H. 112. The gorge long ago eroded along a fracture in the granite of Kinsman Notch, later filling with a jumble of large boulders, forming numerous caverns. Lost River cascades through the resulting half-mile subterranean gorge, swirling within immense glacial potholes, flowing over spectacular falls. Trails, boardwalks, and ladders make the caves accessible.

The society also maintains a garden with 300 varieties of native flowers, ferns, and shrubs, an ecology trail, and a museum. The only fee charged is to enter the gorge.

Road Approaches

Both section ends are accessible from major highways. At the north end, the A.T. crosses U.S. 3 at Whitehouse Bridge.

Park south of the A.T near New Hampshire State Park Flume Complex, 5.8 miles north of North Woodstock and 10.2 miles south of Franconia. At the south end, the A.T. crosses N.H. 112, 6.2 miles west of North Woodstock, 4.8 miles east of Bungay Corner (junction of N.H. 112 and N.H. 116), and 17.7 miles east of Woodsville.

Both ends of the section have experienced theft and vandalism. Do not leave valuables in car.

Maps

Map No. 3 (this guide)
AMC Franconia Map
White Mountain National Forest Map (1:250,000)
Franconia Notch State Park Map
USGS 7 1/2 minute topographic quadrangles:
- Lincoln, N.H.
- Mt. Moosilauke, N.H.
- Franconia, N.H.

Shelters and Campsites

This section has one campsite and one shelter, as well as a public campground on U.S. 3 at the north end of the section.

Lafayette Campground: Operated and maintained by New Hampshire Division of Parks in Franconia Notch State Park; on U.S. 3 approximately 2.5 miles north of Trail crossing; 98 tentsites; fee charged; limited provisions, showers, phone, ample water.

Next shelter or campsite: north 2.4 miles (Liberty Spring Tentsite); south 4.6 miles.

Kinsman Pond Campsite: Built and maintained by AMC 4.6 mi. from north end of section on side trail 0.1 mile from A.T.; accommodates 14; also 5 tent platforms; water from pond should be boiled; good water 1 mile north on A.T.

Next shelter or campsite: north 4.6 miles; south 4.0 miles.

Eliza Brook Shelter: Built and maintained by AMC approximately in middle of section; accommodates 8; water from brook.

Next shelter or campsite: north 4.0 miles; south 7.1 miles (Beaver Brook Shelter).

This section has one mountain hut , which is described under "Public Accommodations."

Regulations

The northern mile of the section and the area around Lonesome Lake (including the hut) lie in Franconia Notch State Park. Camping and fires are prohibited except at Lafayette Campground on U.S. 3.

The rest of the Trail in the section lies within WMNF, where camping and fires are restricted to sites 200 feet or more off the Trail.

Supplies and Services

From the Trail crossing of U.S. 3, at the northern end of the section, it is 2.5 miles north to Lafayette Campground (limited provisions, showers, phone), 4.9 miles to Franconia Notch State Park headquarters (aerial tramway, phone, snacks, souvenirs, bus stop), 10.2 miles to Franconia (P.O. 03580, phone, supermarket, restaurants, laundromat, equipment, bus stop), and 20 miles to Littleton (full services, hospital, cobbler, bus stop).

From the Trail crossing of U.S. 3, it is 0.8 miles south to Flume Store (snacks, phone, souvenirs, bus stop), 5.8 miles to North Woodstock (P.O. 03262, phone, supermarket, restaurants, specialty backpacking store, laundromat), and 6.8 miles to Lincoln (P.O. 03251, groceries, laundromat, phone, Linwood Medical Center).

From the Trail crossing of N.H. 112, at the southern end of the section, it is 6.2 miles east to North Woodstock and 7.7 miles to Lincoln (see above). From this crossing, it is 12.0 miles west to Swiftwater (phone, groceries, restaurant), 15.4 miles to Bath (P.O. 03740, phone, groceries), and 17.7 miles to Woodsville (P.O. 03785, phone, supermarket, restaurant, bus stop).

In an emergency, call any AMC hut or the New Hampshire State Police (603) 846-5500 or (800) 852-3411.

Public Accommodations

One AMC hut, which has dormitory-style lodging and family-style meals (at least one meal must be taken with lodging), is in this section. Reservations are usually necessary and may be made at any AMC hut, or by calling or writing the Reservations Secretary, Pinkham Notch Camp (see "Important Addresses," page 301).

Lonesome Lake Hut Leased from the state of N.H. and operated by AMC 2.8 mi. from N end of section; reservations strongly recommended; accommodates 44; ample water.

From the Trail crossing at U.S. 3, it is 10.2 miles north to Franconia (motels, cabins), 1.6 miles south to a roadway lined with motels and cabins and 5.8 miles north to North Woodstock (motels, guest house). From the Trail crossing at N.H. 112, it is 6.2 miles east to North Woodstock.

Trail Description, North to South

Miles	Data
0.0	At the trailhead of Liberty Spring Trail, turn left onto paved bike trail, cross creek on steel bridge. Turn right (W), and going under U.S. 3 to **Cascade Brook Trail**. Ascend NW into woods on old logging road. The bike trail continues to Whitehouse Trail, which leads 1 mi. to Flume Complex (parking, meals, snacks, phone).
0.2	Cross Whitehouse Brook on rocks.
1.3	**Basin-Cascades Trail** descends right 1.5 mi., past the Kinsman Falls, to The Basin (a large glacial pothole) on U.S. 3. Just beyond this junction, the A.T. crosses Cascade Brook on wooden bridge.
1.8	**Kinsman Pond Trail** diverges left, ascending 2.3 mi. to Kinsman Pond Campsite and 2.4 mi. to Kinsman Junction, where it rejoins the A.T. A.T. continues upstream parallel to Cascade Brook.
2.7	Reach junction at the edge of Lonesome Lake where the Trail turns left onto **Fishin' Jimmy Trail**. The Cascade Brook Trail continues straight ahead 0.2 mi. to Lonesome Lake Trail, which may then be followed left to Kinsman Ridge Trail and right to U.S. 3. The A.T. crosses the outlet brook of Lonesome Lake and ascends.
2.8	Reach AMC **Lonesome Lake Hut** (no camping allowed). From the hut, **Around-Lonesome-Lake Trail** leads right 0.3 mi. to Lonesome Lake

Trail, which may be followed left to Kinsman Ridge Trail or right to U.S. 3. From the hut, the A.T. continues on the Fishin' Jimmy Trail passing W across the lower slopes of the Cannonballs.

3.7 Cross brook, and shortly beyond, climb steeply.

4.2 Cross brook in sag, and ascend steeply.

4.6 Reach **Kinsman Junction** where Fishin' Jimmy Trail ends and the A.T. continues, ascending on **Kinsman Ridge Trail**. The Kinsman Pond Trail leads left 0.1 mi. to **Kinsman Pond Campsite** (for drinking water boil water from pond). To right, **Kinsman Ridge Trail** leads over the Cannonballs to Cannon Mountain and from there descends to U.S. 3 at aerial, tramway base station.

4.9 **Mt. Kinsman Trail** descends right 3.5 mi., past Bald Peak and the Kinsman Flume and Profile (1.5 mi.) to N.H. 116. The A.T. ascends, veering S.

5.2 Reach summit of **North Kinsman Mountain** (4,293 ft.). Near the summit, a short trail leads left (E) to cliff overlooking Kinsman Pond. Descend S through col (water is sometimes found on right), and then ascend.

6.2 Reach summit of **South Kinsman Mountain** (4,358 ft.). Rough, steep descent.

6.5 Pass through small col, where water may be found, and continue descent.

7.1 Cross small brook in100 yds., pass left of Harrington Pond. Descend steeply over wet, rough footway to headwaters of Eliza Brook.

7.5 Cross headwaters of Eliza Brook, descend along E bank, past cascades and falls, eventually entering logging road. Follow it downhill.

8.6 Turn right off road, cross Eliza Brook. Just beyond, a short side trail leads right to **Eliza Brook Shelter,** with water from brook. Continue generally SW. Ascend gradually to powerline.

9.0 Pass under transmission line. Beyond, the **Reel Brook Trail** descends right 4.0 mi. to N.H. 116 near Easton. The Trail ascends the N ridge of Mt. Wolf, steeply at first.

10.3 On the **East Peak of Mt. Wolf** (3,478 ft.), a side trail leads left to outlook on summit.

10.9 Cross knob on south ridge of Mt. Wolf (3,360 ft.), then descend. At the end of the descent, the A.T. follows the ridge with little change in elevation for 3 mi.

11.5 Cross small brook.

12.1 **Gordon Pond Trail** descends left, passes Gordon Pond in 0.3 mi., passes Gordon Falls in 1.3 mi., and reaches N.H. 112 in 4.8 mi.

12.6 Pass just E of high point on ridge (3,009 ft.).

14.2 Pass through col, where water is found to right of Trail, and ascend steeply.

14.5 Begin steep descent. **Dilly Trail** descends left 0.8 mi. past outlook over Kinsman Notch to Lost River Reservation on N.H. 112.

15.3 Unmarked trail leads left 0.5 mi. to the Lost River Reservation's ecology trail, and to parking lot.

15.4 Reach N.H. 112 in Kinsman Notch. Turn left and follow highway.

15.5 Reach Beaver Brook Trail and end of section. To continue on Trail ascend SW on Beaver Brook Trail.

Trail Description, South to North

Miles	Data
0.0	From the junction of N.H. 112 and **Beaver Brook Trail** in Kinsman Notch, cross the highway diagonally left, and turn right to follow the Kinsman Ridge Trail. The Trail soon bears right and ascends steeply.
0.1	Unmarked side trail leads right 0.5 mi. to Lost River Reservation's ecology trail, and to parking lot.
1.0	**Dilly Trail** descends right 0.8 mi. past outlook over Kinsman Notch to Lost River Reservation on N.H. 112. The A.T. continues NE along ridge with little elevational change for the next 3 mi.
1.3	Pass through col to left of the Trail, where water is found.
2.9	Pass E of high point on ridge (3,009 ft.).
3.4	**Gordon Pond Trail** diverges right, passes Gordon Pond in 0.3 mi., passes Gordon Falls in 1.3 mi., and descends in 4.8 mi. to N.H. 112.
4.0	Pass water in small brook on Trail.
4.6	Pass over knob on south ridge of Mt. Wolf (3,360 ft.), where there is a view E to Gordon Pond.
5.2	Side trail leads right 200 ft. to outlook on the summit of **East Peak of Mt. Wolf** (3,478 ft.). Descend along the north ridge of Mt. Wolf.
6.5	Reach junction where **Reel Brook Trail** descends left 4.0 mi. to N.H. 116 near Easton. The A.T. continues on level ground, passing under powerline. Descend NE.
6.9	Reach side trail leading left to **Eliza Brook Shelter** (water from brook). Just beyond, cross Eliza Brook, turn left, upstream, on old logging road.

Turn left again off the logging road after approximately 0.5 mi. The Trail becomes rough and steep, passing falls and cascades to left in Eliza Brook.

8.0 Cross headwaters of Eliza Brook and continue steeply uphill on wet, rough footway.

8.3 Pass to right (E) of Harrington Pond, cross small brook, and climb N.

9.0 Pass through small col where water may be found, and continue ascent.

9.3 Reach open summit of **South Kinsman Mountain** (4,358 ft.). Descend N through scrub and small evergreens to col (water sometimes found on left), and ascend gradually.

10.3 Reach open summit of **North Kinsman Mountain** (4,293 ft.). Near the summit, a short trail leads right (E) to cliff overlooking Kinsman Pond. Descend N from summit.

10.7 **Mt. Kinsman Trail** diverges left, descending 3.5 mi past Bald Peak and the Kinsman Flume and Profile (1.5 mi.), to N.H. 116. The A.T. continues E descending gradually.

10.9 Reach **Kinsman Junction** where the Trail continues ahead on **Fishin' Jimmy Trail**. The **Kinsman Pond Trail** leads right 0.1 mi. to **Kinsman Pond Campsite** (boil water from pond for drinking water), and 2.4 mi. to Cascade Brook Trail to rejoin the A.T. **Kinsman Ridge Trail** (a possible alternate to the A.T.) turns left, passes over the Cannonballs to Cannon Mountain (Profile Mountain) in 3.3 mi. and descends 3.3 mi. more to aerial-tramway base station on U.S. 3. From here, the Greenleaf Trail may be ascended 3.3 mi. to the summit of Mt. Lafayette to rejoin the A.T. From

Kinsman Junction, the A.T. heads E on the Fishin' Jimmy Trail and descends, sometimes steeply.

11.3 Cross small brook and, 0.5 mi. farther, a larger brook. The Trail then passes E across the lower slopes of the Cannonballs.

12.7 Reach AMC **Lonesome Lake Hut** (camping prohibited). From the hut, **Around-Lonesome-Lake Trail** leads left 0.3 mi. to Lonesome Lake Trail, which leads right (E) to U.S. 3 and left (W) to Kinsman Ridge Trail. The A.T. descends from the hut to the lake and then E across its outlet.

12.8 Reach junction where Fishin' Jimmy Trail ends and the A.T. turns right onto **Cascade Brook Trail**, descending parallel to the outlet brook of Lonesome Lake. The Cascade Brook Trail leads left 0.2 mi. to Lonesome Lake Trail, which may be followed left to Kinsman Ridge Trail or right, descending 1.2 mi. to Lafayette Campground.

13.7 Kinsman Pond Trail enters on right from **Kinsman Pond Campsite**. The A.T. continues downstream.

14.2 Cross Cascade Brook on wooden bridge. Just beyond, **Basin-Cascades Trail** descends left 1.5 mi. past Kinsman Falls to The Basin on U.S. 3. The A.T. continues on woods road.

15.2 Cross Whitehouse Brook on rocks. Continue to U.S. 3.

15.4 Go under both lanes of U.S. 3 and reach paved bike path.

15.5 Bear left over steel bridge to junction with **Liberty Spring Trail**. To reach Whitehouse Trail and Flume Complex, bear right on bike path. To continue on Trail follow Liberty Spring Trail.

Kinsman Notch (N.H. 112) to Glencliff (N.H. 25)

Section 6 New Hampshire

8.9 Miles

Brief Description of Section

The Trail in this section traverses the massive, bald Mt. Moosilauke (4,802 feet), which covers an area of 30 square miles. The mountain towers over the southwest corner of the White Mountains.

From Kinsman Notch (1,870 feet) in the north, the Trail follows the Beaver Brook Trail steeply upward past fine cascades, with several stone ladders over cliffs, and then ascends to the summit of Mt. Moosilauke. From the summit, cairns lead into the Carriage Road, which is followed for a mile, then the Glencliff Trail leads steeply down the west slope to Glencliff (1,074 feet). This section is usually hiked in a day.

Use great care when passing over the cliffside section of the Beaver Brook Trail. Mt. Moosilauke is above treeline and subject to the full force of storms, which can be violent. Water is generally abundant in this section.

The mountain and its numerous trails are worth several days' exploration. Side trails are described briefly in the trail data, but, for complete information, consult the *AMC White Mountain Guide*. For information on the flora, fauna, geology, and history, as well as trails on the mountain, refer to the *DOC Trail Guide to Mt. Moosilauke*. The guide and information on trails in the section may be obtained from the Dartmouth Outing Club (see "Important Addresses," page 301).

Mt. Moosilauke

Mt. Moosilauke was a hunting ground for the Pemigewasset Indians, to whom Moosilauke meant "high bald place."

In the eighteenth century, Europeans farmed the Moosilauke area. The Indians retreated before the wave of settlement, the region was opened to land grants, and it was not long before much of the virgin forest was cleared for cultivation and to provide timber for building.

About 1850, agriculture declined, and the mountain became a logging and resort center. Two bridlepaths were built to the summit, and, in 1860, a summit hotel, the Prospect House, was opened. As the tourist business boomed, the Moosilauke Mountain Road Company completed the five-mile Carriage Road to the summit.

Between 1899 and 1914, paper companies stripped all but the most inaccessible timber from the west side of the mountain. Around 1920, this intensive logging ended, and the USFS purchased most of the land.

The Dartmouth Outing Club (DOC) adopted the Prospect House in 1920, maintaining it as a summer hostel until it burned down in 1942; its foundation is still visible. Tourism on the mountain declined with the advent of the automobile. The Carriage Road fell into disrepair years ago and is now used only by hikers. (The A.T. follows the former road for a short distance near the summit.)

The mountain is now used for education and recreation. The flora, fauna, and geology of the summit, now owned by Dartmouth College, are studied by students of the outdoors. The remainder of the massif, now a part of the White Mountain National Forest, is a recreational spot used by hundreds of people each year.

Road Approaches

Both the north and south ends of the section are accessible from major highways. At the north end, the Trail crosses N.H. 112 (ample parking) 6.2 miles west of North Woodstock, 4.8 miles south of Bungay Corner (junction of N.H. 112 and N.H. 116), and 17.7 miles east of Woodsville (near I-91). At the south end, the Trail crosses N.H. 25 approximately 0.5 miles north of Glencliff (cars are best parked in Glencliff).

Maps

Map No. 3 (this guide)
AMC Franconia Map
DOC Mt. Moosilauke Map
DOC Trail Map
White Mountain National Forest Map (1:250,000)
USGS 15 minute topographic quadrangle:
  Rumney, N.H.
USGS 7 1/2 minute topographic quadrangles:
  Mt. Moosilauke, N.H.
  Mt. Kineo, N.H.
  Warren, N.H.

Shelters and Campsites

This section has two shelters.

***Beaver Brook Shelter*:** Built and maintained by DOC 0.2 mile from north end of section on short side trail; accommodates 5; water from brook.

Next shelter or campsite: north 7.1 mile (Eliza Brook Shelter); south 7.6 miles.

***Jeffers Brook Shelter*:** Built and maintained by DOC 1.1 mile from south end of section, 0.1 mile on blue-blazed side trail; accommodates 10; water from brook.

Next shelter or campsite: north 7.6 miles; south14.4 miles (Mt. Cube Shelter).

Regulations

From Kinsman Notch to the Hurricane Trail Junction near Glencliff, the A.T. passes across both White Mountain National Forest (WMNF) and private land. The northern end is part of Lost River Reservation, and the summit of Mt. Moosilauke is owned by Dartmouth College, but the remainder is in WMNF.

From Hurricane Trail Junction south to USFS 19, the Trail is on private land. Camping and fires are prohibited.

Between USFS 19 and N.H. 25, the A.T. crosses WMNF.

Supplies and Services

From the Trail crossing of N.H. 112 at the northern end of the section, it is 6.2 miles east to North Woodstock (P.O. 03262, phone, supermarket, restaurants, specialty backpacking store, laundromat) and 7.7 miles to Lincoln (P.O. 03251, phone, groceries, laundromat, Linwood Medical Center). From this crossing, it is 12.0 miles west to Swiftwater (phone, groceries, restaurant), 15.4 miles to Bath (P.O. 03740, phone, groceries), and 17.7 miles to Woodsville (P.O. 03785, phone, supermarket, restaurant, bus stop).

From the Trail crossing at the southern end, approximately one-half mile north of the center of Glencliff (P.O. 03238, phone), it is five miles south to Warren (P.O. 03279, phone, groceries).

In an emergency, call the New Hampshire State Police (603) 846-5500 or (800) 852-3411.

Public Accommodations

From the Trail crossing at N.H. 112, it is 6.2 miles east to North Woodstock (motels, guesthouse). Public accommodations are not available near the southern end of the section.

Trail Description, North to South

Miles	Data
0.0	From N.H. 112 in Kinsman Notch, ascend SW on **Beaver Brook Trail**.
0.2	Side trail leads left 250 ft. to **Beaver Brook Shelter**. Cross brook and ascend gradually.
0.4	Pass cascade, the lowest in a series of cascades on right, and ascend steeply. At one point, the Trail becomes very steep. Great care must be used here, especially in poor weather.
1.4	Ascend gradually through evergreens.
1.8	Reach col between Mt. Blue and Mt. Jim. **Ridge Trail** descends left 3.5 mi. to Ravine Lodge (private). The A.T. bears right to ascend around the S side of Mt. Blue.
2.3	Pass to left of spring. Descend slightly to swampy col and then ascend through small growth to open, grassy slopes.
3.2	**Gorge Brook Trail** descends left (SE) 2.7 mi. to

Ravine Lodge (water is sometimes found 150 yds. down this trail). The A.T. bears right and ascends to open summit of **Mt. Moosilauke** (4,802 ft.), where the ruins of the summit house are still visible. This peak offers one of the finest views in the White Mountains, particularly NE toward the highest peaks in the region. The **Benton Trail** descends right (NW) 3.5 mi. to Tunnel Brook Trail, which may then be followed N to N.H. 112 or S to Glencliff. From the summit, the A.T. descends on the Carriage Road, marked with prominent rock cairns, and soon passes below treeline.

Path leads left 50 ft.

3.9 Reach junction where Trail turns right onto **Glencliff Trail**. At this point, the **Carriage Road** descends ahead 4.1 mi. to Breezy Point, approximately 2.5 mi. from N.H. 118 on road passable by automobile. Fifty feet farther on the A.T., a side trail leads left 0.2 mi. to South Peak (4,523 ft.). The A.T. steeply descends W on Glencliff Trail.

4.2 Pass stream and continue descent.

6.2 Turn left and enter woods at site of old camp.

6.8 **Hurricane Trail** forks left, passes E over Hurricane Mountain, and reaches Ravine Lodge (private) in 5.1 mi. The A.T. crosses a brook and continues uphill on old woods road through conifers and hardwoods.

7.0 Pass through wooden gate and follow cart track downhill to grove. Bear left and follow old lane through gate and over bridge.

7.2 Turn left onto paved Sanitarium Road and descend.

7.5 Turn right onto dirt USFS 19 and descend.

7.6 Turn left onto Town Line Trail.

7.8 Pass blue-blazed trail on right, which leads 0.1 mi. to **Jeffers Brook Shelter.**

8.8 Cross Oliverian Brook on footbridge.

8.9 Reach N.H. 25 just N of Glencliff and turn left. Follow highway 200 yds. to the section's end. To continue on Trail, turn right and ascend SW into woods.

Trail Description, South to North

Miles **Data**

0.0 From N.H. 25, at the spot where the Trail from the S reaches the highway, just N of Glencliff, proceed NW 200 yds. and turn right (NE) into woods.

0.1 Cross Oliverian Brook on footbridge and bear right.

1.1 Blue-blazed trail on left leads 0.1 mi. to **Jeffers Brook Shelter.**

1.3 Turn right uphill onto USFS 19.

1.4 Turn left uphill onto paved Sanitarium Road.

1.7 Turn right, away from road, onto **Glencliff Trail**. Cross bridge, and continue through gate.

1.9 Bear left onto cart track. Pass through wooden gate and keep to right side of field. After passing through fringe of trees, keep to left side of second field.

2.1 Turn left and enter woods at site of old camp. **Hurricane Trail** forks right, passes E over Hurricane Mountain, and reaches Ravine Lodge (private) in 5.1 mi. The A.T. crosses a brook and continues uphill on old woods road through conifers and hardwoods.

2.8 Pass stream and ascend steeply.

4.7 Side trail leads right 0.2 mi. to South Peak (4,523 ft.). Fifty feet beyond, reach junction where **Carriage Road** descends 4.1 mi. right to Breezy Point, approximately 2.5 mi. from N.H. 118 by road passable by car. The A.T. turns left at this junction and follows the Carriage Road N through woods.

5.0 Path leads right 50 ft. to good view of ravine. Pass above treeline and continue along Carriage Road marked by prominent rock cairns.

5.7 Reach summit of **Mt. Moosilauke** (4,802 ft.), where the ruins of the summit house are still visible. This peak affords one of the finest views in the White Mountains, particularly NE toward the highest peaks in the region. From the summit, the **Benton Trail** descends NW 3.5 mi. to Tunnel Brook Trail, which may then be followed N to N.H. 112 or S to Glencliff. From the summit, the A.T. descends NE following **Beaver Brook Trail**. In 200 ft., the **Gorge Brook Trail** descends SE (right) 2.7 mi. to private Ravine Lodge (water is sometimes found 150 yds. down this trail). The A.T. descends through scrub.

6.3 Pass through swampy col and ascend slightly, skirting around S side of Mt. Blue.

6.6 Pass to right of spring. The Trail affords splendid views over Jobildunk Ravine to S. Descend E.

7.2 Reach col between Mt. Blue and Mt. Jim. **Ridge Trail** descends right 3.5 mi. to private Ravine Lodge. The A.T. descends gradually and then steeply. At one point, it becomes very steep and must be descended very carefully. On the left is a series of cascades.

8.5 Pass lowest cascade and descend gradually.

8.7 Cross brook. Side trail leads right 250 ft. to **Beaver Brook Shelter**.

8.9 Reach N.H. 112 in Kinsman Notch and end of section. To continue on Trail, cross highway diagonally left and turn right onto **Kinsman Ridge Trail**.

Glencliff (N.H. 25) to N.H. 25A

Section 7 New Hampshire

11.6 Miles

Brief Description of Section

The Trail in this section passes through low-country hardwood forests, often along abandoned woods roads, to Glencliff (1,074 feet) across N.H. 25C, and N.H. 25A (1,267 feet). This section has only one low summit, Mt. Mist (2,220 feet).

The A.T. passes Wachipauka Pond and to the east of Upper Baker Pond. The one side trail goes to the summit of Webster Slide Mountain near the northern end. For current information on the Trail in this section, contact the Dartmouth Outing Club (see "Important Addresses," page 301).

Road Approaches

Both ends and the center of the section are accessible from major highways. At the northern end, the Trail crosses N.H. 25 approximately a half mile northwest of Glencliff. N.H. 25C intersects the center of the Section 4 miles west of Warren and 10 miles east of Piermont. At the southern end the Trail crosses N.H. 25A (difficult parking at roadside) 1.8 miles east of the Mt. Cube House, 4.3 miles west of Wentworth, and 26.7 miles west of I-93. This crossing is also 10.7 miles east of Orford (N.H. 10) and 11.2 miles east of Fairlee, Vt. (I-91).

Maps

Map No. 4 (this guide)
DOC Trail Map
USGS 15 minute topographic quadrangles:
Rumney, N.H.
Mt. Cube, N.H.
USGS 7 1/2 minute topographic quadrangle:
Warren, N.H.

Shelters and Campsites

This section does not have shelters or designated campsites. Camping is allowed within White Mountain National Forest (WMNF). (See "Regulations" below.) The first shelter north of this section (1.1 miles) is Jeffers Brook Shelter; the next shelter south (3.2 miles) is Mt. Cube Shelter.

Regulations

The segment of the Trail between Glencliff (N.H. 25) and N.H. 25C lies within WMNF, where camping is permitted only at sites 200 feet or more from the Trail. The office of the Pemigewasset Ranger District, 127 Highland St., Plymouth, N.H. 03264, is the nearest to this section.

From N.H. 25C to N.H. 25A, the Trail passes across private land where camping and fires are prohibited.

Supplies and Services

From the Trail crossing of N.H. 25 at the northern end of the section, approximately half a mile north of the center of

Glencliff (P.O. 03238, phone), it is five miles south to Warren (P.O. 03279, phone, groceries). Warren is also four miles east of the Trail crossing at N.H. 25C in the center of the section. From the Trail crossing at the southern end of the section, it is 4.3 miles east to Wentworth (P.O. 03282, phone, limited groceries), 10.7 miles west to Orford (P.O. 03777, phone, limited groceries), and 11.2 mi. west to Fairlee, Vt. (bus stop).

In an emergency, contact the New Hampshire State Police (603) 846-5500 or (800) 852-3411.

Public Accommodations

This section has no public accommodations.

Trail Description, North to South

Miles	Data
0.0	From N.H. 25 NW of Glencliff follow woods road, cross old railroad bed, then bear left uphill, continue level SE, then swing SW, and climb steeply.
1.5	Pass N of the summit of **Wyatt Hill** and descend gradually W.
2.3	Reach **Wachipauka Pond**. A.T. skirts N and W shores of pond and then ascends W, passing **Hairy Root Spring** (not reliable in summer).
2.8	Reach saddle between Mt. Mist and Webster Slide Mountain, where a side trail climbs right to summit of Webster Slide Mountain. The Trail climbs steeply S passing to right of an outlook.
3.8	Pass over summit of **Mt. Mist** (2,220 ft.) and descend gradually S.
6.8	Cross stream (reliable water source). Reach N.H. 25C, follow it to the right (W) for 100 ft., enter

woods across a puncheon on the W side of the powerline. This is the **Ore Hill Trail**.

8.8 Pass a side trail to a spring.

9.8 Cross a dirt road and continue onto the **Atwell Hill Trail.** This road, the Atwell Hill, was laid out from Dover to Haverhill in 1768. The Trail descends gently, crosses a swampy area, and turns left onto an old woods road.

11.3 Turn right off the woods road and descend into a swampy area.

11.6 Reach N.H. 25A, south of Upper Baker Pond. Cross highway bridge at right, and follow highway 100 yds. to the section's end. To continue on A.T., turn left onto Mt. Cube Trail.

Trail Description, South to North

Miles	Data
0.0	From the **Mt. Cube Trail** on N.H. 25A, turn right, cross over a highway bridge, and enter the woods at left on the **Atwell Hill Trail**, 100 yds. E, through a swampy area.
0.3	Turn left onto an old woods road.
1.3	Turn right off the woods road and cross a swampy area.
1.8	Cross the dirt Atwell Hill Road. Continue straight on the **Ore Hill Trail**. The Trail crosses a swamp and ascends gradually.
2.8	Pass a side trail right to a spring.
4.8	Reach N.H. 25C, turn right and pass under the power line, and turn left onto the **Wachipauka Pond Trail** in 100 feet. Cross stream (reliable water sources) and ascend NE.

7.8 Pass over summit of **Mt. Mist** (2,220 ft.) and descend steeply. Pass outlook on right.

8.8 Reach saddle between Mt. Mist and Webster Slide Mountain where side trail climbs left to the summit of Webster Slide Mountain (views). The A.T. descends E, passing **Hairy Root Spring** (not reliable in summer).

9.1 Reach **Wachipauka Pond**. The Trail skirts the W and N shores of the pond and then ascends gradually E.

10.1 Pass N of the summit of **Wyatt Hill** and then descend steadily NE.

11.6 Reach N.H. 25 and the end of the section, just NW of Glencliff. To continue on A.T., go left 200 yds. on road and turn right into woods.

N.H. 25A to Lyme-Dorchester Road (Dartmouth Skiway)

Section 8 New Hampshire

15.4 Miles

Brief Description of Section

The Trail in this section crosses two outstanding features: Mt. Cube (2,911 feet) and Smarts Mountain (3,240 feet). Ascents of both peaks, from either direction, are quite steep, making travel strenuous. The section, going south, starts on N.H. 25A 0.3 miles east of a brick farmhouse known as Mt. Cube House (1,267 feet), climbs Mt. Cube on a footpath, passes through Quinttown (1,158 feet) on woods roads, climbs over Smarts Mountain, and ends by following the Lyme-Dorchester Road to Dartmouth Skiway (approximately 870 feet). Two days may be needed to hike the section.

This section has two side trails, both of which may be used as alternate routes to the A.T. One is the Quinttown Trail, which bypasses Smarts Mountain. The other is the former A.T., the Clark Pond Loop, a 17.6-mile (approximately five miles longer than the A.T.) low-country trail passing three lakes east of the present Trail. The northern end of the Clark Pond Loop is on the summit of Smarts Mountain. The southern end is on the east flank of Moose Mountain in Section 9, the next section south. These trails are described briefly in the data below. For more information on them, and current information on the A.T., the hiker should contact the Dartmouth Outing Club (see "Important Addresses," page 301).

Road Approaches

The northern end of this section is accessible by car on N.H. 25A (difficult parking at roadside) 4.3 miles west of Wentworth and 22.3 miles west of I-93. This crossing is also 10.7 miles east of Orford (N.H. 10) and 11.2 miles east of Fairlee, Vt. (Interstate 91). A dirt road starting on N.H. 25A, 1.2 miles east of Orfordville, follows Jacobs Brook 1.7 miles east to intersect the Trail at Quinttown, 6.2 miles from the northern end of the section. The southern end is accessible by the Lyme-Dorchester Road. Starting at Lyme on N.H. 10, this paved road leads 2.8 miles east to the Dartmouth Skiway (ample parking) and the Trail. The north fork of this road (the Trail) may be followed as far north as Smarts Ranger Trail Junction (limited parking).

Maps

Map No. 4 (this guide)
DOC Trail Map
USGS 15 minute topographic quadrangle:
  Mt. Cube, N.H.

Shelters and Campsites

This section has three shelters.

Mt. Cube Shelter: Built and maintained by DOC 7 miles from north end of section; accommodates 8; ample water. This shelter, among the oldest on the Trail, is scheduled to be rebuilt in 1989.

Next shelter or campsite: north 17.5 miles (Jeffers Brook Shelter); south 5.3 miles.

Firewarden's Cabin: Closed cabin built by N.H. Forest Service, now maintained by DOC 5.4 miles from south end of section; accommodates 8; water from Mike Murphy Spring 0.1 mile north on A.T.

Next shelter or campsite: north 5.3 miles; south 0.2 mile.

Smarts Mountain Shelter: Built and maintained by DOC 5.2 miles from south end of section on short side trail; accommodates 4; water from Mike Murphy Spring 0.2 mile north on A.T.

Next shelter or campsite: north 5.5 miles; south 6.7 miles (Trapper John Shelter).

Regulations

Camping and fires are prohibited except at Smarts Mountain Shelter, Firewarden's Cabin, and Mt. Cube Shelter, and fires are restricted to fire rings provided at these sites.

Supplies and Services

From the Trail crossing at N.H. 25A at the northern end of the section, it is 4.3 miles east to Wentworth (P.O. 03282, phone, limited groceries), 10.7 miles west to Orford (P.O. 03777, phone, limited groceries), and 11.7 miles west to Fairlee, Vt. (bus stop). From Quinttown, 6.2 miles from the northern end of the section, it is approximately 6 miles west to Orford by dirt road. From the Trail crossing at the Dartmouth Skiway at the southern end of the section, it is 1.2 miles west to Lyme Center (P.O. 02769) and 3.2 miles west to Lyme (P.O. 03768, phone, limited groceries, meals).

In an emergency, contact the New Hampshire State Police, (800) 852-3411 or (603) 846-3411.

Public Accommodations

An inn is located in Lyme, 3.2 miles west of the section's southern end. This section has no other accommodations.

Trail Description, North to South

Miles	Data
0.0	From N.H. 25A, 0.3 mi. E of **Mt. Cube House** and next to Upper Baker Pond, enter the woods on S side of road about 100 yds. W of the metal highway bridge. Cross a small swamp, and ascend on abandoned logging roads.
0.8	Cross a gravel logging road, and ascend.
2.0	Cross **Bracket Brook** on a log bridge, and begin ascending Mt. Cube on switchbacks.
3.4	Reach the saddle between North and South Cube summits. A side trail leaves right to the open summit of **North Cube**. The Trail continues left.
3.5	Reach **South Cube** summit. *The proposed Eastman Ledges relocation will link Mt. Cube and Smarts Mountain via the long ridges between the two. This new section is scheduled for completion in 1989.*
3.7	Cross brook, and descend steeply on worn trail through spruce.
4.5	Pass spring (unreliable) on right, and descend gradually.
4.7	Pass **Mt. Cube Shelter.**
4.9	Turn left onto narrow dirt road, which becomes rougher and more overgrown as it descends across W side of Mt. Cube.

6.3 Enter dirt road, and continue straight over bridge. (The dirt road to right follows Jacob Brook to N.H. 25A east of Orfordville.) This is Quinttown. Continue ahead in flat section. Just beyond, turn right, following second brook, and then dirt road turning left, uphill. Follow valley on left.

7.2 Cross brook. Beyond, reach junction with **Quinttown Trail.** This alternate route to the A.T. leads right, bypasses Smarts Mountain, and rejoins the A.T. in 5.1 mi. on the Lyme-Dorchester Road.

7.4 With house ahead on main road, take right fork onto less-worn woods road. Beyond, road is grass-grown and leads through level section.

8.3 Bear left, ascending with Mousley Brook on left.

8.9 Cross to left bank of Mousley Brook, ascending more steeply on old road, which becomes ingrown and washed-out near headwaters of brook.

9.9 Near crest, turn sharp right, and pass covered **Mike Murphy Spring**, named in honor of the last ranger to be stationed on Smarts Mountain. *This is near the S end of the Eastman Ledges relocation. Follow blazes closely and do not use unfinished relocation.*

10.0 Pass **Firewarden's Cabin**, now a closed shelter maintained by DOC, and continue ahead.

10.1 Pass over summit of **Smarts Mountain** (3,240 ft.). Blue-blazed **Clark Pond Loop**, former A.T. route, descends left 4.4 mi. to Cummins Pond and continues past Clark Pond (9.3 mi.), Goose Pond (13.6 mi.), and **Moose Mountain Shelter** (16.5 mi.), rejoins the A.T. at Moose Mountain col (16.9 mi.) in Section 9, and terminates at the Harris Trail (17.6 mi.). A.T. continues straight ahead (W), descending from summit on **Smarts Mountain Ranger Trail.**

10.2 Side trail leads left 500 ft. to **Smarts Mountain Shelter.** To the right of this junction is an intermittent spring. The Trail descends steeply W.

10.5 Trail turns sharp left and descends steeply over exposed ledges, then less steeply through spruce forest.

10.8 Turn right off **Smarts Mountain Ranger Trail** and onto the **Lambert Ridge Trail.** Descend steeply into a swampy col; water available.

12.5 Cross a swampy section and ascend onto the rocky spine of Lambert Ridge.

14.3 Reach parking lot on **Lyme-Dorchester Road.** The Trail continues right on the dirt road.

15.0 A gravel road diverges right to **Quinttown Trail.**

15.4 At fork in Lyme-Dorchester Road at the Dartmouth Skiway, the section ends. The Trail continues straight ahead into the woods and up Holts Ledge.

Trail Description, South to North

Miles **Data**

0.0 At fork in Lyme-Dorchester Road, 2.8 mi. E of Lyme, and 5.0 mi. E of East Thetford, Vt., the Trail proceeds E on dirt road.

0.4 DOC **Quinttown Trail** follows gravel road leading left, bypasses Smarts Mountain, and rejoins the A.T. in 5.1 mi. The A.T. continues straight on **Lyme-Dorchester Road.**

1.1 Just before bridge over Grant Brook, reach Smarts Mountain Ranger Trail junction. The Trail leaves sharp left from the parking lot. The **Smarts Mountain Ranger Trail** leads straight ahead to the summit of Smarts Mountain.

1.4 Cross the first in a series of open ledges that constitute the rocky spine of Lambert Ridge.

2.7 Descend off Lambert Ridge, cross a stream, and begin ascending Smarts Mountain.

4.6 Join **Smarts Mountain Ranger Trail**, which continues to the summit.

4.9 Trail turns sharp right and ascends steeply toward summit of Smarts Mountain.

5.1 Side trail leads right 500 ft. to **Smarts Mountain Shelter**. An intermittent spring is located just beyond the trail junction. The A.T. continues E.

5.2 Reach summit of **Smarts Mountain** (3,240 ft.). The blue-blazed Clark Pond Loop enters from right, ending here. The Smarts Mountain Ranger Trail also ends here.

5.3 Pass **Firewarden's Cabin**, now maintained as a shelter by DOC.

5.4 Pass covered **Mike Murphy Spring**, named in honor of the last ranger to be stationed on Smarts Mountain, a friend of hikers who developed the spring. *In this area is the S end of the planned Eastman Ledges relocation for 1989. Follow blazes closely; do not use unfinished relocation.* Beyond, Trail turns sharp left, bears right onto grassgrown road, and then follows left bank of Mousley Brook.

6.4 Cross to right bank of Mousley Brook, following old woods road.

7.0 In level section, at base of mountain, bear right onto grass-grown road.

7.9 Woods road comes in on right.

8.1 At edge of field, **Quinttown Trail** comes in on left from Lyme-Dorchester Road. Beyond, cross brook and continue on well-worn road. This dirt road follows Jacob Brook to N.H. 25A E of Orfordville.

8.9 Turn right, downhill, where faint woods road turns left. This is Quinttown. Cross brook 200 ft. farther, with road coming in on right from farmhouse. Cross second brook and leave dirt road. Continue ahead on overgrown road where worn road turns left. Ascend gradually across W slope of Mt. Cube.

10.4 At brook crossing, turn right, uphill.

10.6 Pass **Mt. Cube Shelter**, and ascend.

10.8 Pass spring (unreliable) on left and ascend on worn Trail.

11.6 Cross brook, and continue steep ascent.

11.8 *North end of scheduled Eastman Ledges relocation. Continue straight ahead. Do not use unfinished relocation.*

11.9 Reach **South Cube** summit (2,911 ft.). Bear right across summit. After following the ridge spine a short distance, descend sharp left into woods.

12.0 The Trail leaves right from the col and descends steeply across switchbacks. The side trail to open North Cube is straight ahead.

13.4 Cross **Bracket Brook** on a log bridge and ascend briefly.

14.6 Cross a gravel logging road and descend on abandoned logging road.

15.4 Reach N.H. 25A, where section ends. Trail continues right 200 yds. along highway and reenters the woods on N side of road.

Lyme-Dorchester Road (Dartmouth Skiway) to Connecticut River (Hanover)

Section 9 New Hampshire

19.0 Miles

Brief Description of Section

This section follows the southern end of a broken range of White Mountain foothills, which lie between Mt. Moosilauke and the Connecticut River. From the Dartmouth Skiway, the Trail passes the crest of Holts Ledge (about 1,900 feet), the summit of Holts Ledge (2,100 feet), and then along the ridge of Moose Mountain, including the summit (2,300 feet).

After passing through Hanover, New Hampshire, home of Dartmouth College (see below), the Trail descends to the Connecticut River (400 feet), the southern end of the A.T. in New Hampshire. The Trail in this section often follows woods roads and footpaths through pastures, fields, and forest at low elevations. Except for the steep ascents of Holts Ledge and Moose Mountain, the terrain is easy to hike.

This section has three side trails. The Clark Pond Loop may be used as an alternate route to the A.T. This 17.6-mile loop, the former A.T., is a low-country trail passing three lakes east of the present Trail. The southern end of the loop is on the eastern flank of Moose Mountain. The northern end is on the summit of Smarts Mountain in Section 8. This trail is described briefly in the trail description.

The Harris Trail begins where the A.T. crosses Goose Pond Road. Follow this road one-half mile west, then the old A.T. route 4.1 miles southwest, rejoining the A.T. between the south summit of Moose Mountain and Three Mile Road.

The Velvet Rocks Shelter Loop leaves the A.T. at the junction with the Ledyard Spring Trail (spring is approximately 0.2 mile) and leads 0.4 mile to the shelter. Total length of loop is 0.6 mile.

The Trescott Road spur (the former A.T.) drops 0.6 miles to Trescott Road 23 miles north of Hanover.

For more information on the Clark Pond Loop, guidebooks, maps, and A.T. information for this area, contact the Dartmouth Outing Club (see "Important Addresses," page 301). The DOC office is located on the Green in Hanover.

Note: a Trail relocation is planned in the area between Three Mile Road and Trescott Road. Carefully follow the blazes.

Dartmouth College

Dartmouth College is in the center of the small town of Hanover, New Hampshire. On December 13, 1769, King George III of England approved a charter prepared by Governor John Wentworth of New Hampshire establishing an institution "for the education and instruction of Youth of the Indian Tribes in this Land in reading, writing and all parts of Learning which shall appear necessary and expedient for civilizing and christianizing Children of Pagans as well as in all liberal Arts and Sciences and also of English Youth and any others." Wentworth decided to name the college after the Earl of Dartmouth, the school's sponsor and benefactor.

The Reverend Eleazar Wheelock was the college's actual founder. The year after the charter was approved, Wheelock struck off into the New Hampshire wilderness and built a single log hut as the home of Dartmouth College. It was there that the first class, all of four students, graduated in 1771.

Today, the Ivy League school is primarily a liberal-arts college, but also has graduate schools of medicine, engineering, and business. Hikers may want to take advantage of the many cultural opportunities the college offers to the public.

Road Approaches

The northern end of this section is accessible by the Lyme-Dorchester Road. Starting in Lyme (on N.H. 10), this paved road leads 2.8 miles east to the Dartmouth Skiway (ample parking) and the Trail. The Trail crosses a number of roads in the middle of the section. It crosses the Etna-Hanover Center Road 1.2 miles south of Hanover Center (no convenient parking) and the Goose Pond Road 3.3 miles east of N.H. 10.

The Connecticut River at Hanover is reached from the north and south by I-89 and I-91, U.S. 5, and N.H. 10; from the west, by U.S. 4 and Vt. 14; from the east, by U.S. 4. At the crossing of the Connecticut River, the Trail is 0.2 miles east of U.S. 5 and Interstate 91 in Vermont. The Trail follows West Wheelock Street for the half mile between the Connecticut River and N.H. 10 in Hanover (difficult, metered parking), south on N.H. 10 (Main Street) to the next traffic light, where it turns left (east) onto N.H. 120 (Lebanon Street). It then follows Lebanon Street (N.H. 120) 0.6 mile until reaching a service station. Here, the Trail turns left, leaving Lebanon Street, and skirts the edge of a playing field for a short distance before turning into woods. Parking is not permitted in this area, but a Dartmouth College parking lot is available for hikers, who should stop at the DOC office in Robinson Hall for instructions.

Maps

Map No. 4 (this guide)
DOC Trail Map
USGS 15 minute topographic quadrangles:
  Mt. Cube, N.H.
  Mascoma, N.H
USGS 7 1/2 minute topographic quadrangle:
  Hanover, N.H./Vt.

Regulations

Camping and fires are prohibited except at Trapper John, Moose Mountain, and Velvet Rocks shelters.

Shelters and Campsites

This section has three shelters.

Trapper John Shelter: Built and maintained by DOC 1.5 miles from north end of section on 0.2 mile side trail; accomodates 8; ample water.

Next shelter or campsite: north 6.7 miles (Smarts Mountain Shelter); south 5.3 miles.

Moose Mountain Shelter: Built and maintained by DOC 6.8 miles from north end of section 1.1 miles up side trail; accomodates 6; ample water.

Next shelter or campsite: north 6.2 miles (Smarts Mountain Shelter); south 9.3 miles.

Velvet Rocks Shelter: Built and maintained by DOC 2.0 miles from south end of section on 0.2 mile side trail; accommodates 4; water 0.6 mile east on Velvet Rocks Loop and Ledyard Spring Trail.

Next shelter or campsite: north 9.3 miles; south 7.0 miles (Happy Hill Cabin).

Supplies and Services

From the Trail crossing of Lyme-Dorchester Road at the Dartmouth Skiway at the north end of the section, it is 1.2 miles west to Lyme Center (P.O. 03769) and 3.2 miles to Lyme (P.O. 03768, phone, limited groceries, meals). From the Trail crossing of the Etna-Hanover Center Road, 5.4 miles from the south end of the section, it is approximately two miles south to Etna (P.O. 03750, limited groceries). The educational and cultural facilities of Dartmouth College (see "Dartmouth College"), as well as the largest shopping area directly on the Trail in New Hampshire and Vermont, are in Hanover (P.O. 03755, phone, supermarket, specialty backpacking stores, bookstore, restaurants, Mary Hitchcock Memorial Hospital, bus stop).

In an emergency, contact the New Hampshire State Police, (800) 852-3411 or (603) 846-5500.

Public Accommodations

An inn is located in Lyme, 3.2 miles west of the north end of this section.

Accommodations are available toward the south end of the section in Hanover. Norwich, Vt. has an inn one mile south of the southern end of the section (Vermont Section 1). Motels, hotels, and rooming houses near White River Junction, Vt., and Lebanon, N.H., five miles south of Hanover, provide services over a wide price range.

Trail Description, North to South

Miles	Data
0.0	From the Dartmouth Skiway (880 ft.), at a fork in the Lyme-Dorchester Road, the Trail ascends gradually SW into woods paralleling the right side of a ski trail. (Do not walk on the ski trail.)
1.5	Side trail leads right 0.2 mi. to **Trapper John Shelter** (water). The A.T. continues to climb parallel to ski trail.
2.1	Turn sharp right at start of fence and reach crest of Holts Ledge (1,900 ft.). The Trail descends through woods.
2.2	Continue straight uphill past where the old A.T. leaves right (blocked).
2.3	Summit of **Holts Ledge**. Note: the Trail to the overlook may be closed during the nesting season of the endangered peregrine falcon, several pairs of which have recently been seen in the area.
3.3	Cross old logging road, then descend to cross beaver pond dam to road.
4.5	Reach **Goose Pond Road** bear left 50 ft., then turn right off road into woods and ascend, at first gradually, then steeply to the **North Peak of Moose** Mountain (2,300 ft.). Following the ridgeline and rocky outcroppings at North Peak. The Trail eventually descends to a col between North and South peaks.
7.7	Reach woods road. A.T. continues straight ahead. **Moose Mountain Shelter** also to left 0.5 mi. Blue-blazed **Clark Pond Loop** descends to **Goose Pond** on woods roads. continues in low country to **Clark Pond** and **Cummings Pond**, then climbs

to rejoin A.T. on Smarts Mountain summit, a total of 17.6 mi., A.T. ascends to South Peak's summit (2,290 ft.).

8.2 From **South Peak of Moose Mountain.** Trail descends gradually with one steep section to woods road.

9.6 Cross woods road and continue descent to small stream. Ascend gradually to Three Mile Road.

10.0 Reach **Three Mile Road.** Turn right and after 100 yds., turn left off road into field, and follow left edge of field.

10.1 Cross stone wall and descend on Trail through woods and overgrown pasture with scattered large trees. Cross old woods road with two wire fences.

10.7 Bear right onto woods road. Turn right onto another woods road and descend. Pass across hill on Trail and old woods road. Descend to wire fence and follow it to its left. Enter field and descend along its edge.

11.7 Turn sharp right onto private road, cross bridge, and turn right onto **Etna-Hanover Center Road.** After 150 ft., turn left onto old lumber road, and ascend through mature woods. Descend on Trail.

12.3 Turn left on wide dirt road.

12.4 Turn right onto paved **Dogford Road.**

12.5 Turn left onto dirt Paine Road, follow 150 yds., turn left into woods.

13.4 Turn right onto **Trescott Road** (E. Wheelock St.) and follow NW.

13.7 Turn left, away from Trescott Road, pass through a conifer plantation, cross over a small knoll, and continue in level section. Reach large beaver pond, which the Trail crosses on the dam. The Trail switchbacks up ledges and turns sharp left on an old logging road. Ascend, then descend, and bear right then right again. Begin climbing again, then switchback left, contouring between ledges to reach a ridge. Follow this ridge N through a clearing near the summit of Velvet Rocks.

15.9 Reach **Trescott Road** spur on right. This trail, the former A.T., drops to **Trescott Road** at a point about 2.3 mi. E of Hanover. Length, 0.6 mi.

16.5 Reach E end of **Velvet Rocks Shelter Trail** loop on right. Here, the **Ledyard Spring Trail** leaves right (spring approximately 0.2 mi.). The A.T. bends left around the hill and continues W.

17.0 Reach W end of **Velvet Rocks Shelter Loop** on right (0.2 mi. to shelter). Trail continues on the crest of a ridge then descends and passes a spring (pool on left unreliable; last water in section). Trail slabs the ridge SW, then leaves the woods and bears left following the S edge of a playing field.

17.8 Reach **N.H. 120** (Lebanon Street) at a service station. Trail turns right and follows road to **N.H. 10** (N. Main Street traffic light). Trail turns right (N) on N. Main Street.

18.5 Reach intersection of North Main and East Wheelock Street Trail turns left (W). The offices of **Dartmouth Outing Club** are located in Robinson Hall, the second building on the left N on Main St. The Trail descends W on West Wheelock St.

19.0 Reach the E end of bridge over **Connecticut River** (400 ft. above sea level) and the end of section. To continue on Trail, cross bridge and follow Vt. 10A W.

Trail Description, South to North

Miles	Data
0.0	From the E end of the bridge over the **Connecticut River** (400 ft. above sea level), follow hard-surfaced West Wheelock St. E into Hanover.
0.5	Reach intersection of North Main St. and East Wheelock St. The offices of **Dartmouth Outing Club** are in Robinson Hall, second building on left (N) on North Main St. The A.T. turns right (S) on **N.H. 10** (North Main St.) to the next traffic light at N.H. 120 (Lebanon St.); it then turns left (E) and follows this route.
1.2	Reach a service station. Trail turns left, following the S edge of a playing field until it bears right into the woods. Shortly, it bears left (NE) and slabs the ridge. Soon, it passes a spring (pool on right not reliable).
2.1	Reach W end of **Velvet Rocks Shelter Loop** on left (0.2 mi. to shelter). The Trail bends right around a hill.
2.6	Reach E end of Velvet Rocks Shelter Loop at a junction with the **Ledyard Spring Trail**, both on left (spring about 0.2 mi.). Trail turns right (E) and continues over a number of knolls.
3.1	Reach **Trescott Road** spur. This trail, the former A.T. route, drops to Trescott Road at a point about 2.3 mi. E of Hanover (length 0.6 mi.). The Trail swings S through a clearing near the summit of Velvet Rocks, then follows a ridge SE, makes a sharp bend left, slabbing down amid fine ledges. It then follows an old logging road for some distance until it turns sharp right. Switchbacking down

through more ledges, it soon reaches a large beaver pond, which it crosses on the dam. The Trail continues almost level for some distance, then crosses over a small knoll, and passes through a conifer plantation.

5.3 Turn right onto **Trescott Road** (E. Wheelock St.).

5.6 Turn left from road onto Trail bypassing the Hanover watershed. Descend through mature woods on old lumber road.

6.1 Turn right onto **Paine Road**.

6.2 Turn right onto paved **Dogford Road**.

6.3 Turn left onto wide dirt road.

6.4 Turn off dirt road onto Trail.

7.2 Turn right onto hard-surfaced **Etna-Hanover Center Road**. After 150 ft., turn left over bridge onto private road.

7.3 Just beyond bridge, turn sharp left, and ascend to field. Follow edge of field with fence on left to corner. Turn left, and enter woods, still with wire fence on left. Leave fence, and ascend on woods road and Trail across hill.

8.0 Enter woods road, and ascend to wire fence. Just beyond, turn left, and follow woods road.

8.3 Where woods road makes sharp right turn, the A.T. follows trail on left. Cross old woods road with two wire fences. Ascend on Trail through woods and overgrown pasture with scattered large trees.

8.9 Cross stone wall, and follow right edge of field.

9.0 Turn right onto dirt road. Turn left after 100 yds. into woods. Cross stream.

9.4 Reach woods road, and cross immediately. **Harris Trail** follows this road left and reaches the A.T., at

Goose Pond Road in 4.6 mi. Begin ascending gradually, sometimes steeply toward South Peak of Moose Mountain.

10.8 Reach summit of **South Peak of Moose Mountain.** (2,290 ft.). Descend to woods road in col between South and North peaks.

11.3 Reach woods road A.T. continues straight ahead. **Moose Mountain Shelter** is 0.5 mi. to the right. Blue-blazed **Clark Pond Loop Trail** descends right to Goose Pond as woods road continues in low country to Clark Pond and Cummings Pond, then climbs to rejoin A.T. on the summit of Smarts Mountain, a total of 17.6 miles). A.T. follows ridge of **Moose Mountain.** Trail descends steeply after North Peak (2,300 ft.), then gradually as it approaches Goose Pond Road.

14.5 Reach **Goose Pond Road** (920 ft.). Turn left on road, follow 50 ft., then bear right on narrow road through old log landing. Follow road to its end, then cross beaver dam. Bear left in about 100 yds., and then begin climbing, first gradually, then steeply.

15.7 Cross old logging road, then continue climbing steadily.

16.7 Summit of **Holts Ledge** (wooded). Begin descending along cliff edge in woods. Note: the Trail to the overlook may be closed during the nesting season of the endangered peregrine falcon, several pairs of which have recently been seen in the area.

16.8 Turn sharp left, ascending into woods.

16.9 Reach crest of Holts Ledge (1,900 ft.). Descend by turning sharp left at start of fence. Trail parallels left side of ski trail for 0.5 mi. Do not hike on the ski trail.

17.5 Side trail leads left 0.2 mi. to **Trapper John Shelter** (water). The A.T. continues to parallel ski trail, gradually descending.

19.0 Reach **Lyme-Dorchester Road** (880 ft.) at a fork in the road, the end of the section. The Dartmouth Skiway, with its ski trails on the N side of Holts Ledge, is located here. To continue on Trail, cross road and bear right onto dirt road.

The Appalachian Trail in Vermont

The Trail in Vermont is 137.0 miles long. The northern part runs east to west, mostly through lowland hardwood country. This part of the Trail rolls across a series of wooded hills dotted with fields, pastures, and abandoned roads and farms of an earlier era. The Trail in the southern part of Vermont, from Sherburne Pass to the Massachusetts border, follows the central ridgecrest of the Green Mountains. For this entire distance (97 miles), the Trail coincides with the Long Trail.

The Dartmouth Outing Club (DOC) maintains the Trail from the Connecticut River west to Vt. 12. This section is blazed with standard, white A.T. blazes in addition to the orange-and-black blazes marking all DOC trails. The responsibility for maintenance of the section from Vt. 12 south to the Massachusetts border lies with the Green Mountain Club (GMC), although parts of this are maintained by the U.S. Forest Service (USFS).

The terrain of the northern part of the Trail in Vermont, from the Connecticut River Valley west to Sherburne Pass, is much like the terrain from the Connecticut River north to Glencliff, N.H. It is a succession of pastures, cleared hills, patches of timber, ravines, and peaks. The route does not follow a continuous ridgecrest, as in the southern Appalachians, but crosses a series of high, strenuous peaks. Griggs Mountain is the dominating feature of this portion of the Trail. It is a land of high wooded ridges and abandoned farms. Stone walls and cellar holes, evidence of former inhabitants, are found even in the woods. Everywhere are indications of the area's history and its gradual reversion to forest after intensive farming.

Beginning at the Connecticut River, the Trail passes west through the small town of Norwich, Vt., on roads. It then ascends across Mosley Hill (1,180 feet) and passes over the wooded crest of Griggs Mountain (1,570 feet) to descend along Podunk Brook to the White River at West Hartford. It crosses the White River on a highway bridge and passes over Bunker Hill (1,480 feet) on old roads before reaching the abandoned Kings Highway. West of Kings Highway, the Trail begins its traverse of the open slopes and abandoned farmlands so characteristic of this portion of the Trail in Vermont (Sections 2 and 3). It first passes over Thistle Hill (1,800 feet). Then, it crosses a series of cleared ridges, descends through several valleys, crosses a number of roads, and reaches Vt. 12.

Vt. 12 to Sherburne Pass is the most western link between the White and Green Mountains. It involves considerable exertion; the route crosses numerous ridges with ascents and descents. From Vt. 12, the route ascends to The Lookout (2,439 feet) and continues west for some distance across rugged terrain into Ottauquechee Valley, hemmed in by high ridges. The autumn foliage in this section is outstanding. From this valley, the Trail follows the gravel Thundering Brook Road past Kent Pond and then a trail around the pond to Vt. 100. It crosses Vt. 100 into Gifford Woods State Park , which has an interesting virgin hardwood forest. After passing through the park, the Trail rises steeply to its junction with the Long Trail, just north of Sherburne Pass. From this junction, the A.T. follows the Long Trail south to the Massachusetts border.

The Long Trail of Vermont follows the main ridge of the Green Mountains some 263 miles, from the Canadian border to the Massachusetts state line. Like the A.T., the Long Trail is a primitive footpath. It is steep, boggy, and rugged in the tradition of other early New England trails, like those the A.T. follows in the White Mountains of New Hampshire. The A.T. on the southern part of the Long Trail passes over a number of high summits and through low points in the Green Mountains where major highways cross the range. The route winds through wilderness terrain, densely forested with evergreens in higher elevations and northern hardwood trees in lower areas. It also passes a number of scenic mountain lakes. Although not as rough as the route in the White Mountains, the Long Trail terrain is strenuous and rewarding.

From Sherburne Pass, the Trail climbs south across the Coolidge Range. Short side trails lead to the summits of Pico Peak (3,957 feet) and Killington Peak (4,235 feet). The Trail reaches its highest point in Vermont just below Killington Peak, the second highest summit in Vermont, next to Mt. Mansfield (4,393 feet). From the Coolidge Range, the Trail continues south across rolling foothills, crosses a number of roads, and reaches Vt. 103.

Just south of Vt. 103, the Trail crosses a suspension bridge over Clarendon Gorge and continues to Vt. 140. South of Vt. 140, the Trail ascends the ridge of White Rocks Mountain (2,680 feet), passes Little Rock Pond, then descends along Little Black Branch to the Danby-Landgrove Road (USFS 10) at a low point on the Green Mountain crest. The Trail rises again to the summit of Baker Peak (2,850 feet). It then descends past Griffith Lake. South of Griffith Lake, the Trail passes over Peru Peak (3,429 feet) and Styles Peak (3,394 feet), before descending to Mad Tom Notch (2,446 feet).

South of Mad Tom Notch, the Trail steadily climbs Bromley Mountain (3,260 feet). The Trail descends to cross Vt. 11 south of Bromley Mountain, then climbs to Spruce Peak (approximately 2,060 feet) via a short side trail. South of Spruce Peak, the Trail reaches Prospect Rock (2,079 feet) and enters

Green Mountain National Forest Lye Brook Wilderness, a primitive tract of Vermont woodland. The Trail passes for some 6.2 miles through the wilderness, reaching Bourn Pond, which has camping as well as a shelter. The Trail leaves the wilderness on the western slope of Stratton Mountain and reaches scenic Stratton Pond. The Stratton Mountain Trail, an alternate loop to the A.T., can be followed from the pond or from the Arlington-West Wardsboro Road, to which the Trail descends not far south of the pond.

From the Arlington-West Wardsboro Road, the Trail ascends south along the ridge, rising to Glastenbury Mountain (3,748 feet), the highest point reached by the A.T. in southern Vermont. South of Glastenbury Mountain, the Trail continues along a wooded ridge. It drops steeply to Vt. 9, but then rises even more steeply to follow a rolling ridge.

The short section of Trail from the Massachusetts-Vermont line to North Adams, Mass., is covered in this guide as a part of Section 9 for the hiker's convenience. Here the Trail passes over the open and rocky ridge of East Mountain, then drops to the Hoosic River and Mass. 2 in North Adams.

Additional information on the Trail from Vt. 12 south is available in the *Day Hikers Guide to Vermont* or *Guide Book of the Long Trail.* These guides and current information on the A.T. are available from the Appalachian Trail Conference or the Green Mountain Club. For information on the Trail from Vt. 12 east to the Connecticut River, contact the Dartmouth Outing Club (see "Important Addresses," page 301).

Private Lands

From the Connecticut River west to the Long Trail (Sections 1-3), and on the Long Trail from Sherburne Pass south to Vt. 140 (Section 4), from the Arlington-West Wardsboro Road to North Adams, Mass. (Sections 8-9), the Trail passes across some private land. In these sections, camping and fires are permitted only at designated sites. Using private lands is permitted through the landowners' generosity, and the hiker is asked to respect their rights.

Green Mountain National Forest

For about one- quarter of its length, primarily in Sections 5 and 7, the Trail passes through Green Mountain National Forest (GMNF). The national forest covers some 250,000 acres, stretching almost 100 miles north from the Massachusetts line. It is not only a recreational resource, but provides timber, wildlife, grazing, and water. In each section of the guide, under "Regulations," are instructions for using the forest in that particular area. Camping is permitted in the forest.

In recent years, recreational use of GMNF's backcountry has increased dramatically. In some places, shelters and trails are traveled by greater numbers of hikers than the local environment can support. Trail erosion, loss of vegetation, water pollution, and disposal of human waste have developed into major concerns. The heavy use around Little Rock Pond is a good example. Here, intense use by hikers and others has damaged the fragile shoreline. Such problems necessitate regulations aimed at reducing the impact camping and hiking have on plant life, soils, and water.

Throughout GMNF, fires at designated sites must be built in the fireplaces provided. Other fires, although ill-advised, may be kindled in the forest. No campfire permits are required. Hikers are encouraged to use portable stoves, to reduce the impact on the campsites.

All visitors to GMNF are asked to keep the trailside and

overnight sites clean. Some GMC sites have facilities for composting food waste. All trash should be carried out.

For further information on policies in GMNF, the hiker should contact the Supervisor's Office, Green Mountain National Forest (see "Important Addresses," page 301).

Plant Life

Throughout the A.T. in Vermont, cutting or damaging living trees, shrubs, and plants is prohibited. Only dead material on the ground may be used for fires.

Lye Brook Wilderness

In Section 7, the Trail passes through Lye Brook Wilderness, a tract of primitive woodland in GMNF preserved by Congress. No entry permit is required; however, the regulations concerning the remainder of GMNF also apply here.

Caretakers

Full-time summer caretakers maintain and supervise a number of backcountry shelters and campsites in the Green Mountains, both within and outside the national forest. At these areas, mentioned in the trail description, a fee is charged to defray costs.

State Parks

The A.T. passes through Gifford Woods State Park (Section 3), which was established to ensure the preservation of certain virgin hardwood forest stands. Camping is permitted within the park at campsites and shelters (see Section 3).

Overnight Facilities

The A.T. hiker has a number of alternatives when planning to spend the night out on the Trail in Vermont. For part of its length in Vermont the A.T. passes across private land where camping is permitted only at designated sites. Heavy use of trail shelters causes space to fill quickly. Hikers should come prepared to camp out. South of Sherburne Pass, shelter stays are limited to two consecutive days. When considering designated sites, the hiker has the following options.

Campsites

A campsite generally refers to a site with water, toilet facilities, fireplace, and sometimes tent platforms. Several campsites are referred to as "primitive." Instead of platforms, sites are simply spots cleared for tents. Both platforms and cleared areas allow concentrated use of an area with localized soil compaction. (Compaction alters water drainage and hinders plant growth.) Some campsites have a caretaker and and charge a fee.

Shelters

The Trail has a number of Adirondack (three walls, open front) shelters that can accommodate four to eight people. Shelters are located near water and have fireplaces and toilet facilities. Camping is permitted in the vicinity of most shelters. At some sites, a caretaker is in residence and a fee is charged.

Cabins

A cabin is simply a closed shelter, which may have bunks. In Vermont, cabins are often called "camps." Cabins are located near water and also have fireplaces and privies. At some sites, a caretaker is in residence, and a fee is charged.

Public Accommodations

A wide range of commercial accommodations is located along the public roads the Trail crosses, although sometimes these are some distance from the Trail. They are described under "Public Accommodations" in each section.

Connecticut River (Norwich) to White River (Vt. 14 at West Hartford)

Section 1 Vermont

9.1 Miles

Brief Description of Section

The Trail in this section traverses the partly forested, partly cleared mountains between the Connecticut River and the White River in Vermont. From the Connecticut River bridge (400 feet), at the northern end of the section, the A.T. follows hard-surfaced roads 1.8 miles to Norwich, then follows trails and woods roads. It is a moderate climb around Mosley Hill (Trail elevation 1,180 feet) through white pine woods, timber, and pastures and along woods roads to DOC Happy Hill Cabin (1,460 feet). Climbing is moderate over the wooded flank (1,570 feet) of Griggs Mountain and a descent through forests and along a dirt road parallel to Podunk Brook, which leads to the White River in West Hartford (400 feet).

Tucker Trail is the only side trail in the section. It can be used as an alternate route to the A.T. between Norwich and DOC Happy Hill Cabin, but it is mostly on roads. For more information on this trail and current information on the A.T. in this section, write the Dartmouth Outing Club (see "Important Addresses," page 301).

Road Approaches

Both the north and south ends of this section are accessible from major highways. The north end of the section (the Connecticut River at Norwich, Vt., and Hanover, N.H.) is reached from the north and south by I-89 and I-91, U.S. 5, and N.H. 10; from the west by U.S. 4 and Vt. 14; and from the east by U.S. 4. Cars can be left in Norwich, where the Trail leaves the paved road.

The south end of the section, the White River at West Hartford, is reached by Vt. 14, about eight miles west of the junction of I-89 and I-91 in White River Junction, Vt. Vehicles are usually left 2.3 miles north of the end of the section, where the road becomes impassable by automobile.

Maps

Map No. 5 (this guide)
DOC Trail Map
USGS 7 1/2 minute topographic quadrangles:
  Hanover, N.H./Vt.
  Quechee, Vt.

Shelters and Campsites

This section has one cabin.

Happy Hill Cabin: Built and maintained by DOC approximately in the center of section; accommodates 8; water from brook; also reached from the north by DOC Tucker Trail.

Next shelter or campsite: north 6.8 miles (Velvet Rocks Shelter); south 9.7 miles (Cloudland Shelter).

Regulations

Camping and fires are prohibited, except at Happy Hill Cabin.

Supplies and Services

A half-mile east of the Connecticut River in Hanover, N.H. (P.O. 03755) are phones, a supermarket, specialty backpacking stores, bookstore, restaurants, bus stop, and Mary Hitchcock Memorial Hospital. For more information on Hanover, refer to Section 9 in New Hampshire. Near the north end of this section, the hiker passes through Norwich, Vt. (P.O. 05055, phone, groceries, restaurant). At the southern terminus of the section, the Trail passes through West Hartford (P.O. 05084, phone, groceries).

In an emergency, contact the Vermont State Police, (802) 773-9101.

Public Accommodations

Hanover, N.H. is one half mile north of the Connecticut River on the A.T. (motels, inns; see Section 9 in New Hampshire). Near the north end of the section, the Trail passes through Norwich, Vt. (inn). The south end has no public accommodations. Motels, hotels, and rooming houses in the White River Junction, Vt., and Lebanon, N.H., areas, four miles south of the northern end of the section and eight miles south of the southern end of the section, provide lodging over a wide price range.

Trail Description, North to South

Miles	Data
0.0	From east bank, cross **Connecticut River** into Vermont. Ascend on Vt. 10A, and pass under I-91.
0.6	Reach and follow U.S. 5 N into Norwich.
1.0	Opposite bandstand (gazebo) in park, turn sharp left onto Elm Street, and gradually descend SW.
1.2	Cross **Bloody Brook**, and ascend.
1.5	Cross **Hopson Road**, and ascend more steeply.
1.8	Fifty yards after passing Hickory Ridge Road on left, Trail enters woods on left and follows the contour to a small stream before climbing steadily.
2.5	Cross power line opening. About 15 yds. south along the power line is a view of Wilder Dam.
2.9	Cross old woods road (former A.T.).
3.5	Cross **Newton Lane.**
4.7	Turn left onto abandoned road and ascend. To the right, the blue-blazed **William Tucker Trail** descends to the upper end of a maintained gravel road (0.8 mi.), descends on the road to Bragg Hill Road (1.3 mi.), and continues down Bragg Hill Road and Meadow Brook Road to Main Street (U.S. 5) in Norwich (3.5 mi.).
5.0	Reach **Happy Hill Cabin**. With cabin on left, cross small stream, swing left into woods, and ascend on old woods road.
5.4	Cross wooded shoulder of **Griggs Mountain** (approximately 1,570 ft.), and descend in woods, soon reaching and following traces of former road.
5.7	Enter large, overgrown field, and follow faint track near upper edge. Pass old foundations, which may be obscured by high grass.

5.8 Leave clearing, turn left onto woods road, and descend.

5.9 Pass road to right.

6.3 Pass entrance to camp on left.

6.6 Cross small stream, then turn sharp right, and recross stream three more times.

6.8 Turn right at road junction (critical turn). Descend gradually across brook, and then ascend.

6.9 Turn left onto **Podunk Road** at junction (beginning of passable road). Make brief ascent, then dip into hollow before resuming ascent.

7.2 Pass road leading right to house on hill. Begin long descent on good gravel road.

7.3 Turn sharp right into woods, and climb steeply uphill. Cross over a hardwood ridge, then descend through forests and overgrown pastures.

8.1 Return to Podunk Road, cross road bridge, turn left onto **Tigertown Road,** and follow under I-89 bridges.

8.6 At road junction, turn sharp right across Central Vermont Railway tracks.

8.7 Turn left onto Vt. 14, and follow highway S into West Hartford.

9.1 Reach E end of **West Hartford-Quechee Road** at bridge over White River. Turn right and cross bridge to continue on Trail.

Trail Description, South to North

Miles **Data**

0.0 Follow Vt. 14 N from West Hartford Bridge.

0.4 Turn right onto **Tigertown Road** (sign).

0.5 Cross Central Vermont railroad tracks, immediately turn left at junction. Continue under I-89.

0.6 Turn sharp right onto **Podunk Road**, cross bridge, then immediately bear left into woods. Follow Trail steeply uphill through overgrown pastures, then cross a hardwood ridge, and descend.

1.8 Turn left onto Podunk Rd.

1.9 Pass road leading left to house.

2.2 Reach end of driveable road. Turn sharp right and descend across stream.

2.3 Turn sharp left on old woods road; ascend with three small stream crossings.

2.5 Turn sharp left, recross brook, continue ascent.

2.8 Pass entrance to camp on right.

3.2 Pass road to left.

3.3 Turn right off woods road into clearing; follow track on upper edge.

3.4 Leave clearing; ascend on old road, then on Trail.

3.7 Pass over shoulder of **Griggs Mountain**.

4.1 Reach **Happy Hill Cabin**, descend, follow old road.

4.4 Turn right off road into woods. Trail begins to drop, then climbs gently through hardwood and pine stands. Road (**William Tucker Trail**) descends to gravel road (0.8 mi.) and downhill to public roads to U.S. 5 in Norwich (3.5 mi.)

5.6 Cross **Newton Lane**.

6.2 Cross old woods road (former A.T.).

6.6 Cross power line. About 15 yds. S along power line is view of Wilder Dam on Connecticut River. Begin descent.

7.3 Join paved **Elm Street.** Descend steadily.

7.6 Cross **Hopson Road** and descend on easier grades.

7.9 Cross **Bloody Brook**.
8.1 Turn right onto **U.S. 5** in Norwich opposite park and bandstand. Follow highway S.
8.5 Bear left onto **Vt. 10A**, pass under Interstate 91 bridges, and descend.
9.1 Reach east bank of **Connecticut River**. Continue uphill on highway.

White River (Vt. 14 at West Hartford) to Vt. 12

Section 2 Vermont

12.0 Miles

Brief Description of Section

In this section, the Trail rolls across a patchwork of wooded and cleared hills, ridges, and valleys. The extensive farming that once covered the area is evident frequently. From White River in West Hartford (400 feet), at the north end of the section, the Trail ascends for 1.4 miles on road, passable by car, then on woods roads and trails, and over Bunker Hill (1,480 feet). It continues with minor elevational changes, passes over Thistle Hill (1,800 feet), and reaches Cloudland Shelter. South of Cloudland Shelter, the Trail crosses a number of ridges and valleys, and two hard-surfaced roads before reaching Vt. 12 (882 feet).

This section has no side trails, but the Trail is intersected by numerous woods roads and abandoned roads. For current information on the A.T. in this section, contact the Dartmouth Outing Club (see "Important Addresses," page 301).

Road Approaches

Both ends of this section are accessible from major highways. At the northern end the A.T. crosses Vt. 14 in West Hartford, eight miles west of White River Junction (on I-91) and five miles south of Sharon (on I- 89). At the southern end, the Trail crosses Vt. 12, 4.4 miles north of Woodstock.

The Trail also crosses three roads passable by car in the southern half of the section. At 6.1 miles from the southern end of the section, it crosses the dirt Cloudland Road about four miles north of Woodstock. At 4.3 miles from the southern end of the section, it crosses the South Pomfret-Pomfret Road 1.6 miles north of South Pomfret and 4.6 miles north of Woodstock. At 1.7 miles from the southern end of the section, it crosses the Barnard Brook Road about one mile north of South Pomfret and four miles north of Woodstock.

Maps

Map No. 5 (this guide)
DOC Trail Map
USGS 7 1/2 minute topographic quadrangies:
  Quechee, Vt.
  Woodstock North, Vt.

Shelters and Campsites

This section has one shelter.

Cloudland Shelter: Built and maintained by DOC; accommodates 8; ample water.

Next shelter or campsite: north 9.4 miles (Happy Hill Cabin); south 9.5 miles (Wintturi Shelter).

Regulations

Camping and fires are prohibited, except at Cloudland Shelter.

Supplies and Services

The northern end of the section lies in West Hartford (P.O. 05084, phone, groceries). From the Trail crossing at Vt. 12, at the southern end of the section, it is 4.4 miles south to Woodstock (P.O. 05091, phone, supermarket, equipment, laundromat, restaurants, bus stop).

In an emergency, call the Vermont State Police, (802) 773-9101.

Public Accommodations

The northern end of the section in West Hartford has no public accommodations, but from here it is eight miles south to the White River Junction, Vt. and Lebanon, N.H. areas, which have motels, hotels, and rooming houses over a wide price range. The southern end of the section on Vt. 12 is 4. miles north of Woodstock (motels, inn).

Trail Description, North to South

Miles	Data
0.0	From Vt. 14 in the center of West Hartford, cross **White River** on West Hartford-Quechee Road highway bridge (400 ft.). Pass Pomfret Road, which runs along west bank of White River. *Note: A relocation is planned for the next three miles. Follow the blazes carefully.*
0.2	Turn right, and follow good unpaved town road.
0.7	Pass red- brick house on left; continue to meadow.
0.8	Turn left onto narrow town road, and ascend.
1.4	Reach end of maintained road at house on right. Continue straight ahead, ascend abandoned road.

2.1 Turn right onto old town road, and ascend.
2.4 Cross ridge of **Bunker Hill,** and descend W.
2.6 Reach end of maintained road opposite driveway left to house on hill—no parking allowed. Descend on road.
2.7 Reach junction with old **King's Highway**, just beyond house and barn. Descend to right on road.
2.9 Opposite Bunker Hill Burying Ground, turn left off road across old fence and ascend through forest growth into birch grove. Continue into woods.
3.3 Reach knob NE of Thistle Hill (1,626 ft.). Bear right, descend beside old fence below ridgeline.
3.6 Turn right onto woods road, continue, ascend.
3.7 Bear left at fork, briefly follow old road, and then turn right onto Trail and descend into gap.
3.8 At low point in gap, reach and follow old woods road uphill to right. Bear right onto main woods road through gap, and ascend.
3.9 At height of land in gap, bear left off road, and begin slabbing ascent of W slope.
4.3 Reach high point on ridge (ill-defined), and descend.
4.5 Cross shallow sag.
4.8 Cross and recross small stream.
5.0 Turn right onto woods road, and descend for 125 ft. before turning left into woods on Trail.
5.1 Turn left, and rejoin woods road, descending.
5.2 Turn right off road onto Trail in woods.
5.3 Turn right onto road, and descend. Cross small brook 125 ft. beyond junction.
5.4 Reach blue-blazed spur on right leading to **Cloudland Shelter**. Trail continues on road.
5.7 Pass under power line and reach upper end of

field. Follow road to right; then along lower edge of field.

5.9 Reach **Cloudland Road** at entrance to field, E of red house. Follow road right for 200 ft., turn left, and ascend on A.T. through overgrown pasture.

6.1 Enter woods on easier grade, and soon resume slabbing ascent of W slope of hill.

6.4 Cross shallow W sag, and ascend E slope.

6.5 Cross stone wall in overgrown pasture. Ascend gradually in increasingly open area.

6.6 Reach summit of nameless hill (1,730 ft.) at cairn. From summit, descend steadily in open near edges of field.

6.8 Reach blue-blazed spur on left leading 50 ft. uphill to small spring. Follow spur 75 ft. beyond, reach and follow town road. Minor elevation changes.

7.1 Turn right at old four-way junction, and descend on old town road.

7.3 Bear left off road to avoid wet area, cross two narrow woods roads, then bear right again to rejoin old road.

7.4 Reach end of maintained, unpaved town road opposite house on right. Descend on road, past private roads and drives to right and left.

7.7 Reach paved **South Pomfret-Pomfret Road**; turn left and follow road W for 250 ft., then turn right onto narrow unpaved road.

7.8 Turn left from dirt road, cross field uphill, turn right on cart track, follow 200 ft., turn right into field. Follow edge of woods on right to crest. Descend.

8.1 Cross wire fence by large maples in field, and descend right downhill to fence. Follow fence.

8.3 Cross wire fence and field to house.

8.4 Cross **Bartlett Brook**, then cross narrow dirt road, passable by automobile in dry weather, and pass between barn and farmhouse. Ascend through field.

8.6 Bear right onto old woods road and continue ascent through stand of evergreens.

8.8 Where road bears right, climb left, uphill, through overgrown field and barway just below crest.

9.0 Pass over crest. To left is Totman Hill (1,560 ft.). Descend slightly on cart track.

9.1 Cross grass-grown road, continue on overgrown woods road past ruined farmhouse.

9.2 Reach crest of sag. Enter fine hardwood forest.

9.4 Cross barway.

9.5 Enter overgrown fields.

9.7 Cross brook, and continue downhill beside brook.

10.0 Bear right on path along hillside.

10.1 Enter field, descend steeply. Cross fence to paved **Barnard Brook Road**; turn right onto road.

10.5 Turn right into woods. Climb to top of Dana Hill.

11.4 Pass a field facing W, and ascend through woods to Vt. 12.

12.0 Turn right onto **Vt. 12**, reaching the end of the section. To continue on Trail, turn left (W) onto unpaved road.

Trail Description, South to North

Miles **Data**

0.0 From **Vt. 12**, the A.T. turns E up hill into woods.

0.6 Near top of Dana Hill, come to field. Continue E to Barnard Brook Road.

1.5	Turn left on **Barnard Brook Road** (South Pomfret 1.0 mi. right).
1.9	Turn right, leaving road, and ascend to upper right corner of field.
2.0	Take path to left along hillside.
2.1	Bear left onto woods road beside brook, and ascend.
2.3	Cross brook, and continue ascent through fields.
2.5	Enter hardwood forest.
2.6	Cross barway, and turn left onto woods road.
2.8	Reach crest of sag with overgrown high point on left, and descend into overgrown field. Turn right, and pass to right of old ruined farmhouse.
2.9	Cross grass-grown road lined with maples, and ascend through field on cart track.
3.0	Pass over crest. To right is Totman Hill (1,560 ft.). The Trail bears right through barway where old woods road bears left, descends through field.
3.2	Reach woods. Follow old woods road on left. Descend woods road through evergreens.
3.5	Enter field and pass between barn and farmhouse.
3.6	Cross narrow unpaved road, where brook comes in on left. In 50 ft., cross Bartlett Brook and bear left across field.
3.7	Cross wire fence, follow it on left side, then slab left uphill toward large maples.
3.9	At large maples, cross wire fence, and continue uphill at woods. Follow edge of woods down.
4.1	Enter cart track, follow 200 ft., cross field right.
4.2	Enter unpaved road, and descend.
4.3	Turn left (N) onto paved **South Pomfret-Pomfret Road**, follow 250 ft., turn right, follow unpaved road E.

4.6 Approaching large farmhouse on left, continue onto overgrown lane leading into woods road.
4.9 Reach open crest. Trail bears left (N) onto another woods road. Cross stream and climb over hilltop.
5.1 Descend E.
5.2 Reach view to N. Follow abandoned town road. Reach blue-blazed spur on right leading 50 ft. uphill to small spring. Ascend near edge of field. Reach summit of nameless hill (1,730 ft.) at cairn.
5.4 From summit, descend gradually.
5.5 Cross stone wall in overgrown pasture. Descend.
5.9 Leave woods, descend through pasture.
6.1 Turn right onto **Cloudland Road** for 200 ft., then turn left, off road into field E of red house.
6.3 Pass under powerline, continue on old road.
6.6 Reach blue-blazed spur on left leading to **Cloudland Shelter**. Continue on old road.
6.7 Cross small brook; turn left (125 ft.) onto woods trail.
6.8 Turn left onto woods road, ascend.
6.9 Turn right onto woods trail.
7.0 Turn right onto woods road, ascend for 125 ft., and turn left into woods.
7.2 Cross and recross small stream.
7.5 Cross shallow sag. Ascend, follow old woods road.
7.7 Reach high point on ridge, descend W slope.
8.2 Bear right onto woods road and descend to low point in gap. Ascend on woods trail.
8.4 Turn left onto woods road, turn left onto Trail.
8.7 Reach knob NE of **Thistle Hill** (1,626 ft.). Continue through woods, then across overgrown clearings.
9.1 Opposite Bunker Hill Burying Ground, turn right

onto unpaved **King's Highway**, ascend on road.

9.3 Leave King's Highway, and ascend on maintained road; no parking allowed.

9.4 Reach end of maintained road, and ascend E.

9.6 Cross ridge of **Bunker Hill,** and descend.

9.9 Descend on old road, turn left onto another abandoned road, and continue descent.

10.6 Reach maintained road at house on left. Descend.

11.2 Turn right onto good unpaved road (Randy Road).

11.3 Pass through meadow, continue past brick house.

11.8 Turn left onto paved **West Hartford-Quechee Road**. Pass **Pomfret Road** on W bank of White River and cross bridge over river (400 ft.).

12.0 Reach paved **Vt. 14** in the village of West Hartford, the end of the section. The Trail continues left (N) on Vt. 14 past general store and across Podunk Brook, then turns right (E) onto unpaved road.

Vt. 12
to Sherburne Pass
(U.S. 4)

Section 3 Vermont

18.5 Miles

Brief Description of Section

The Trail in this section travels south between two mountain ranges, the White Mountains of New Hampshire and the Green Mountains of Vermont. It crosses many ridges, and the terrain is rugged, with steep ascents and descents. The Lookout (2,439 feet) in the northern end of the section provides a panoramic view.

Much of the footpath follows old logging roads, which are often rough and overgrown. Consequently, the main ridge of the Green Mountains to the south has less traffic, providing a greater chance for solitude. The Trail also passes through Gifford Woods State Park (see below). Water is readily available in this section.

The northernmost two miles and the section from the River Road to Kent Pond are on dirt roads passable by car.

The northern junction of the Long Trail and the A.T. is one-half mile north of the southern end of this section. From this point south for 97 miles to the Massachusetts-Vermont state line, the Long Trail and the A.T. coincide. The northbound hiker leaves the Long Trail at this junction as the A.T. veers east toward the White Mountains of New Hampshire.

For information on the Long Trail and the A.T. in this section, refer to *Guide Book of the Long Trail* , available from the ATC and GMC (see "Important Addresses," page 301).

Note: the Trail between Vt. 12 and Vt. 140 (Section 5) is scheduled for relocation onto National Park Service lands acquired for the A.T. Carefully follow the white blazes.

Gifford Woods State Park

The Trail passes through Gifford Woods State Park near Vt. 100. The state park was created in 1931 to preserve natural forest. Within its 114 acres is a 12-acre plot of virgin forest dominated by sugar maples, Vermont's state tree. In addition, elders of many species, including an eastern hemlock more than 400 years old, are scattered over the park's remaining acres. The park protects one of the few remaining examples of undisturbed northern hardwoods in New England. The name is taken from an early area farm operated by the Giffords, whose house still stands just north of the park.

The park is on a major migratory route, and bird watchers gather in the spring and fall to study the many species passing through the park.

The park, containing 47 campsites plus overflow facilities and 21 lean-to shelters, also serves as a base camp for day hikes on the A.T. and the Long Trail. Fishing at Kent Pond and Deer Leap are short hikes away.

Road Approaches

Both the northern and southern ends of this section are accessible from major highways. At its northern end, the Trail crosses Vt. 12, 4.4 miles north of Woodstock. At its southern end, the Trail crosses U.S. 4 at Sherburne Pass (ample parking), 10.3 mi. east of Rutland, and 3.6 miles west of Sherburne. About two miles from the southern end, the Trail crosses Vt. 100 at the maintenance driveway of Gifford Woods State Park, 0.3 mile north of the intersection of U.S. 4 and Vt. 100. From the maintenance driveway, it is 12.2 miles west to Rutland via U.S. 4, 2.3 miles south to Sherburne via U.S. 4, and 7.7 miles north on Vt. 100 to Pittsfield.

Four secondary roads also provide access to the Trail: Lookout Farm Road, Chatauguay Road, River Road, and Thundering Brook Road. Lookout Farm Road intersects the A.T. 3.9 miles west northwest of Vt. 12. The Chatauguay Road (pronounced Shat-a-gee) approaches to within 0.6 mile of the A.T. at a point 8.6 miles from Vt. 12. To reach the A.T. via the Chatauguay Road, proceed 2.2 miles north on hard-surfaced road from Bridgewater Corners at U.S. 4 to Bridgewater Center; continue north on dirt road along the North Branch of the Ottauquechee River to fork at 7.1 miles; follow right fork to house on right at 7.8; continue beyond on foot to trail junction at 8.4 miles. From the fork, the road may be too wet to be passable by car.

The A.T. reaches River Road 14.4 miles from the northern end of the section. Sherburne on U.S. 4 is 1.5 miles south. Four hundred feet north, River Road is met by Thundering Brook Road and the A.T. follows Thundering Brook Road west to Kent Pond. It is approximately 0.3 mile south to U.S. 4 from Kent Pond Road.

Maps

Map No. 5 (this guide)
GMC *Guide Book of the Long Trail*
USGS 7 1/2 minute topographic quadrangles:
  Woodstock North, Vt.
  Delectable Mountain, Vt.
  Pico Peak, Vt.

Shelters and Campsites

This section has three shelters.

Winturri Shelter: Log shelter 25 miles north end of section; accommodates 8; water from spring 100 yards north of shelter.

Next shelter or campsite: north 9.5 miles (Cloudland Shelter); south 8.2 miles.

Stony Brook Shelter: Log shelter maintained by GMC 7.8 miles from south end of section; accommodates 6; water from stream ten yards west.

Next shelter or campsite: north 8.2 miles; south 6.2 miles.

Gifford Woods State Park: At Trail crossing of Vt. 100 near south end of section; 21 shelters and numerous campsites (see "Gifford Woods State Park" on page 224); fee charged for overnight use ($6.50 for tentsite, $9.00 for lean-to); showers; ample water.

Next shelter or campsite: north 6.2 miles; south 4.3 miles (Pico Camp).

Regulations

Camping and fires are prohibited, except at Wintturi Shelter, Stony Brook Shelter, and Gifford Woods State Park.

Supplies and Services

From the Trail crossing at Vt. 12 at the northern end of the section, it is 4.4 miles south to Woodstock (P.O. 05091, phone, supermarket, equipment, laundromat, restaurants, bus stop).

From the Trail crossing of Vt. 100 near the southern end of the section, it is 2.3 miles south to Sherburne on U.S. 4 (Killington P.O. 05751, bus stop) and 7.7 miles north to Pittsfield (P.O. 05762, phone, limited groceries, laundromat). The Inn at Long Trail (limited supplies, lodging, meals, bus stop) is located at the southern terminus of this section and will accept and hold parcels marked, "Hold for Appalachian Trail Hiker," if sent via United Parcel Service (Inn at Long Trail, Sherburne Pass, Route 4, Killington, Vt. 05751). From the southern end of the section, it is 10.3 miles west to Rutland (P.O. 05701, phone, supermarket, backpacking store, restaurants, laundromats, airport, Rutland Hospital (802) 775-7111), bus stop) 1.6 miles east to a store with limited supplies, 3.6 miles east to Sherburne (Killington P.O. 05751), and 3.6 miles east, then south via the Killington Access Road, to a grocery store and delicatessen.

In an emergency, call the Vermont State Police, (802) 773-9101).

Public Accommodations

The northern end of the section on Vt. 12 is 4.4 miles north of Woodstock (motels, inn). North of the crossing of Vt. 100 at Kent Pond is an inexpensive lodge offering bed, bath, and breakfast. The Inn at Long Trail (lodging, meals; hiker's special: see "Supplies and Services" for address and more information) is located at the southern terminus of the section on U.S. 4 at Sherburne Pass. Numerous other motels and inns are found to the west along U.S. 4 and in Rutland.

Trail Description, North to South

Miles	Data
0.0	From **Vt. 12** (Barnard Gulf Rd., 882 ft.), turn W (right) onto unpaved road. Cross brook, passing large white house and barn on right. Ascend through woods, with brook on left, on road passable by car.
1.1	Continue past public road leading to right between house and small pond.
1.9	Turn left onto woods road 125 ft. beyond tree farm sign, and immediately cross small brook.
2.0	Turn right at fork, and ascend W on woods road. between old fields on left and brook on right. Recross brook. Ignore skid roads to left.
2.5	Reach blue-blazed spur trail leading 0.4 mi. left to **Wintturi Shelter**. Water available from spring 100 yds. N of shelter.
2.9	After reaching high point, continue with little elevation change through gap between Pinnacle and Cobb Hill. Descend through woods into wet area.
3.2	Reach gravel **Lookout Farm Road** immediately after crossing Atwood Brook. Turn left, and ascend on road.
3.4	At sharp right turn in Lookout Farm Road, bear left (straight) onto woods road. Continue past steel-gated woods road to right (former route), and ascend.
3.8	Cross woods road near top of knoll, and continue on woods roads. Minor elevation changes.
4.6	Reach junction with spur trail. Trail forks left and descends SW in woods. Spur trail to right ascends to woods road and trail register in 325 ft., then

continues to The Lookout, 600 ft. Private camp on summit (2,439 ft.) has observation deck on the roof.

4.7 From low point S of The Lookout, ascend, and then descend around S flank of ridge, then ascend toward ridge.

5.3 Reach high point of ridge, and descend through large stand of white birches.

5.8 Descend more steeply, following wide switchbacks.

6.4 Cross logging road and small stream, then ascend.

6.6 Pass over high point of low ridge.

7.1 Descend, and cross second brook, and reach gravel **Chatauguay Road.** Turn left, and ascend on road beside brook.

7.3 Reach height of land at Chatauguay Gulf, and descend along unmaintained road.

7.9 Pass road to left and then jeep road to right. Continue straight ahead down old road, which brook follows for the next 0.3 mi.

8.3 Reach gravel road forking uphill to left. Bear right on road, and descend.

8.5 Turn right off road onto Trail across clearing. Cross headwaters of **North Branch of Ottauquechee River** at far end of clearing, and begin steady ascent.

9.0 Reach high point on north shoulder of ridge, and descend, soon reaching and following old woods roads.

9.4 Bear left at uphill fork, and descend steadily.

9.5 Turn sharp right onto woods road, continue 100 ft. across tributary of Mink Brook. Turn left, and follow woods road downstream beside Mink Brook.

10.3 Pass **Stony Brook Shelter** (1,380 ft.) on right. Just beyond, cross Mink Brook and bear right into Notown Clearing. Bear left across clearing, and enter old road. (To right, road, which is passable by car in season follows Stony Brook downstream to Vt. 107.)

10.4 Cross Stony Brook, and follow north bank upstream on woods road.

10.9 Reach washed-out section of road followed by brook for next 500 feet. It may be necessary to cross and recross brook or go high up on right bank before regaining Trail on north (right) bank.

11.1 Bear right from brook, still on old woods road. Cross tributary (Windfall Brook). Short detour on downhill side may be necessary.

11.9 Turn right off woods road, ascend on series of former logging roads before beginning steep ascent.

12.4 Reach crest of ridge a short distance beyond Trail register (2,370 ft.). Descend gradually through hardwoods.

12.5 Turn left onto grassy woods road, and descend westerly. Continue past two woods roads to right.

13.6 Join maintained gravel woods road (**Quimby Road**), and descend beside Quimby Brook. Continue across powerline clearing.

14.0 Turn sharp right off Quimby Road, and continue 150 feet through woods to truck road. Turn right, and follow truck road N and then W.

14.1 Cross Quimby Brook, pass through chain, and swing left (S) on road; 250 feet beyond, turn right into woods.

14.2 Cross access road leading right to sand pit, and reach **River Road**, opposite Sherburne municipal offices (former Sherburne Valley School). (To left, it is 1.5 mi. to Sherburne Center.) In a few yds., bear right from road, follow path paralleling road. When path ends, continue on road for 400 ft.

14.5 Turn left onto **Thundering Brook Road** across Ottauquechee River. Begin long ascent.

15.0 Cross brook on bridge. Pass over ridge, and descend long hill.

15.7 Reach **Kent Pond**, and continue on road over Kent Pond Dam.

15.9 At end of pond, leave road, and bear right into open field. Pass near edge of pond, then bear diagonally left through field.

16.0 Reach fence at edge of field and enter woods on woods road. Soon bear left onto trail.

16.4 Cross small brook, follow trail through mature hardwoods along shore of pond. At mouth of inlet brook, bear left upstream. Cross inlet brook on bridge. Bear left from pond, and cross meadow.

16.6 Reach **Vt. 100** at the Kent Pond Road (boat launching ramp). Turn right onto Vt. 100. After 100 yds., bear left onto path into **Gifford Woods State Park.** Continue on gravel road leading to caretaker's house, where open shelters and tentsites with fireplaces may be rented.

16.7 Turn left from gravel road onto trail through picnic areas, rejoin gravel road, turn right. Continue on gravel road, passing road on left to stone building (toilets and showers). Ascend camping area.

16.9 Opposite Tent Platform No. 11, turn right on path past park boundary, climb through forest.

17.0 Turn right onto woods road, climb steeply for 100 yds., and then turn left onto Trail.

17.2 Turn left onto woods road.

17.3 Reach swampy area, then ascend steeply on Trail. Pass Trail register and spur trail on left leading 20 yds. to Ben's Balcony.

17.8 Reach summit of knob.

17.9 Reach **Maine Junction** where **Long Trail** meets from the right. (On Long Trail to right, it is 0.7 mi. to the N end of the Deer Leap Mountain Trail and 1.3 mi. to **Tucker-Johnson Shelter**, a frame shelter with bunks for 8.) Continuing straight ahead from junction on combined A.T. and Long Trail, descend steadily SW for 0.2 mi., then steeply over boulders.

18.4 Turn sharp left where blue-blazed **Deer Leap Trail** goes to right and ascends steeply 0.3 mi. to Deer Leap Cliffs (2,500 ft.) and continues over Deer Leap Mountain, rejoining the Long Trail in 1.3 mi. Descend from junction for 50 yds.

18.5 Cross U.S. 4, just E of the summit of **Sherburne Pass** (2,150 ft.). This ends the section. To continue on Trail, enter woods S of highway.

Trail Description, South to North

Miles **Data**

0.0 Just E of the summit of **Sherburne Pass** (2,150 ft.) on U.S. 4, enter woods on white-blazed trail. Climb for 50 yds. to trail junction. The blue-blazed **Deer Leap Trail** climbs very steeply 0.3 mi. straight ahead to Deer Leap Cliffs (2,500 ft.) and continues N over Deer Leap Mountain to the Long Trail in 1.3 mi. Turn sharp right at this junction and continue on white-blazed trail, ascending steeply over boulders, then more gradually on rough footway.

0.5 Reach **Maine Junction,** where A.T. and Long Trail separate. To the left, the **Long Trail** leads 0.7 mi. to the N end of the Deer Leap Mountain Trail, 1.3 mi. to **Tucker-Johnson Shelter**, and on to Canada. Bear right on the A.T., climb spur, and descend, passing on the right a 50-ft. side trail to Ben's Balcony (2,100 ft.).

1.1 Pass swampy area, continue on old woods road.

1.2 Turn right from woods road.

1.4 Rejoin woods road, and turn right at fork. Descend 250 ft., and bear left from woods road onto trail past **Gifford Woods State Park** boundary.

1.6 Turn left on gravel road opposite Tent Platform No. 11, and descend, passing road on right to stone building with toilets and showers.

1.7 Turn left onto path through picnic area. (To left is caretaker's house, where shelters and tentsites with fireplaces may be rented.)

1.8 Turn right onto gravel road, then left onto path leading 100 ft. to **Vt. 100**. Turn right onto highway, and follow S a short distance.

1.9 Turn left (E) onto **Kent Pond Road** (boat launching ramp), then immediately bear right from road into overgrown meadow. Cross meadow to bridge over Kent Pond inlet brook. Turn left and follow inlet brook to shore of Kent Pond. Continue through woods along shore.

2.1 Cross small brook.

2.4 Reach woods road entering from left, follow it to fence and open field. Bear left through field, passing near edge of pond.

2.6 Bear left onto **Thundering Brook Road**. Proceed over Kent Pond Dam and across outlet of pond.

2.8 At end of pond, begin ascent of long hill. Continue on road over crest, descend into Ottauquechee Valley.

3.4 Cross brook on bridge.

3.9 Reach end of descent and cross Ottauquechee River by bridge.

4.0 Turn right onto **River Road.** To left is North Sherburne on Vt. 100, and 1.5 mi. to right is Sherburne Center. Proceed 135 yds., and, just before bending road and hemlock trees, bear left onto path paralleling road.

4.3 Opposite Sherburne municipal offices (former Sherburne Valley School), cross road leading left to sand pit and enter overgrown field. Turn left onto truck road.

4.4 Cross Quimby Brook, follow road, then turn left into woods.

4.5 Turn left onto **Quimby Road** (unpaved), and ascend beside brook.

4.8 Cross powerline clearing with views of Pico Peak and Killington Peak.

4.9 About 100 yds. after passing woods road on right, take the upper right fork onto overgrown woods road, where lower road leads toward stream.

5.1 Take left fork of woods road, and ascend steadily on Trail leading to notch in ridge, passing through forest.

6.0 Pass Trail register, and reach crest of ridge (2,370 ft.). Descend steeply E.

6.6 Turn left onto woods road.

7.4 Cross tributary (Windfall Brook) of **Stony Brook**

where short detour on downhill side may be advisable to bypass poor crossing.

7.5 Reach washed-out road followed by brook for next 500 ft. It may be necessary to cross and recross brook or go high on left bank. Follow brook downstream.

8.1 Cross Stony Brook, and come into Notown Clearing, used for logging operations. Avoid road to left leading down Stony Brook to Notown and Vt. 107 (in good weather this road is passable by car).

8.2 Bear right across clearing and cross Mink Brook to **Stony Brook Shelter** (1,380 ft.) on left. Climb steadily SE on logging road beside Mink Brook, passing through hardwoods.

8.9 Cross to left bank (E) of brook, take left fork above brook.

9.0 Turn sharp left from woods road, and ascend.

9.1 Turn right at fork.

9.5 Reach high point on N shoulder of ridge, descend.

10.0 Cross headwaters of **North Branch of Ottauquechee River** at far end of clearing, cross clearing, and turn left onto gravel **Chatauguay Road**.

10.2 Bear left off road onto washed-out woods road, ascend.

10.5 Leave washout area and rejoin Chatauguay Road. Continue on road with brook on right.

10.6 Pass jeep road to left and road to right. Ascend on Chatauguay Road (unmaintained here).

11.2 Pass over height of land at Chatauguay Gulf, and descend along road, returning to gravel surface.

11.4 Turn right off road, cross stream, and ascend through woods.

11.7 Reach high point of low ridge.

11.9 Descend, cross a second brook and logging road, and begin steady climb.
12.1 Switchback up steep slope.
12.7 Pass through large stand of white birches.
13.2 Reach high point of ridge.
13.8 Reach low point S of **The Lookout**, then swing left, and ascend.
13.9 Reach junction with spur trail to left, which ascends to woods road and Trail register in 325 ft., then continues to **The Lookout** after 600 ft. A private camp is on the summit (2,439 ft.) with a small observation deck on roof. Trail bears S. Minor elevation changes.
14.7 Cross woods road near top of knoll, and descend.
14.9 Pass steel-gated woods road to left (former route).
15.1 Reach **Lookout Farm Road** at curve, descend.
15.3 Turn right off Lookout Farm Road, and cross **Atwood Brook** into wet area.
15.6 Continue through gap between Pinnacle and Cobb Hill. Reach high point, and descend.
16.0 Blue-blazed trail leads 0.4 mi. right to **Wintturi Shelter**. Water from spring 100 yds. N of shelter. Trail continues E; ignore skid roads to right, and cross brook.
16.5 Turn left at road junction.
16.6 Turn right on road; in 125 ft., pass tree farm sign.
17.4 Continue past public road leading to left between house and small pond.
18.5 Reach paved **Vt. 12** (Barnard Gulf Road 882 ft.) and the end of section. To continue on Trail, turn left, proceed 500 ft. Turn right, cross Vt. 12, and go up unpaved driveway.

Sherburne Pass (U.S. 4) to Vt. 103

Section 4 Vermont

16.7 Miles

Brief Description of Section

The northern part of this section traverses the Coolidge Range of the Green Mountains, including the highest elevations crossed by the A.T. in Vermont. Two short side trails provide access to Pico Peak (3,957 feet) and Killington Peak (4,235 feet). Much of this section is dense hardwood and evergreen forests. The Trail is often rocky and can become muddy. The southern part of the section descends into foothills, winding through pastures, fields, open woods, and thick second-growth conifers.

This section has several side trails in the north, in addition to the loop over Pico Peak and the side trail to Killington Peak. Cooper Lodge is reached from the west via the Bucklin Trail. Side trails are described briefly in the trail description; for more information, refer to *Day Hikers Guide to Vermont* or *Guide Book of the Long Trail*, available from the Appalachian Trail Conference and the Green Mountain Club (see "Important Addresses," page 301).

The summit of Killington Peak can be reached by the Killington Gondola, which leaves from Vt. 100.

Note: much of this section will be rerouted onto National Park Service lands acquired for the A.T. Follow blazes carefully.

Road Approaches

Both the northern and southern ends of this section are accessible from major east-west highways crossing the Green Mountains. At the northern end, the Trail crosses U.S. 4 (parking by permission only) 10.3 miles east of Rutland and 3.6 miles west of Sherburne. At the southern end, the Trail crosses Vt. 103 (ample parking) at the Green Mountain Railroad crossing by Clarendon Gorge, 2.2 miles east of U.S. 7, 7.7 miles east of Rutland, and 3.2 miles west of Cuttingsville.

In the southern half of the section, three secondary roads intersect the Trail: Upper Road, 11.1 miles from the northern end of the section; Cold River Road (Lower Road), 12.7 miles from the northern end; and Lottery Road, 15.0 miles from the northern end. Upper and Cold River roads connect North Clarendon, on U.S. 7 to the west of the A.T., and North Shrewsbury, to the east of the A.T. Lottery Road travels southwest from the Trail to Shrewsbury.

Maps

Map No. 6 (this guide)
GMC *Guide Book of the Long Trail*
USGS 7 1/2 minute topographic quadrangles:
  Pico Peak, Vt.
  Killington Peak, Vt.
  Rutland, Vt.

Shelters and Campsites

This section has four shelters. A GMC caretaker may be in residence at Cooper Lodge in the summer to supervise shelter use; a small fee may be charged to defray costs.

Pico Camp: Closed frame cabin built in 1959 and maintained by the GMC 2.6 miles from north end of section; accommodates 12; water 45 yards north on Trail; 0.4 mile side trail to summit of Pico Peak.

Next shelter or campsite: north 4.5 miles (Gifford Woods State Park); south 2.9 miles.

Cooper Lodge: Built in 1939 by Vermont Forest Service 5.5 miles from north end of section, now maintained by GMC; closed stone-and-frame cabin; fires prohibited; accommodates 16; water from spring 100 feet south and also on Trail north; 0.2 mi. steep side trail to summit of Killington Peak, also joins with the Bucklin Trail.

Next shelter or campsite: north 2.9 miles; south 4.2 miles.

Governor Clement Shelter: Built in 1929 by family of William H. Field of Mendon, named for Percival W. Clement, Governor of Vermont; 7.0 miles from south end of section; maintained by GMC; stone shelter accommodates 12; water from stream across road.

Next shelter or campsite: north 4.2 miles; south 6.2 miles.

Clarendon Shelter: Built in 1952 and malntained by GMC 0.8 mile from south end of section; accommodates 8; water from stream 50 feet east.

Next shelter or campsite: north 6.2 miles; south 3.4 miles (Minerva Hinchey Shelter).

Regulations

Camping and fires are prohibited except at designated sites. Fires are also prohibited at Cooper Lodge.

Supplies and Services

The Inn at Long Trail (limited supplies, lodging, meals, bus stop) is located at the northern terminus of this section and will accept and hold parcels marked,"Hold for Appalachian Trail Hiker," if sent via United Parcel Service (Inn at Long Trail, Sherburne Pass, Route 4, Killington, Vt. 05751). From the northern end of the section, it is 0.3 mile west to Rutland (P.O. 05701, phone, supermarkets, backpacking stores, restaurants, laundromats, airport, bus stop, Rutland Hospital 802-775-7111). It is 1.6 miles east to a store with limited supplies, 3.6 miles east to Sherburne (Killington P.O. 05751, bus stop) and 3.6 miles east then south via the Killington Access Road to a grocery store and delicatessen.

From the Trail crossing at Vt. 103 at the southern end of the section, it is one mile west to a small store with limited supplies, 4.2 miles west to North Clarendon (P.O. 05759, groceries, bus stop) and 7.7 miles west to Rutland (see above). It is also 3.2 miles east to Cuttingsville (P.O. 05738, phone, groceries, bus stop).

In an emergency, call the Vermont State Police, (802) 773-9101.

Public Accommodations

The Inn at Long Trail (lodging, meals, hiker's special with dorm and dinner; see "Supplies and Services" for address and more information) is located at the northern terminus of the section on U.S. 4 at Sherburne Pass. Other motels and inns are to the west along U.S. 4 and in Rutland.

From the Trail crossing at Vt. 103 at the southern end of the section, it is 3 miles west to lodging, 4.2 miles west to North Clarendon (motels), and 7.7 miles west to Rutland (motels, inns). Rutland and North Clarendon may also be reached to the west from the A.T. junctions on Cold River and Upper roads.

Trail Description, North to South

Miles	Data
0.0	Just E of summit of **Sherburne Pass** (2,150 ft.), enter woods, cross section of old highway, and pass E of ruins of former Long Trail Lodge.
0.8	Pass trail leading right 0.1 mi. to upper station of the Alpine Lift Mountain. Ascend through hardwoods on NE slope of Pico Peak.
1.3	Pass stream, which disappears into sink hole on right.
2.1	Pass spring 70 ft. to right of Trail, and continue 150 ft. to Pico Junction. Follow ski trail uphill 300 ft., turn left into woods.
2.6	Pass **Pico Camp**. A spring 100 ft. N on A.T. supplies water. Behind the camp, the blue-blazed **Pico Link Trail** climbs steeply 0.4 mi. to Pico Peak (3,957 ft.) and the summit station of the Pico Peak Ski Resort chair lift. Continue S; minor elevation changes occur.
3.7	Pass gully and, in 200 ft., a spring. Trail climbs gradually S, passes to the right of West Glade Ski Trail, and climbs steeply.
5.5	Turn right, and, in 200 ft., pass **Cooper Lodge** (3,900 ft.). Water from a spring 100 ft. S of the cabin and on the Trail N. In front of the lodge, the **Bucklin Trail** descends W 3.2 mi. to Wheelerville Road at a point 4 mi. S of U.S. 4. Behind the lodge,

the A.T. ascends 100 ft. to where a spur trail climbs very steeply left 0.2 mi. to **Killington Peak** (4,235 ft.), the second highest mountain in Vermont. From the summit the Green Mountains from Glastenbury Mountain in the S to Mt. Mansfield in the N are visible, as well as the Taconic and the Adirondack ranges in New York and the White Mountains in New Hampshire. To the SE is Mt. Ascutney, and to the W is Rutland. Killington is part of the Coolidge Range, which includes, N to S, Pico Peak, Little Pico, Mendon Peak, Little Killington, Shrewsbury Peak, Smith Peak, Bear Mountain, and Salt Ash Mountain. From the spur trail, the A.T. continues S through forest along W slope of Killington. *Note: A reroute is planned between Cooper Lodge and Governor Clement Shelter, W of present Trail. Follow blazes carefully.*

6.6 **Shrewsbury Peak Trail** leads left 2 mi. to Shrewsbury Peak and 3.8 mi. to dirt road 3 mi. NE of North Shrewsbury.

6.9 Reach **Consultation Point** (3,760 ft.) E of Little Killington. Descend steeply on rough trail.

7.4 Descend steadily through hardwoods, passing several overgrown logging roads.

9.4 Turn right onto wide logging road.

9.7 Turn right off road, follow Trail to **Governor Clement Shelter** (1,860 ft.) in overgrown field on right (W). Water in large stream E of road. Continue across clearing into woods.

9.8 Turn right onto woods road, and, in 25 ft., turn left off road. Cross **Robinson Brook,** ascend. Turn left, slab west bank, and continue. Minor elevation changes.

10.1	Cross stone wall, and ascend in old clearing.
10.3	Cross stone wall to left of deer camp, and descend.
10.5	Reach old road, turn sharp left (E), cross Sargent Brook, turn sharp right, follow brook downstream.
11.1	Cross **Upper Cold River Road** on old logging roads. Descend beside **Sargent Brook**.
11.8	Cross **Gould Brook**, and descend along left bank, entering wide trail.
12.7	Turn right to **Cold River Road** (Lower Road). Cross concrete bridge. Turn left into woods, follow west bank of **Northam Brook** uphill.
12.9	Leave brook, and soon cross a field.
13.0	Leave field, and turn left onto **Keiffer Rd**.
13.1	Turn right off road, and ascend beside stone wall.
14.0	Reach crest of ridge.
14.5	Pass **Hermit Spring** (unreliable) on right.
14.8	Enter pasture.
15.0	Cross unpaved **Lottery Road** (passable by car), and ascend through another pasture into a grove of sugar maples.
15.4	Reach airplane beacon on top of **Beacon Hill** (1,760 ft.). Trail drops steeply.
15.9	Cross brook and reach **Clarendon Shelter**. Ascend from shelter.
15.9	Turn left on old town road, then descend gradually through open woods. Pass sign marking a point on the Crown Point Military Road, built during the French and Indian Wars.
16.5	Pass under power line.
16.6	Reach **Vt. 103** (869 ft.). Turn right and follow W.
16.7	Turn left, reach end of section at railroad tracks. To continue on Trail, cross tracks and descend to Clarendon Gorge.

Trail Description, South to North

Miles	Data
0.0	Follow **Vt. 103** (869 ft.) 830 ft. E from the Green Mountain Railroad crossing. Bear left onto a town road, and ascend. The Trail passes sign marking a point on the Crown Point Military Road.
0.9	Reach **Clarendon Shelter**. Cross brook 90 ft E of shelter and climb steeply.
1.4	Reach airplane beacon on top of **Beacon Hill** (1,760 ft.). Descend through grove of sugar maples and across a pasture.
1.7	Cross unpaved **Lottery Road,** and pass through another pasture into the woods.
2.2	Pass **Hermit Spring** (unreliable) on left. Climb, pass over crest of ridge, and descend.
3.3	Cross small brook.
3.6	Turn left onto unpaved **Keiffer Road**. Bearing left on road, enter field to right.
3.8	After crossing field, reenter woods, and reach W bank of Northam Brook. Follow brook to left.
3.9	Reach **Lower Cold River Road**. The Trail follows this road right, crosses a concrete bridge, then bears left and follows old road.
4.4	Enter woods road. Follow left bank of river upstream.
4.9	Cross **Gould Brook**. Ascend hogback between two streams, and follow Sargent Brook upstream.
5.7	Cross **Upper Cold River Road**; continue, paralleling stream.
6.3	Enter logging road with bridge on left. Turn sharp left across bridge, and, 200 ft. beyond, turn sharp right off road, and ascend into woods.

6.4 Cross stone wall.

6.5 Enter old clearing, and descend to stone wall.

6.9 Follow west bank, turn right, cross **Robinson Brook,** and turn right onto woods road.

7.0 Turn left off woods road and continue across clearing to **Gov. Clement Shelter** (1,860 ft.) in overgrown field on left (W). Water is available in a stream 200 ft. E. Continue 125 ft. to woods road and turn left.

7.4 Turn left from logging road onto Trail (important turn). Climb steadily NE through hardwoods and into spruce forest. Ascend steeply over rough trail. *Note: A reroute is planned between Gov. Clement Shelter and Cooper Lodge. New route will be W of present Trail. Follow blazes carefully.*

9.3 Cross the S flank of Little Killington.

9.8 Reach **Consultation Point** (3,760 ft.), and descend slightly along E slope of Littie Killington.

10.1 **Shrewsbury Peak Trail** leads right 2 mi. to **Shrewsbury Peak** and 3.8 mi. to dirt road 3 mi. NE of North Shrewsbury. Continue through evergreen forest along W slope of Killington Peak.

11.2 Spur trail on the right climbs 0.2 mi. steeply to **Killington Peak** (4,235 ft.), the second highest mountain in Vermont. From the summit the Green Mountains from Glastenbury Mountain to Mt. Mansfield are visible, as well as the Adirondack and the Taconic ranges in New York and the White Mountains in New Hampshire. To the SE is Mt. Ascutney, to the W is Rutland. Killington is a part of the Coolidge Range, which includes, N to S, Pico Peak, Little Pico, Mendon Peak, Little Killington, Shrewsbury Peak, Smith Peak, Bear Mountain, and Salt Ash Mountain. Reach **Cooper Lodge** (3,900 ft.) just beyond spur trail to Killington Peak. Water can be found in a spring 100 ft. S of the cabin, and on the Trail N. In front of the lodge, the **Bucklin Trail** descends W 3.2 mi. to Wheelerville Road at a point 4 mi. S of U.S. 4. Seventy yds. N of Cooper Lodge, the A.T. turns left and drops steeply for 0.5 mi. Continue N, pass to the left of the West Glade Ski Trail. Bear left to avoid several ski trails and lifts.

13.0 Pass spring, and cross to E flank of Pico Peak.

14.2 Pass **Pico Camp.** A spring 100 ft. N on Trail furnishes water. Behind the camp, the Pico Link climbs steeply 0.4 mi. to Pico Peak (3,957 ft.). The summit station of the Pico Peak Ski Area chair lift is located here. From Pico Camp, continue N.

14.6 Reach Pico Junction. Follow ski trail down hill 300 ft. Turn right into woods. The Trail zigzags down NE slope, passing a brook that disappears into a sink hole on left.

16.0 Pass trail leading left 0.1 mi. to upper station of the Alpine Lift. Descend to Sherburne Pass.

16.7 Reach end of section at U.S. 4, just E of the summit of **Sherburne Pass** (2,150 ft.). To continue on Trail, cross highway into woods.

Vt. 103 to Danby-Landgrove Road (USFS 10)

Section 5 Vermont

14.2 Miles

Brief Description of Section

In the northern part of this section, between Vt. 103 (869 feet) and Vt. 140 (approximately 1,280 feet), the Trail passes through open woods and fields. Adjacent to Vt. 103, the Trail crosses Clarendon Gorge, which was cut by the Mill River. In the southern part of the section, the Trail passes across White Rocks Mountain, passing by Little Rock Pond (1,854 feet) in a hardwood forest. Between Little Rock Pond and the Danby-Landgrove Road (approximately 1,500 feet), at the southern end of the section, the Trail follows the left bank of the Little Black Branch. Between Greenwall Shelter and USFS 10 (Danby-Landgrove), the Long Trail/A.T. passes through the White Rocks National Recreation Area.

This section has three side trails. The Homer Stone Brook Trail provides access to the A.T. at Little Rock Pond from South Wallingford on U.S. 7. The Green Mountain Trail leads 5.1 miles to USFS 10 (Danby-Landgrove) 100 yards west of Long Trail/A.T. to the summit of Green Mountain. The Keewaydin Trail provides access to White Rocks Mountain from USFS White Rocks Picnic Area on USFS 52.

For information on these trails and the area, refer to *Day Hikers Guide To Vermont* and the *Guide Book of the Long Trail.* Both guides and current Trail information are available from the Appalachian Trail Conference and the Green Mountain Club (see "Important Addresses," page 301).

Road Approaches

The northern end of this section is on Vt. 103, a major east-west highway crossing the Green Mountains, 1.2 miles east of U.S. 7, 7.7 miles east of Rutland (via U.S. 7), and 3.2 miles west of Cuttingsville.

The southern end of the section is accessible by car by the Danby-Landgrove Road, 0.6 miles east of Big Branch Picnic Area, 3.5 miles east of Danby on U.S. 7, and 10.3 miles west of North Landgrove. The road, not maintained during winter, is paved from the Trail crossing west to Danby, but is gravel east to North Landgrove.

Vt. 140 intersects the Trail 5.4 miles from the northern end of the section. This point is 2.1 miles east of White Rocks Picnic Area, 3.5 miles east of U.S. 7 in Wallingford, and three miles west of East Wallingford (junction of Vt. 155 and Vt. 103).

Maps

Map No. 6 (this guide)
GMC *Guide Book of the Long Trail*
USGS 15 minute topographic quadrangle:
  Wallingford, Vt.
USGS 71/2 minute topographic quadrangle:
  Rutland, Vt.

Shelters and Campsites

Shelters between Vt. 140 and the Massschusetts/Vermont line are jointly maintained by USFS and GMC. This section has four shelters and one campsite. GMC stations a caretaker at some shelters from mid-May through October. Fee $2.00 per person per night.

Minerva Hinchey Shelter: Frame, open-front structure built 1969 by GMC; 2.6 miles south of north end of section; accommodates 10; on short side trail; water from spring 150 feet south.

Next shelter or campsite: north 3.4 miles (Clarendon Shelter); south 4.4 miles.

Greenwall Shelter: Built 1962 by USFS 7.0 miles from north end of section; accommodates 8; 600 feet northeast on side trail is spring which may fail in dry seasons.

Next shelter or campsite: north 4.4 miles; south 4.7 miles.

Little Rock Pond Shelter: Built in 1962 by USFS 2.2 mi. from south end of section; accommodates 8; caretaker in residence; fee charged; spring 0.3 mile south on A.T.

Next shelter or campsite: north 4.7 miles; south 0.3 mile.

Little Rock Pond Campsite: 2.2 miles from south end of section; tent platforms only; Clivus Multrum composting toilet; caretaker in residence, fee charged; spring 0.1 mile north on A.T.

Next shelter or campsite: north 0.3 mile; south 0.3 mile.

Lula Tye Shelter: Built 1962 by USFS; named for corresponding secretary of the GMC from 1926 to 1955; on short side trail 1.9 miles from south end of section; accommodates 8; caretaker in residence; fee charged; water from spring 0.3 mile north on A.T.

Next shelter or campsite: north 0.3 mile; south 3.1 miles (Big Branch Shelter).

Regulations

Camping and fires are restricted to shelters and designated campsites.

The southern half of the section, from Greenwall Shelter (including the shelter) to Danby-Landgrove Road, lies within Green Mountain National Forest (GMNF). Throughout GMNF, dispersed camping is allowed at least 200 feet from water and 100 feet from any trail; fires must be built in the fireplaces provided. No campfire permits are required.

Cutting or damaging living trees, shrubs, and plants is prohibited. Only dead material on the ground may be used for fires. All trash must be carried out.

Supplies and Services

From the Trail crossing at Vt. 103 at the northern end of the section, it is one mile west to a small store with limited supplies, 4.2 mile west to North Clarendon (P.O. 05759, groceries, bus stop), and 7.7 miles west to Rutland (P.O. 05701, phone, supermarkets, backpacking stores, restaurants, laundromats, airport, bus stop, Rutland Hospital (802) 775-7111). From this crossing, it is also 3.2 miles east to Cuttingsville (P.O. 05738, phone, groceries, bus stop).

From the Trail crossing at Vt. 140, it is 3.5 miles west to Wallingford (P.O. 05773, phone, groceries, meals, bus stop) and 3.0 miles east to East Wallingford and the junction of Vt. 155 (P.O. 05742, phone, groceries).

From the Trail crossing of the Danby-Landgrove Road, it is 3.5 miles west to Danby (P.O. 05739, phone, groceries, bus stop).

In an emergency, contact the Vermont State Police, (802) 773-9101.

Public Accommodations

From the A.T. crossing at Vt. 103 at the north end, it is three miles west to accommodations, 4.2 miles west to North Clarendon (motels), and 7.7 miles west to Rutland (motels, inns). From the crossing at Vt. 140, it is 3.5 miles west to Wallingford (motel). From the A.T. crossing of the Danby-Landgrove Road, it is 3.5 miles west to Danby (motels).

Trail Description, North to South

Miles	Data
0.0	Where **Vt. 103** crosses the Green Mountain Railroad, 2.1 mi. E of U.S. 7, the Trail descends S to Clarendon Gorge.
0.2	At the head of **Clarendon Gorge,** cross Mill River on high suspension bridge dedicated to the memory of Robert Brugmann. Climb steeply S up ridge, pass two lookouts, and follow crest of ridge.
2.0	Reach Spring Lake Clearing (1,620 ft.).
2.2	Reenter woods and climb ridge. Descend to clearing.
2.6	A spur trail leads left 200 ft. to **Minerva Hinchey Shelter;** a spring is 150 ft. S. Cross clearing, enter woods, and pass under power line.
2.9	Turn right onto road, and after 100 yds., turn left onto trail. Ascend S through hardwoods.
3.4	Cross brook and pass over summit ridge of Button Hill (approimately 2,010 ft.). Descend W side **Button Hill.**
4.0	Turn right onto farm road, which passes through open area.
4.2	Turn left at ruins, and pass to right of site of Buf-

fum Lodge, destroyed by fire in 1966. A nearby brook furnishes water.

4.7 Turn left onto gravel road passable by car, and descend.

5.2 Reach **Vt. 140**. Turn left on highway and immediately right onto Trail. Ascend, passing W of minor peak. Cross grass-grown road and continue S through woods and pastures.

6.1 Cross gravel **Sugar Hill Road.** To right (W), road descends 3.7 mi. to Wallingford; to left, it is 3.1 mi. to East Wallingford. Trail continues straight on dirt road passable by car about 0.4 mi. to house, then descends.

6.5 Cross brook, then boundary line of Green Mountain National Forest. Ascend through fields.

6.9 Reach end of pasture, continue on woods road.

7.0 Reach **Greenwall Shelter**. Spring, which may fail in dry seasons, is 200 yds. NE. Ascend W, climbing N side of **White Rocks Mountain.**

7.5 **Keewaydin Trail** leaves right, descending 0.8 mi. to USFS White Rocks Picnic Area.

7.8 Spur trail descends steeply right 0.2 mi. to White Rocks Cliff. The A.T. ascends to ridge of White Rocks Mountain.

8.1 Pass side trail leading 100 yds. right to spring.

8.6 Pass through spruce woods just W of summit of **White Rocks Mountain** (2,680 ft.). Descend steadily along ridge through hardwoods.

10.6 Cross overgrown South Wallingford-Wallingford Pond Road.

10.8 Cross Homer Stone Brook.

11.1 Pass through clearing, the old Aldrich Job. Continue SW. Little elevational change.

11.7 Side trail leads 100 ft. left (E) to **Little Rock Pond Shelter**. Water is 0.3 mi. S on Trail. About 100 yds. beyond path to shelter. **Homer Stone Brook Trail** descends right (W) 2.5 mi. to South Wallingford and U.S. 7.

11.8 At N end of **Little Rock Pond Green Mountain Trail** leaves right, follows the N and W shores of pond, reaches the summit of **Green Mountain** (2,500 ft.) in 1 mi., and continues 4.1 mi. to USFS 10 (Danby-Landgrove) 100 yds. W of Long Trail/ A.T. Trail takes left fork here, skirting along E shore of pond.

12.0 Pass spring that supplies water for Little Rock Pond Shelter, Lula Tye Shelter, and the Little Rock Pond Campsite. Soon pass spur trail leading left (E) 100 ft. to **Little Rock Pond Campsite.**

12.2 Reach S end of Little Rock Pond at junction with Little Rock Pond Loop Trail, which skirts W side of pond and connects with **Green Mountain Trail**, which intersects Trail at N end of pond (mile 11.8).

12.3 Path leads left 100 ft. uphill to **Lula Tye Shelter**. Water is 0.3 mi. N on Trail, from the same spring that supplies Little Rock Pond Shelter and the pond campsite. Descend gradually through hardwoods and along brook.

13.3 Cross Little Black Branch, and recross it in 0.2 mi. where Trail turns right onto old logging road.

14.2 Reach the **Danby-Landgrove Road** (USFS 10) just W of bridge over Black Branch (1,500 ft.), 3.5 mi. W of Danby and U.S. 7. To continue on Trail, turn left (E) over bridge, and continue 300 yds. before bearing right onto Trail.

Trail Description, South to North

Miles	Data
0.0	From **Danby-Landgrove Road** (USFS 10), just W of bridge over Black Branch (1,500 ft.), enter woods on old logging road.
0.7	Cross Little Black Branch, and recross it in 0.2 mi.
1.8	A path leads right 100 ft. (E) uphill to **Lula Tye Shelter**. Water from spring 0.3 mi. N on Trail.
2.0	Reach S end of Little Rock Pond at junction with **Little Rock Pond Loop Trail,** which skirts W side of pond and rejoins A.T. via **Green Mountain Trail** at N end of pond (mile 2.4). Skirt E shore of pond. In 100 yds., reach spur trail leading right (E) 100 ft. to **Little Rock Pond Campsite.**
2.1	Pass spring that supplies water for Little Rock Pond Shelter, Lula Tye Shelter, and the campsites.
2.4	At N end of Little Rock Pond, **Green Mountain Trail** leaves left, following N and W shores of pond, reaches Green Mountain summit (2,500 ft.) in 0.8 mi., and continues 4.3 miles to USFS 10 (Danby-Landgrove) 100 yds. W of Long Trail/A.T. The **Homer Stone Brook Trail** descends left (W) 2.5 mi. to South Wallingford and U.S. 7.
2.5	Path leads 100 ft. E to **Little Rock Pond Shelter.** Water is 0.3 mi. S on Trail from the same spring that supplies Lula Tye Shelter. Continue NE; little elevational change.
3.1	Pass through clearing, the old Aldrich Job.
3.4	Cross Homer Stone Brook.
3.5	Cross overgrown South Wallingford-Wallingford Pond Road. Climb steadily along ridge of White Rocks Mountain.

5.5 Pass just W of the summit of **White Rocks Mountain** (2,680 ft.).

6.1 Pass side trail leading to spring 100 yds. left.

6.4 Spur trail descends very steeply left 0.2 mi. to viewpoint at brink of **White Rocks Cliff**. Trail bears E.

6.6 **Keewaydin Trail** leaves left, descending 0.8 mi. to USFS White Rocks Picnic Area. Turn right (E) down N side of White Rocks Mountain.

7.1 Reach **Greenwall Shelter**. Spring, which may fail in dry seasons, is 200 yds. NE.

7.3 Trail enters pasture, curves left, and passes Green Mountain National Forest boundary line.

7.7 Reach farmhouse after crossing brook, and follow narrow road passable by car.

8.1 Cross gravel **Sugar Hill Road.** To left (W), road descends 3.7 mi. to Wallingford; to right,it is 3.1 mi. to East Wallingford. Continue N through woods and pastures, and cross grass-grown road. Pass W of a minor summit, and descend.

9.0 Cross Roaring Brook, and immediately reach **Wallingford Gulf Road, Vt. 140**. Turn left on highway, then immediately right (N) up a dirt road passable by car.

9.5 Turn right (N) uphill onto old farm road.

9.8 Pass to right of site of Buffum Lodge, destroyed by fire in 1966. A nearby brook furnishes water.

9.9 At old ruins in large clearing, take right fork, and ascend overgrown slope. Enter woods, and climb steeply.

10.6 Reach summit ridge of **Button Hill** (approximately 2,010 ft.). Cross brook, and descend N through hardwoods.

11.2 Turn right onto road, and after 100 yds. turn left onto Trail.

11.5 Pass under power line.

11.7 A spur trail leads right 200 ft. to **Minerva Hinchey Shelter**. A spring is 150 ft. S. Ascend hill behind camp.

12.0 After descent, reach Spring Lake Clearing (1,620 ft.) with views of the Coolidge Range to the NE and the Taconic Range in New York to the W.

12.2 Reenter woods where power line emerges, and follow ridge N.

13.3 Reach lookout. Drop steeply N passing another lookout.

14.0 Reach Mill River at the head of **Clarendon Gorge**. Cross the gorge on high suspension bridge. Ascend briefly.

14.2 Cross Green Mountain Railroad tracks and reach the **Rutland-Bellows Falls Highway,** Vt. 103, at end of section (869 ft.). To continue, follow Vt. 103 briefly E (right), then turn left onto old town road.

Danby-Landgrove Road (USFS 10) to Vt. 11 and 30

Section 6 Vermont

17.0 Miles

Brief Description of Section

The Trail in this section closely follows the crest of the Green Mountains through hardwood and spruce forests. From the Danby-Landgrove Road (1,500 feet) in the north to Vt. 11 & 30 (1,840 feet) in the south, the Trail passes over four summits: Baker Peak (2,850 feet), Peru Peak (3,429 feet), Styles Peak (3,394 feet), and Bromley Mountain (3,260 feet). The Trail also passes scenic Griffith Lake, which has one shelter and a campsite. This section passes through Green Mountain National Forest (GMNF); the section between USFS 10 (Danby-Landgrove) and Griffith Lake passes through the Big Branch Wilderness; and the section between Griffith Lake and USFS 21 (Mad Tom Notch) passes through Peru Peak Wilderness.

This section has three side trails. The Lake Trail provides access to Griffith Lake from U.S. 7. The Baker Peak Trail, coinciding with the Lake Trail from their beginning at U.S. 7, meets the A.T. just south of the summit of Baker Peak. The third trail, the Old Job Trail, is the former A.T. and is now used as a lowland alternate between Big Branch Bridge and Griffith Lake, covering a distance of 5.3 miles. Leaving the A.T. just south of the Big Branch Bridge, this trail follows Big Branch then Lake Brook upstream, passes Old Job Shelter, and rejoins the A.T. at Griffith Lake. For complete information on these side trails and the area, the hiker should refer to

Day Hikers Guide to Vermont and *Guide Book of the Long Trail.* Both guides and Trail information are available from the Appalachian Trail Conference and Green Mountain Club (see "Important Addresses," page 301).

Road Approaches

The northern end of the section is accessible by car on the Danby-Landgrove Road, 0.6 miles east of Big Branch Picnic Area, 3.5 miles east of Danby on U.S. 7, and 10.3 miles west of North Landgrove. The road, not maintained in winter, is paved from the Trail crossing west to Danby, but it is gravel east to North Landgrove.

The southern end of the section is on Vt. 11 and 30, a major highway crossing the Green Mountains, 5.3 miles east of Manchester Depot on U.S. 7 and 4.4 miles west of Peru. In addition to access by car at each end, gravel USFS 21 intersects the Trail 11.9 miles from the northern end of the section. From this point it is 2.5 miles east to GMNF Hapgood Pond Recreation Area and 4.3 miles east to Peru on Vt. 11.

Maps

Map No. 7 (this guide)
GMC *Guide Book of the Long Trail*
USGS 15 minute topographic quadrangles:
  Wallingford, Vt.
  Londonderry, Vt.

Shelters and Campsites

Shelters in this section are jointly maintained by USFS and GMC. This section has five shelters and two campsites. The

GMC stations a caretaker in summer at Peru Peak Shelter and at the campsites on Griffith Lake, to help hikers and supervise shelters and camping in the vicinity of the pond (see "Regulations"). At these sites, a fee is charged to defray costs.

Big Branch Shelter: Built 1963 by USFS 1.2 miles from north end of section; accommodates 8; water from Big Branch.

Next shelter or campsite: north 3.1 miles (Lula Tye Shelter); south 0.3 mile.

Old Job Shelter: Built 1935 by CCC 1.5 miles from north end of section on 1.0 mile side trail; bunks accommodates 8; water from Lake Brook.

Next shelter or campsite: north 0.3 mile; south 1.4 miles.

Lost Pond Shelter: Gift of Louis Stare, Jr., built 1965 on Cape Cod, dismantled, trucked to Vermont to present site 2.9 miles from north end of section, and assembled; bunks accommodates 8; water from brook in ravine below shelter.

Next shelter or campsite: north 1.4 miles; south 4.2 miles.

Griffith Lake Campsite: A number of designated sites, one with tent platforms, supervised by GMC caretaker; fee charged; water from Peru Peak Shelter.

Next shelter or campsite: north 4.2 miles; south 0.5 mile.

Peru Peak Shelter: Built 1935 by CCC 7.6 miles from north end of section; accommodates 10; caretaker in residence; fee charged; water from adjacent brook.

Next shelter or campsite: north 0.5 mile; south 6.1 miles.

Mad Tom Shelter: Built 1962 by USFS, moved to its

present location in 1980, on a spur trail 0.1 mile west of A.T., 3.3 miles from south end of section; accommodates 8. Water from spring 200 feet north.

Next shelter or campsite: north 6.1 miles; south 2.7 miles.

Bromley Tentsite: Primitive, with toilet.

Next shelter or campsite: north 2.7 miles; south 3.6 miles (Spruce Peak Shelter).

Regulations

This section lies within Green Mountain National Forest (GMNF). Camping is restricted to shelters and designated campsites or dispersed camping at least 200 feet from any water and 100 feet from trail. Fires at designated sites must be built in the fireplaces provided. Campfire permits are not required. Cutting or damaging living trees, shrubs, and plants is prohibited. Only dead materials on the ground may be used for fires. All trash must be carried out.

Supplies and Services

From the Trail crossing at Danby-Landgrove Road, it is 3.5 miles west to Danby on U.S. 7 (P.O. 05739, phone, groceries, bus stop). From the Trail crossing of USFS 21, it is 2.5 miles east to USFS Hapgood Pond Recreation Area (camping) and 4.3 miles east to Peru on Vt. 11 (P.O. 05152, phone, groceries). From the Trail crossing of Vt. 11 and 30, it is 5.5 miles west to Manchester Center (P.O. 05255, phone, supermarket, equipment, restaurants, laundromat, bus stop in Manchester) and 4.4 miles east to Peru (see above).

In an emergency, contact the Vermont State Police, (802) 773-9101.

Public Accommodations

From the Trail crossing at Danby-Landgrove Road, it is 3.5 miles west to Danby (motel). From the Trail crossing of Vt. 11 and 30, it is 5.5 miles west to Manchester Center (motels). Inns, motels, and tourist homes are available on Vt. 11 between Manchester Center and Peru, not far from the Trail crossing.

Trail Description, North to South

Miles	Data
0.0	The section begins on **Danby-Landgrove Road** (USFS 10) 3.5 mi. E of Danby and U.S. 7. Cross bridge over Black Branch, and ascend SE on road.
0.2	Just beyond wide turnout on right, bear right onto trail. At this point, it is 10.4 mi. E to Landgrove and from there, 2.5 mi. to Vt. 11. Continue E on ridge high above Big Branch, and eventually descend to north bank of Big Branch (water).
1.2	Reach **Big Branch Shelter**. Ascend along N side of river, passing the stone foundation of an old water wheel.
1.3	Cross Big Branch on suspension bridge, and follow S bank upstream.
1.5	Reach junction with the **Old Job Trail**. The Old Job Trail continues straight ahead, passes **Old Job Shelter** in 1.0 mi., then climbs along Lake Brook to rejoin the A.T. at Griffith Lake in 5.3 mi. The Old Job Trail is often used as an alternate to the A.T. between Big Branch and Griffith Lake. At this junction, the A.T. bears right uphill.

1.6 Bear right onto woods road, and ascend steadily.
2.6 Bear right onto wide woods road.
2.9 Spur trail leads right to **Lost Pond Shelter** with water from Stare Brook in ravine below shelter.
3.1 Turn right onto wide fire road, follow for 100 yds., and turn left onto Trail in woods. Ascend S.
3.3 Bear right on A.T.
3.6 Bear right onto trail and cross a small stream (for southbound hikers, the last sure water until reaching Griffith Lake). Ascend W side of ridge.
4.4 Emerge onto N end of ridge.
4.9 Reach summit of **Baker Peak** (2,850 ft.). From the summit, the A.T. coincides with the Baker Peak Trail in a steep descent over open rocks. Pass S end of summit, bypass trail on left.
5.0 Reach junction. **Baker Peak Trail** descends straight SW 1.0 mi. to Lake Trail, which leads 2.5 mi. farther to U.S. 7. The A.T. bears left and continues descent of Baker Peak.
5.6 Cross woods road, and traverse W side of ridge.
6.0 Cross swampy woods road and ascend.
6.7 The **Lake Trail** descends right (W) 3.5 mi. to a public road which leads right 0.5 mi. to U.S. 7, 2.0 mi. S of Danby. The A.T. descends straight ahead through a small cleft.
6.9 Reach N end of Griffith Lake. The Old Job Trail's southern terminus enters from left. Continue S on woods road along E side of Lake.
7.1 Pass to left of **Griffith Lake Campsite**.
7.2 Cross Lake Brook, then another stream, then follow winding trail through evergreen forest.
7.6 Reach **Peru Peak Shelter;** water from adjacent brook. Ascend E.

8.9 Reach wooded summit of **Peru Peak** (3,429 ft.); a short side trail leads left to lookout. Pass S over several knobs.

10.4 Pass through col. Climb steeply.

10.6 Reach summit of **Styles Peak** (3,394 ft.). Follow ridge SW.

11.1 Drop steeply S to SE.

11.9 Reach former Mad Tom Shelter site; water from pump located at USFS 21. Cross gravel USFS 21 at the height of land in **Mad Tom Notch** (2,446 ft.). From the notch, it is 2.5 mi. E to Hapgood Pond (a USFS camping area) and 4.3 mi. E to Vt. 11. From road ascend S to ridge through hardwoods and spruce.

13.7 Reach spur trail on right which leads 0.1 mi. W to **Mad Tom Shelter**. Note: water may dry up during dry seasons.

14.0 Pass over northern summit of **Bromley Mountain** (3,120 ft.). Descend into col. Climb steeply toward Bromley.

14.5 Reach **Bromley Mountain** summit (3,260 ft.). To the right 100 ft. is the summit station of the Big Bromley Chair Lift and an observation tower. The Trail descends on a wide ski trail (the westernmost of several trails leaving the mountain).

14.7 Bear right (important turn) into woods on trail. Descend steadily and sometimes steeply.

15.2 Turn sharp right near small brook on left.

16.1 Reach Bromley Brook.

16.4 Pass trail leading left 150 ft. to **Bromley Tentsite**. Just beyond, cross Bromley Brook on bridge. Continue on wide trail, descending gradually, pass under power line, and cross bridge.

16.9	Turn right onto gravel road.
17.0	Pass through parking lot. Cross **Vt. 11 and 30** (1,840 ft.) at end of section.

Trail Description, South to North

Miles	Data
0.0	From **Vt. 11 and 30**, 5.3 mi. E of Manchester Depot and 4.4 mi. W of Peru, follow gravel road NW 0.1 mi., then turn left onto Trail into woods. Cross brook by bridge, pass under power line, and ascend gradually.
0.7	Cross Bromley Brook (water) on bridge. Just beyond, spur trail leads right 150 ft. to **Bromley Tentsite**. The Trail climbs steadily NE.
1.8	Near small brook (last water), turn sharp left, and begin steady and, in some places steep ascent of Bromley Mountain.
2.4	Enter wide novice ski trail, and follow left uphill.
2.6	Reach summit of **Bromley Mountain** (3,260 ft.). To right 100 ft. is the summit station of the Big Bromley Chair Lift and an observation tower. Continue along the W edge of the clearing, turn sharp left just beyond the end of the chair lift, pass to the left of some outbuildings, leaving the N side of the open summit, then descend steeply into col.
3.1	Pass over northern summit of Bromley Mountain, (3,120 ft.) and follow ridge N.
3.4	Reach spur trail on left which leads 0.1 mi. W to **Mad Tom Shelter**. Note: water may dry up during dry seasons.
5.1	Cross gravel USFS 21 at the height of land in **Mad Tom Notch** (2,446 ft.). From the notch, it is 2.5 mi.

E to Hapgood Pond (USFS camping area) and 4.3 mi. to Vt. 11. One hundred yds. beyond USFS road is old Mad Tom Shelter site on left; water is from pump located at USFS 21. Ascend steeply to ridge of Styles Peak.

6.4 Reach summit of **Styles Peak** (3,394 ft.), with view E and S toward Bromley. Drop steeply N.

6.6 Pass col. Continue N over several knobs.

8.1 Reach wooded summit of **Peru Peak** (3,429 ft.); a short side trail leads right to lookout. Make zigzag descent.

9.4 Reach **Peru Peak Shelter;** water from adjacent brook. Proceed W, cross several streams, then, at woods road, turn right.

9.9 Reach Griffith Lake and follow eastern shore.

10.0 Pass to right of **Griffith Lake Campsite**.

10.2 The **Old Job Trail** descends right (NE) along Lake Brook. It passes Old Job Shelter in 4.3 mi. and then swings W to rejoin the A.T. at Big Branch in 5.3 mi. The Old Job Trail is frequently used as an alternate to the A.T. between Griffith Lake and Big Branch. At this point, at the northern end of Griffith Lake, A.T. continues straight ahead (N).

10.3 The **Lake Trail** bears left and descends W 3.5 mi. to a public road, which leads N (right) 0.5 mi. to U.S. 7, 2 mi. S of Danby. A.T. follows ridge N.

11.0 Cross swampy woods road.

11.4 Cross another woods road, and begin ascent of Baker Peak.

12.0 Reach junction with **Baker Peak Trail,** which descends left (SW) 1 mi. to Lake Trail that leads 2.5 mi. farther to U.S. 7. The A.T. and the Baker Peak Trail bear right and coincide for the final rocky scramble to the summit of Baker Peak. A bad-weather bypass trail is on the right and is recommended in windy or slippery conditions.

12.1 Reach summit of **Baker Peak** (2,850 ft.). Leave summit, reenter woods, and pass N end of bypass trail on right.

12.6 Pass over N end of ridge and begin descent.

13.5 Cross small stream.

13.9 Turn right onto wide fireroad, follow for 100 yds., and then turn left into woods on old woods road.

14.1 Spur trail leads left to **Lost Pond Shelter** with water from Stare Brook in ravine below shelter. The A.T. continues N along the woods road.

14.5 Bear left onto a narrow woods road, descending steadily.

15.6 Reach Big Branch and the northern terminus of the Old Job Trail entering from right, which leads to **Old Job Shelter** in 1.0 mile. Bear left along Big Branch.

15.7 Cross Big Branch on suspension bridge. Bear left on old road down N side of river, passing stone foundation of old water wheel.

15.8 Reach **Big Branch Shelter**. Water from stream. The Trail ascends the ridge behind the shelter and continues W high above Big Branch.

16.9 Reach **Danby-Landgrove Road** (USFS 10). It is 10.4 mi. E (right) to Landgrove and 2.5 mi. farther to Vt. 11. Turn left.

17.0 Cross bridge over Big Black Branch and reach end of section. At this point, it is 3.5 mi. W to Danby on U.S. 7. To continue on Trail turn right (N) into woods on old logging road.

Vt. 11 and 30 (Manchester-Peru Highway) to Arlington-West Wardsboro Road

Section 7 Vermont

14.4 Miles

Brief Description of Section

Note: work is scheduled to begin in 1988 to reroute the Trail over Stratton Mountain. Follow the blazes in this area carefully.

The most notable feature in this section is Stratton Pond (2,555 feet) on the western slope of Stratton Mountain. The pond is the largest body of water on the Long Trail. Stratton Pond is the most heavily used location on the Vermont A.T., which has had serious impact on the pond's fragile shoreline. To keep user impact to a minimum and to allow damaged areas to rehabilitate, GMC stations caretakers at the pond's shelter sites to supervise use. Please cooperate with them to preserve the beauty of the pond and its environs.

Between Vt. 11 and 30 (1,840 feet) in the north and the Arlington-West Wardsboro Road (2,340 feet) in the south, the Trail passes over Spruce Peak (2,060 feet) and Prospect Rock (2,079 feet). For 2.9 miles in the middle of the section, the Trail passes through Lye Brook Wilderness, a 14,300-acre tract of primitive Vermont woodland.

This section has four side trails. The Lye Brook Trail provides access from Manchester on Vt. 11 to the A.T. at Bourn Pond. The Branch Pond Trail gives access to Bourn Pond from the Arlington-West Wardsboro Road 1.2 miles west of the Trail crossing (at its southern end). The North Shore Trail is a short loop around Stratton Pond. The fourth trail,

Stratton Mountain Trail, may be used as an alternate to the A.T. between Stratton Pond and the Arlington-West Wardsboro Road, if the hiker wishes to climb Stratton Mountain (3,936 feet).

For complete information on the side trails and the area, refer to *Day Hikers Guide to Vermont* and the *Guide Book of the Long Trail.* Both guides and Trail information are available from the Appalachian Trail Conference and the Green Mountain Club (see "Important Addresses," page 301).

Stratton of the Past

In the mid-nineteenth century, Stratton Mountain was a prosperous farming community. The area has since reverted to woodland, but cellar holes, apple trees, and lilac bushes are reminders that people once lived in this remote part of the Green Mountains.

Arlington-West Wardsboro Road (formerly the Stratton Turnpike, locally known as the Kelley Stand Road) was once used for travel between Boston and Saratoga Springs, New York. West of the A.T. crossing is Kelley Stand, a former stage stop for travelers and a picnic site.

Road Approaches

The northern end of this section is on Vt. 11 and 30, a major highway crossing the Green Mountains, 5.3 miles east of Manchester Depot on U.S. 7 and 4.4 miles west of Peru.

At the southern end of the section, the Trail crosses the Arlington-West Wardsboro Road at Black Brook. This road does not have parking, but USFS 7 has a parking lot just south of this point, which is 1.2 miles east of the Branch Pond Trail's trailhead; 3.8 miles east of Kelley Stand; 12.2 miles east of Arlington on U.S. 7; 5 miles west of Stratton; and nine miles west of West Wardsboro on Vt. 100. Much of the road east to West Wardsboro is paved, but west to Arlington it is narrow, gravel, and sometimes impassable in wet weather. The road is not maintained in winter from Arlington to Stratton.

Maps

Map No. 7 (this guide)
GMC *Guide Book of the Long Trail*
USGS 15 minute topographic quadrangle:
Londonderry, Vt.
USGS 7 1/2 minute topographic quadrangles:
Manchester, Vt.
Sunderland, Vt.

Shelters and Campsites

Shelters in this section are jointly maintained by USFS and GMC. This section has six shelters, all on side trails. GMC stations caretakers at the shelters and campsites around Stratton Pond to help hikers and supervise camping and shelter use (see "Regulations"). At these sites a small fee is charged to defray costs.

Spruce Peak Shelter: A log shelter 0.1 mile on side trail 2.8 miles from north end of section; constructed in 1983 by the Brattleboro Section of GMC, USFS, and a work crew from the Rutland Community Correctional Center; accommodates 14; spring 100 feet south at the end of a spur trail.

Next shelter or campsite: north 3.4 miles; (Bromley Tentsite); south 3.0 miles.

William B. Douglas Shelter: Built 1956 by GMC, is 5.8 miles from north end of section, 0.5 mile on Branch Pond Trail; bunks accommodates 10; spring 50 feet south.

Next shelter: north 3.0 miles; south 3.6 miles on side trail.

South Bourn Pond Shelter: Built 1966 by USFS; bunks accommodate 8; spring 250 feet east on side trail.

Next shelter: north 3.6 miles on Branch Pond Trail; south 1.8 miles.

Stratton View Shelter: Built 1937 by GMC 0.1 mile on side trail from Lye Brook Trail at the outlet of Stratton Pond.

Next shelter: north 1.8 miles; south 0.1 mile on A.T.

Vondell Shelter: Built 1967 by International Paper Company 3.9 miles from south end of section; bunks accommodate 8; caretaker in residence; fee charged; water from Willis Ross Spring 0.2 mile south at A.T.

Next shelter or campsite: north 0.1 mile; south 0.1 mile.

Bigelow Shelter: Built 1961 by GMC 3.9 miles from south end of section; bunks accommodates 6; caretaker in residence; fee charged; water from Willis Ross Spring 0.1 mile south at A.T.

Next shelter or campsite: north 0.1 mile; south 5.7 miles (Story Spring Shelter).

The last five campsites are in two clusters on the side trails. Consult Map 7 for a better idea of distances than A.T. mileage indicates.

Stratton Pond has a number of designated sites maintained and supervised by GMC caretaker; fee charged.

Regulations

Prospect Rock to Winhall River, 2.9 miles of the route in the middle of the section, is in GMNF's Lye Brook Wilderness. Camping and fires are regulated in the GMNF. Camping in the wilderness is restricted to designated campsites and shelters or dispersed to sites 200 feet from water and 100 feet from any trail. Throughout GMNF, fires at designated sites must be built in the fireplaces provided. Campfire permits are not required.

Cutting or damaging living trees, shrubs, and plants is prohibited. Only dead material on the ground may be used for fires. All trash must be carried out.

Supplies and Services

From the Trail crossing of Vt. 11 and 30, it is 5.5 miles west to Manchester Center (P.O. 05255, phone, supermarket, backpacking equipment, restaurants, laundromats, bus stop in Manchester) and 4.4 miles east to Peru (P.O. 05152, phone, groceries). From the crossing of the Arlington-West Wardsboro Road, it is 12.2 miles west to Arlington (P.O. 05250, phone, groceries, bus stop), and 9 miles east to West Wardsboro (P.O. 05360, phone, groceries).

In an emergency, contact the Vermont State Police, (802) 773-9101.

Public Accommodations

From the Trail crossing of Vt. 11 and 30, it is 5.5 miles west to Manchester Center (motels). Inns, motels, and tourist homes are available on the highway between Manchester Center and Peru, not far from the Trail crossing. From the

Trail crossing of the Arlington-West Wardsboro Road, it is 12.2 miles west to Arlington (inns).

Trail Description, North to South

Miles	Data
0.0	From parking area 5.3 mi. E of Manchester Depot and 4.4 mi. W of Peru, cross **Vt. 11 and 30**. Climb highway bank, and continue through hardwoods and a boulder field.
0.5	Cross a stream and overgrown old Vt. 11 and 30.
0.8	Cross another stream, ascend steeply.
1.0	Pass two vistas (NW and S), and reach ridge top. Gradually descend narrow ridge, through hardwoods.
1.9	Cross old woods road. Cross small brook, and ascend W and then S.
2.3	Reach side trail leading right 400 ft. to **Spruce Peak** (2,060 ft.). Bear left and continue. Minor elevation changes.
2.8	Reach spur trail leading 0.1 mi. W to **Spruce Peak Shelter.** Spring 100 ft. S.
3.1	Cross small stream in gully, bear sharp left, and ascend toward ridge.
3.3	Reach high point on W flank of ridge, and continue S. Minor elevation changes.
4.4	Cross small stream, and descend.
4.9	Reach spur trail bearing right 150 ft. across road to **Prospect Rock.** Bear left on Trail, and continue 150 ft. to dirt **Old Rootville Road**. Road descends W (right) 1.5 mi. to maintained road, which leads 0.7 mi. to Vt. 11 and 30, 2 mi. E of Manchester Cen-

ter. At junction, blue-blazed spur trail descends right (W) 200 ft. to Prospect Rock (2,079 ft.). Trail follows road E from junction.

5.8 Reach end of dirt road at end of clearing, and enter Lye Brook Wilderness at crossing of brook. Turn sharp right, and continue 100 ft. to junction. Trail turns sharply to left. The former A.T. (now **Branch Pond Trail**) leads to the right to **William B. Douglas Shelter** in 0.5 mile; at junction with the Lye Brook Trail, to **South Bourn Pond Shelter** in 4.1 mi.; and Stratton Pond (via the Lye Brook Trail) in 6.5 mi. From junction, head E on or beside former Rootville Road.

6.0 Bear left into woods, ascend for short distance, then continue to SE (minor elevation changes).

6.5 Cross wet sag on puncheon, and gradually ascend.

7.2 Cross twin brooks.

7.6 Swing S on high ground on W side of Winhall River Valley, continue. Minor elevation changes.

8.4 Turn sharp left from high point on W slope, and descend to W bank of Winhall River. Follow river downstream.

8.7 Turn right onto old woods road and cross **Winhall River** on footbridge. Trail leaves Lye Brook Wilderness. One hundred ft. beyond, turn sharp right off road, pass over low knoll into wet area, ascend N slope of nameless ridge.

9.1 Reach high point on N slope; gradually descend S. Cross small stream and ascend to ridge. Continue minor elevation changes for some distance, then descend.

10.4 Reach NE corner of **Stratton Pond** at trail junction. **North Shore Trail** leads to the right, continuing around pond to **Stratton View Shelter** in 0.6 mi. and junction with **Lye Brook Trail** at Stratton Pond outlet in 0.7 mi. A.T. continues S along E shore of pond.

10.5 Reach Willis Ross Clearing at SE corner of Stratton Pond, 175 ft. beyond N end of **Stratton Mountain Trail**, and 50 ft. beyond **Willis Ross Spring**. To right (W), **Lye Brook Trail** (formerly the A.T.) follows S shore of pond to **Bigelow Shelter** in 0.1 mi., **Vondell Shelter** in 0.2 mi., junction with **North Shore Trail** in 0.6 mi. at outlet of pond (Stratton View Shelter is 0.1 mi. E). Lye Brook Trail continues to crossing of Branch Pond Trail at **South Bourn Pond Shelter** in 2.4 mi., and down Lye Brook Hollow to public road in 9.8 mi., S of Manchester Depot. From Willis Ross Clearing, A.T. ascends S. See Note on page 267.

10.7 Turn sharp right on high ground above pond and continue SW. Minor elevation changes.

12.2 Cross well-defined woods road after ascending from spruce swamp. Continue ascent to low ridge.

12.9 Reach high point on ridge and begin long, gradual descent on ridge.

14.4 Reach gravel **Arlington-West Wardsboro Road**. Turn right and follow road W past woods road to right and cross bridge over Black Brook (2,340 ft.). To continue on Trail, turn left into woods.

Trail Description, South to North

Miles	Data
0.0	From point where Black Brook crosses **Arlington-West Wardsboro Road** (2,340 ft.), Trail heads E along road 150 ft. and turns left into woods. **Stratton Mountain Trail** (blue-blazed), an alternate to the A.T., continues E on Arlington-West Wardsboro Road past the Daniel Webster marker; it turns N into the woods in 2.9 mi., passes **Webster Shelter**, rises to **Stratton Mountain** summit (3,936 ft.), and descends, rejoining A.T. at Stratton Pond in 8.6 mi. From junction where Stratton Mountain Trail diverges, A.T. climbs into woods from Arlington-West Wardsboro Road.
1.5	Reach high point on ridge, and descend.
2.1	Cross well-defined woods road, and descend into spruce swamp. Continue NE. Minor elevation changes.
3.7	Turn sharp left and descend to Stratton Pond.
3.9	Reach Willis Ross Clearing at SE corner of Stratton Pond. To left (W), **Lye Brook Trail** (formerly the A.T.) follows S shore of pond to **Bigelow Shelter** in 0.1 mi., **Vondell Shelter** in 0.2 mi., junction with **North Shore Trail** in 0.6 mi. at outlet of pond (**Stratton View Shelter**, 0.1 mi. E). Lye Brook Trail continues to crossing of **Branch Pond Trail** (former A.T.) at South Bourn Pond Shelter in 2.4 mi., and then down Lye Brook Hollow to public road in 9.8 mi., S of Manchester Depot. A.T. follows the E shore of pond. In 50 ft., pass Willis Ross Spring, and in another 125 ft., pass on right N end of **Stratton Mountain Trail**.

4.0 Reach NE corner of Stratton Pond at trail junction. North Shore Trail leads to left, continuing around pond to Stratton View Shelter (0.6 mi.) and junction with Lye Brook Trail at Stratton Pond outlet (0.7 mi.). Ascend N from pond then continue, with elevational changes.

4.3 Descend from ridge.

4.6 Cross small stream, gradually ascend N.

5.3 Reach high point on N slope; descend into wet area.

5.7 Turn sharp left onto road, and in 100 ft., cross **Winhall River** on footbridge. Trail enters the **Lye Brook Wilderness Area**. Turn left off old woods road, and follow river upstream.

5.8 Begin ascent away from river.

6.0 Reach high point, and turn sharp right, continue. Minor elevation changes.

6.8 Swing N on high ground on W side of Winhall River Valley.

7.2 Cross twin brooks. Gradually descend.

7.9 Cross wet sag on puncheon, continue NW.

8.4 Bear right onto former Rootville Road. Trend W on or beside road.

8.6 Reach trail junction. Trail turns sharp right. **Branch Pond Trail** (former A.T.) goes left (S) to **William B. Dougias Shelter** (0.5 mi.), junction with **Lye Brook Trail** at **South Bourn Pond Shelter** (4.1 mi.), and **Stratton Pond** (via Lye Brook Trail, 6.5 mi.). Continue 100 ft., turn sharp left, and leave Lye Brook Wilderness at crossing of brook. Reach dirt road at end of clearing. Trail follows road W.

9.5 Turn right (N) away from dirt road. Straight

ahead, Old Rootville Road descends 200 ft. to **Prospect Rock** (2,079 ft.). The old road continues 1.5 mi. to maintained road, which leads 0.7 mi. to Vt. 11 and 30, 2 mi. E of Manchester Center. In 150 ft., pass spur trail to left leading 150 ft. to Prospect Rock. Ascend away from dirt road.

10.0 Cross small stream and continue. Minor elevation changes.

11.1 Reach high point on W flank of ridge, and descend.

11.3 Bear sharp right and cross small stream in gully; continue with minor elevation changes.

11.6 Reach spur trail leading 0.1 mi. W (left) to **Spruce Peak Shelter**. Spring 100 ft. S.

12.1 Bear right, and pass side trail leading left 400 ft. to **Spruce Peak** (2,060 ft.). Descend to N.

12.5 Cross small brook and power line. Begin gradual descent through mixed hardwoods, and climb narrow ridge.

13.5 Pass two vistas, descend steeply, then more gradually.

13.7 Cross stream.

14.0 Cross old Vt. 11 and 30 (overgrown) and another stream. Continue through a boulder field.

14.4 Reach Vt. 11 and 30 and entrance to parking area where section ends. To continue on A.T., pass through parking area and onto gravel road.

Arlington-West Wardsboro Road to Bennington-Brattleboro Highway (Vt. 9)

Section 8 Vermont

20.6 Miles

Brief Description of Section

From both ends of this section, the Trail ascends to and follows a rolling ridge through a wilderness of hardwoods and evergreens leading to the summit of Glastenbury Mountain (3,748 feet) in the center of the section. The summit is completely covered with tall spruce. The unused firetower at the top, which should be climbed with care, provides a view of the area. Between Story Spring Shelter and South Alder Brook, the Trail passes through an area of beaver activity, where the footway can be quite wet. Nonetheless, in dry weather, water can be in short supply along the ridges.

One side trail in this section can be used as an alternate route to the A.T. between Goddard Shelter and Vt. 9. This is the West Ridge Trail, which follows a prominent ridge west of the A.T. It is described briefly in the north-to-south Trail description. For complete information on this trail and more information on the area, refer to *Day Hikers Guide to Vermont* and the *Guide Book of the Long Trail.* Both are available from the Appalachian Trail Conference and the Green Mountain Club (see "Important Addresses," page 301).

Note: the northern 1.5 miles of this section may be rerouted in 1988 as the Trail is moved onto Stratton Mountain. Pay close attention to blazes.

Road Approaches

At its northern end, the Trail in this section crosses the Arlington-West Wardsboro Road by Black Brook (ample parking). This point is 1.2 miles east of the trailhead of Branch Pond Trail, 3.8 miles east of Kelly Stand, 12.2 miles east of Arlington on U.S. 7, five miles west of Stratton, and nine miles west of West Wardsboro on Vt. 100. The road is paved for most of its distance east to West Wardsboro but is narrow, graveled, and sometimes impassable west to East Arlington during mud season. It is not maintained in winter from East Arlington to Stratton.

The southern end of the section on Vt. 9—the Bennington-Brattleboro Highway (ample parking), a major highway crossing the Green Mountains—is 5.2 miles east of Bennington, 2.8 miles west of Woodford, and 4.8 miles west of Woodford State Park. Roadside theft and vandalism have occurred frequently at this crossing. Do not leave valuables in vehicles.

Maps

Map No. 8 (this guide)
GMC *Guide Book of the Long Trail*
USGS 15 minute topographic quadrangle:
  Londonderry, Vt.
USGS 7 1/2 minute topographic quadrangles:
  Sunderland, Vt.
  Woodford, Vt.

Shelters and Campsites

This section has five shelters, all jointly maintained by USFS and GMC.

Story Spring Shelter: Built in 1963 by GMC; 1.7 miles from north end of section; bunks accommodate 8; spring 150 feet north on A.T.

Next shelter: north 5.6 miles (Bigelow Shelter); south 4.6 miles.

Caughnawaga Shelter: Built in 1931 by Camp Najerog 6.3 miles from north end of section; bunks accommodate 4; water from brook 30 feet in front of shelter.

Next shelter or campsite: north 4.6 miles; south 4.2 miles.

Kid Gore Shelter: Built in1971 by GMC and Camp Najerog alumni: 6.3 miles from north end of section on 0.1 mile side trail; accommodates 8.

Next shelter or campsite: north 4.6 miles; south 4.2 miles.

Goddard Shelter: Log lean-to built in 1985 by the GMC and USFS; 10.5 miles from north end of section; accommodates 12; spring 40 feet east on Trail.

Next shelter or campsite: north 4.2 miles; south 8.3 miles.

Melville Nauheim Shelter: Built in 1977 by GMC; 1.8 miles from south end of section; bunks accommodate 8; water from stream where side trail leaves A.T.

Next shelter or campsite: north 8.3 miles; south 5.5 miles (Dunville Hollow Campsite).

Regulations

This entire section passes through Green Mountain National Forest. No camping is allowed near Hell Hollow Brook. Camp at least 200 feet from water and 100 feet from trails. Fires at designated sites must be built in the fireplaces provided. Elsewhere, use camping stoves. Cutting or damaging living trees and plants is prohibited. Only dead wood on the ground may be used for fires. All trash must be carried out.

Supplies and Services

From the crossing of the Arlington-West Wardsboro Road, it is 12.2 miles west to Arlington (P.O. 05250, phone, groceries, bus stop) and nine miles east to West Wardsboro (P.O. 05360, phone, groceries). From the Trail crossing of Vt. 9, the Bennington-Brattleboro Highway, it is 3.9 miles west to a store (groceries) and 5.1 miles west to Bennington business district (P.O 05201, phone, supermarkets, backpacking equipment, restaurants, laundromat, cobbler, bus stop).

In an emergency, call the Vermont State Police, (802) 773-9101.

Public Accommodations

From the Trail crossing of the Arlington-West Wardsboro Road, it is 12.2 miles west to Arlington (inns). From the Trail crossing at Vt. 9, it is 2.4 miles west to a motel and 5.1 miles west to Bennington (wide range of tourist accommodations). Two motels are east of the Trail crossing.

Trail Description, North to South

Miles	Data
0.0	Just W of bridge over Black Brook on **Arlington-West Wardsboro Road,** Trail turns left (S) into woods. Turn right at old junction, and ascend to E end of Trail parking area. Skirt N edge of parking area.
0.1	Cross USFS 77 (parking); ascend SW in woods.
0.9	Reach and follow spur ridge. Minor elevation changes for some distance, then ascend around W slope of main ridge.
	Reach high point on W slope, and descend.
1.5	Pass **Story Spring** on left, and continue 150 ft. to
1.7	**Story Spring Shelter.** Bear sharp right opposite shelter, and descend SW.
2.1	Skirt edge of meadow, and bear left onto higher ground.
2.6	Cross two adjacent branches of South Alder Brook. Bear left 250 ft. beyond second brook opposite old beaver pond, and ascend SW.
4.6	Cross shoulder of nameless ridge, and descend gradually SW.
5.6	Turn sharp right below summit of nameless peak (3,412 ft.), and descend S.
6.0	Cross two small streams.
6.3	Reach Glen Haven and **Caughnawaga Shelter.** Water available from brook 30 ft. in front of shelter. Just beyond, a side trail leads left 0.1 mi. to **Kid Gore Shelter.** The A.T. climbs along ridge.
6.9	Reach Big Rock. Trail ascends, generally SW, along ridge.
9.9	Pass spring.

10.2 Reach spruce-covered summit of **Glastenbury Mountain** (3,748 ft.). The abandoned firetower was renovated by the USFS as an observation deck. From the tower, one can see the Berkshires to the S; the Taconics to the W; Equinox and Stratton mountains to the N; and Somerset Reservoir, Mt. Pisgah (Mt. Snow), and Haystack Mountain to the E. Descend S from summit.
Note: Camping is not permited on the summit.

10.5 Reach **Goddard Shelter** with spring 40 ft. E on the A.T. This is the last sure water until Hell Hollow Brook, 6.7 mi. S on A.T. The blue-blazed **West Ridge Trail** leaves the A.T. at this point and leads 7.8 mi. SW along a ridge (no water on S half) to the **Bald Mountain Trail**, which can be followed E 2.6 mi. to Vt. 9, 1.2 mi. W of the Trail crossing of Vt. 9, or W 3.5 mi. to Bennington. The A.T. descends very steeply E from the shelter.

10.8 Descend to old woods road, and follow it up ridge.

11.5 Leave woods road.

11.7 Pass large rectangular boulder near the summit of nameless peak (3,150 ft.), and descend steadily S.

12.0 Cross woods road, and continue descent.

12.4 Cross another old woods road in shallow sag, and ascend S.

12.9 Reach **Glastenbury Lookout** and the ridge connecting it to Bald Mountain. Ascend S along ridge. Trail swings off ridge and climbs steeply up the W side of the ridge.

14.0 Pass just W of summit of nameless peak (3,331 ft.), and descend steadily SW.

14.6 Pass **Little Pond Lookout** (3,060 ft.), and continue SW along narrow ridge.

14.9 Reach summit of **Little Pond Mountain** (3,100 ft.), and continue southward on ridge.

16.1 Reach summit of **Porcupine Ridge** (2,815 ft.), descend steadily SW, and pass through a balsam and spruce swamp on puncheon.

17.2 Cross bridge over **Hell Hollow Brook.** Camping along the brook is prohibited.

17.6 Cross **Twin Brooks**, and ascend SW.

18.1 Reach high point E of the summit of Maple Hill.

18.3 Cross under power line where it reaches its highest point on the S side of Maple Hill (2,620 ft.). From here can be seen Bennington and Mt. Anthony to the W and Mt. Snow, Haystack Mountain, and the N end of the Hoosac Range to the E. The Trail descends southward.

18.8 Cross **Black Brook**. Just beyond, trail leads left 300 ft. to **Melville Nauheim Shelter**; the A.T. descends SW.

19.5 Cross woods road, descend gradually, and cross another woods road.

19.7 Pass through the fissure of **Split Rock**, pass a lookout, and descend steeply.

20.3 Cross old woods road, descend very steeply to **City Stream**, and follow upstream (left) briefly.

20.5 Cross City Stream on the William A. MacArthur Memorial Bridge.

20.6 Reach the **Bennington-Brattleboro Highway** (Vt. 9; 1,360 ft.) and the end of the section. To continue on the Trail, cross road.

Trail Description, South to North

Miles	Data
0.0	On **Bennington-Brattleboro Highway** (Vt. 9; 1,360 ft.), 5.2 mi. E of Bennington and 2.8 mi. W of Woodford, the Trail heads E into the woods.
0.1	Cross **City Stream** on the William A. MacArthur Memorial Bridge. The Trail follows the N bank briefly downstream before bearing uphill for a steep climb to Split Rock.
0.3	Cross old woods road, and climb to a lookout.
0.9	Pass through the fissure of **Split Rock**.
1.1	Cross woods road, climb gradually, and cross another woods road.
1.8	Side trail leads right 300 ft. to **Melville Nauheim Shelter**. A.T. ascends N, crossing Black Brook.
2.3	Cross under power line where it reaches its highest point on the S side of Maple Hill. From this point (2,620 ft.) can be seen Bennington and Mt. Anthony to the W, and Mt. Snow, Haystack Mountain, and the northern end of the Hoosac Range to the E.
2.5	Reach high point E of the wooded summit of Maple Hill, then descend.
3.0	Cross Twin Brooks.
3.4	Cross bridge over **Hell Hollow Brook.** This is the last sure water until Glastenbury Shelter. Camping along the brook is prohibited.
3.6	Cross old woods road, pass through a balsam and spruce swamp on puncheon. Climb steadily NE.
4.5	Reach summit of **Porcupine Ridge** (2,815 ft.). Follow ridge NE to lookout. The Trail continues on ridge, descending somewhat, then climbing.

5.7 Reach summit of **Little Pond Mountain** (3,100 ft.), descend briefly, and then continue along narrow ridge.

6.0 Pass **Little Pond Lookout** (3,060 ft.). Continue NE along ridge, and then climb steadily toward an unnamed peak.

6.6 Pass just W of summit of nameless peak (3,331 ft.). Descend steeply NW along the W side of the ridge. The grade becomes moderate, and the Trail swings back onto the ridge.

7.7 Reach **Glastenbury Lookout** and the connecting ridge to Bald Mountain. Descend N.

8.2 Cross old woods road in shallow sag and ascend gradually.

8.6 Cross another woods road and climb steadily.

8.9 Pass large rectangular boulder near the summit of nameless peak (3,150 ft.).

9.1 Enter woods road and follow down ridge, then leave road, and ascend at moderate grade.

9.8 Cross old skid road. The Trail climbs very steeply, then levels off.

10.1 Reach **Goddard Shelter** with spring 40 ft. E on the A.T. The blue-blazed **West Ridge Trail** leaves the A.T. at this point and leads 7.8 mi. SW along a ridge (no water on S half) to the Bald Mountain Trail, which may be followed E 2.6 mi. te Vt. 9 or W 3.5 mi. to Bennington. From shelter, climb N.

10.4 Reach summit of **Glastenbury Mountain** (3,748 ft.). The abandoned firetower was renovated by the U.S. Forest Service as an observation deck. From the tower can be seen the Berkshires to the S, the Taconics to the W, Equinox and Stratton mountains to the N, and Somerset Reservoir, Mt.

Pisgah (Mt. Snow), and Haystack Mountain to the E. From the summit, the A.T. descends N along the ridge.

Note: No camping permitted on summit.

13.7 Reach Big Rock, and descend generally N.

14.3 In Glen Haven, a side trail leads right 0.1 mi. to **Kid Gore Shelter**. Just beyond pass is **Caughnawaga Shelter** with water from brook 30 ft. in front of shelter. From the shelter, the Trail climbs to a small ridge, then drops steeply.

14.6 Cross two small streams.

15.0 Ascend N, and turn sharp left below summit of nameless peak (3,412 ft.)

16.0 Ascend gradually NW, and cross shoulder of nameless ridge.

18.0 Bear right opposite old beaver pond, then cross two adjacent branches of South Alder Brook.

18.5 Bear right and skirt edge of meadow.

18.9 Pass **Story Spring Shelter** on right, and in 150 ft., pass **Story Spring.**

19.1 Ascend, to high point on W slope. Descend.

19.4 Follow ridge. Minor elevation changes.

19.7 Begin descent from ridge.

20.5 Descend and cross USFS 77. Skirt parking area, enter woods.

20.6 Reach **Arlington-West Wardsboro Road** at Black Brook (2,340 ft.). From this point, it is 1.2 mi. W to the **Branch Pond Trail** and 3.8 mi. W to the site of Kelley Stand. To continue on Trail, follow Arlington-West Wardsboro Road 150 ft. E (right), and then turn left into woods.

Bennington-Brattleboro Highway (Vt. 9) to Massachusetts 2 (North Adams)

Section 9 Vermont

18.5 Miles

Brief Description of Section

This section covers the Trail from Vt. 9 (approximately 1,360 feet) to Mass. 2 (approximately 630 feet), including Section 1 of the *Appalachian Trail Guide to Massachusetts-Connecticut,* in addition to the southernmost part of the Trail in Vermont.

The Trail route in Vermont passes through rolling hardwood terrain at elevations ranging from 2,000 to 2,500 feet, but also passes along ridgelines. On the ridge, the route traverses Harmon Hill (2,325 feet) and a nameless ridge (summit 3,025 feet). In Massachusetts, the A.T. traverses East Mountain (2,340 feet). In this section, the Trail also follows logging roads, often passing through lowland hardwood forests. The climb from Vt. 9 to Harmon Hill is the steepest of the section.

This section has three side trails, which are noted in the trail data. Dunville Hollow Trail crosses the A.T. a half-mile north of Congdon Camp, providing access to the Trail from Bennington to the west and from the Dunville Hollow Road to the east. The Broad Brook Trail provides access to the A.T. near Seth Warner Shelter from White Oak Road in Williamstown (difficult stream crossings in high water). Pine Cobble Trail (which may be rerouted) provides access to the A.T. on East Mountain from Mass. 2 in Williamstown. For hikers wishing to pass through Williamstown, Pine Cobble Trail is an alternate route.

For further information on these trails and the A.T. in this section, refer to *Guide Book of the Long Trail,* available from the ATC and the GMC (see "Important Addresses," page 301). For descriptions of the Pine Cobble Trail and the A.T. south of this section, refer to the *Appalachian Trail Guide to Massachusetts-Connecticut*, available from the ATC.

Road Approaches

Both the northern and southern ends of this section are accessible from major highways. The northern end is on Vt. 9—the Bennington-Brattleboro Highway (ample parking), a major highway crossing the Green Mountains—5.2 miles east of Bennington, 2.8 miles west of Woodford, and 4.8 miles west of Woodford State Park. The southern end of this section is on Mass. 2 at the A.T. footbridge over the Hoosic River, opposite Phelps Avenue, at a point 2.4 miles east of the Williamstown business area and 2.4 miles west of the center of North Adams. Cars may be parked with permission and at owner's risk at Scarafoni's Ford dealership on Mass. 2, 0.8 mile east of the Trail crossing.

Maps

Map No. 8 (this guide)
GMC *Guide Book of the Long Trail*
Williams College Outing Club Guide Book
USGS 15 minute topographic quadrangle:
  Bennington, Vt.
USGS 7 1/2 minute topographic quadrangles:
  Woodford, Vt.

Bennington, Vt.
Stamford, Vt.
Pownal, Vt.
Williamstown, Mass.

Maps accompanying *Appalachian Trail Guide to Massachusetts-Connecticut.*

Shelters and Campsites

Shelters in this section are maintained jointly by USFS and GMC. This section has two shelters and two primitive campsites with tentsites and toilet facilities.

Dunville Hollow Primitive Camping Area: 3.7 miles from north end of section on short side trail; tentsites and toilet facilities only; water from adjacent stream.

Next shelter or campsite: north 5.5 miles (Melville Nauheim Shelter); south 0.8 mile.

Congdon Camp: Frame cabin built in 1967 by GMC 4.5 miles from north end of section; bunks accommodate 12; tentsites on ridge behind camp; water from nearby brook.

Next shelter or campsite: north 0.8 mile; south 7.2 miles.

Seth Warner Shelter: Built in 1965 by trainees under Manpower Development Act, 6.8 miles from south end of section on 0.2-miles side trail; bunks accommodate 8; water from brook 350 feet west (may fail in dry seasons).

Next shelter or campsite: north 7.2 miles; south on A.T. 9.8 miles (Wilbur Clearing Shelter).

Seth Warner Primitive Camping Area: 200 feet south

of Seth Warner Shelter on side trail; tentsites and toilet facilities.

Next shelter or campsite: north 7.2 miles; south 9.8 miles (Wilbur Clearing Shelter).

Regulations

Although parts of this section pass through Green Mountain National Forest (GMNF), most of the A.T. is in the state-owned Stamford Meadows Wildlife Management Area. In accordance with Vermont law and GMC-landowner agreements, camping and fires are permitted only at designated sites, even on GMNF and Vermont state lands.

Supplies and Services

From the A.T. crossing of Vt. 9, the Bennington-Brattleboro Highway, it is 3.9 miles west to a grocery store and 5.1 miles west to Bennington business district (P.O. 05201, phone, groceries, supermarkets, backpacking equipment, restaurants, laundromat, cobbler, bus stop). Less than one mile east of the Trail crossing of Mass. 2, are services (phone, supermarket, fast food, laundromat, hiking equipment), one mile to YMCA (showers, pool; members free), and 2.5 miles east to the center of the North Adams business district (P.O. 01247, cobbler, bus stop). Phones, restaurants, and a supermarket are west of the Trail crossing. It is 2.9 miles west to the Williamstown business district (P.O. 01267, bus stop, and all other services except cobbler).

In an emergency, call the Vermont State Police, (802) 773-9101, or the Massachusetts State Police, Pittsfield Barracks, (413) 445-5511.

Public Accommodations

From the Trail crossing at Vt. 9, it is 2.4 miles west to a motel and 5.1 miles west to Bennington (wide range of accommodations). Two motels are east of the Trail crossing. In Williamstown, west of the Trail crossing at Mass. 2, are a number of motels.

Trail Description, North to South

Miles	Data
0.0	From **Bennington-Brattleboro Highway** (Vt. 9) Trail climbs steeply W on rock and log steps.
0.9	Bear SW, and climb more gradually.
1.8	Enter clearing.
2.0	Reach open summit of **Harmon Hill** (2,325 ft.). The Trail descends S.
2.3	Cross small brook, and continue S on near level ground.
3.0	Pass through large clearing, and then cross wide woods road. Soon descend and cross small stream.
3.7	Blue-blazed side trail leads right 150 ft. to **Dunville Hollow Primitive Camping Area**.
4.0	Cross **Dunville Hollow Trail** leading 5.0 mi. W to Bennington and 1.0 mi. E to the Dunville Hollow Road (which leads N 3.0 mi. to Vt. 9). Skirt former beaver pond, and descend E.
4.5	Reach **Congdon Camp;** water from nearby brook. Descend E to **Stamford Stream,** follow S (R) upstream. Trail, climbs away from stream.
5.3	Cross old logging road, and continue SW.
5.6	Pass old building foundations on a knoll.

6.1 Cross **Sucker Pond Outlet Brook.** Ascend S gradually.

6.5 Cross woods road; to right, it is 0.2 mi. to Sucker Pond (public water supply; no swimming or camping allowed); left, 5.9 mi. to Vt. 9.

6.7 Side trail leads 0.1 mi. W to the E shore of Sucker Pond. Climb S.

7.6 Reach NW summit (2,840 ft.) of nameless peak. Veer SE, then S, over several minor knobs.

8.8 Cross **Roaring Branch** at the base of beaver dam. Trail skirts right side of old beaver pond.

9.4 Pass over the N summit of a nameless ridge (2,900 ft.) and then under power line.

10.0 Reach the S summit (3,025 ft.) of nameless ridge Descend steadily, passing lookout with views.

11.4 Cross **County Road.** It is 4 mi. W to the Barber Pond Road and 6.4 mi. to Pownal Center (U.S. 7) on rough roadway. It is 4.2 mi. E to Stamford on Vt. 8 and Vt. 100 on road passable by car under favorable conditions. In Stamford, it is called Mill Road. Pass under power line shortly beyond County Road.

11.7 Blue-blazed side trail leads right (W) 0.2 mi. to **Seth Warner Shelter.** Brook 350 ft. to the W has water except in dry seasons. **Seth Warner Primitive Camping Area** is 200 ft. S on a side trail.

11.9 Cross narrow dirt road. **Broad Brook Trail** at first follows this road, then descends W 4.0 mi. to White Oaks Rd., 3.0 mi. N of Williamstown. Continue generally S along ridge, crossing three old logging roads and two small streams.

12.8 Bear right (W), follow an old woods road some distance, and then pass to the E side of a low ridge.

14.1 Cross brook, and climb gradually SW.

14.5 Reach the **Massachusetts-Vermont state line.** This is the southern terminus of the Long Trail. The A.T. continues S.

15.3 Leave woods, enter open area on ridge. Just beyond, reach **Eph's Lookout** (2,254 ft.). Descend S along ridge.

16.0 On rocky knoll, the blue-blazed **Pine Cobble Trail** descends right 0.2 mi. to Pine Cobble (1,894 ft.) and 1.9 mi. farther to Cole Avenue in Williamstown. The Trail turns sharp left, passes to the left of a marshy pond, and descends steeply and circuitously around an old rock slide.

16.4 Turn right onto old woods road.

16.6 Turn left onto trail, and descend SE.

16.8 Reach old bridge abutments on **Sherman Brook,** ascend gradually away from brook, and then drop steeply back to it, and follow downstream.

18.2 Reach a small reservoir on Sherman Brook.

18.3 Turn left onto private road, and soon enter driveway leading 50 ft. to Massachusetts Ave., which the Trail follows to the right.

18.5 Turn left, cross foot bridge over railroad track and **Hoosic River.** Reach Mass. 2 in North Adams, the end of the section. To continue on the A.T., proceed straight ahead (S) on Phelps Avenue.

Trail Description, South to North

Miles **Data**

0.0 In North Adams, Mass. on **Mass. 2**, opposite Phelps Avenue, proceed N crossing footbridge over **Hoosic River** and railroad track. Turn right

(E) onto Massachusetts Avenue. Just before reaching a stone bridge, turn left up driveway, and after 50 ft. turn W onto a private road.

0.2 Leave road, heading N into woods.

0.3 Reach a small reservoir on **Sherman Brook** and follow brook upstream.

1.3 The Trail makes a short, steep ascent away from the brook, then descends gradually back to it at old bridge abutments.

1.7 Bear NW, and ascend.

1.9 Trail reaches an old woods road which it follows for some distance.

2.3 Trail swings W to climb steeply and circuitously around an old rock slide (views).

2.5 Skirt marshy pond, and ascend to high point of open, rocky ridge. The blue-blazed **Pine Cobble Trail** descends left 0.2 mi. to Pine Cobble (1,894 ft.) and 1.9 mi. farther to Cole Avenue in Williamstown. A.T. bears right ascending along the ridge.

3.2 Near end of open area, reach **Eph's Lookout** (2,254 ft.), named for Ephraim Williams, founder of Williams College. Just beyond, enter woods.

4.0 Cross the **Massachusetts-Vermont state line**. This is the southern terminus of the Long Trail, maintained by GMC. The A.T. and the Long Trail coincide for the next 97.1 mi. to Sherburne Pass on U.S. 4. The Trail descends gradually NE from the state line.

4.4 Cross brook and pass to the E side of a low ridge following an old woods road for some distance.

5.7 Bear left, return to ridge. Cross three old logging roads and two smsll streams.

6.6 Cross narrow dirt road, **Broad Brook Trail** at

first follows road, then descends W 4.0 mi. to White Oaks Rd., 3.0 mi. N of Williamstown. A.T. continues N.

6.8 Blue-blazed side trail leads left 0.2 mi. W to **Seth Warner Shelter,** with brook 350 ft. to the W furnishing water except in dry seasons. **Seth Warner Primitive Camping Area** is 200 ft. S on a side trail. The A.T. continues NE.

7.1 Cross **County Road** after passing under a power line. Under favorable conditions, this road is passable by car. It is 4.0 W mi. to the Barber Pond Road and 6.4 mi. W to Pownal Center (U.S. 7). It is 4.2 mi. E to Stamford on Vt. 8 and Vt. 100. In Stamford, it is called Mill Road. Climb steadily NE.

8.4 Pass lookout.

8.5 Reach S summit of nameless ridge (3,025 ft.). Follow the ridge N.

8.9 Pass under power line and then over the N summit of the nameless ridge (2,900 ft.). Begin steady and sometimes steep descent N.

9.6 The Trail follows along the left side of an old beaver pond.

9.7 Cross **Roaring Branch** at the base of a beaver dam. Trail then passes over several minor knobs.

10.9 Reach NW summit (2,840 ft.) of nameless peak, then descend.

11.8 Side trail leads 0.1 mi. W to the E shore of Sucker Pond (public water supply; no swimming or camping allowed).

12.0 Cross woods road; to the left, it is 0.2 mi. to Sucker Pond, and to the right, it is 5.0 mi. to Vt. 9. Descend gradually, heading generally N.

12.4 Cross Sucker Pond Outlet Brook. Ascend ridge.

12.9 On wooded knoll, pass old building foundations said to be the remains of a 19th-century hotel.

13.2 Cross an old logging road, and descend.

13.4 Reach **Stamford Stream** and follow down, eventually bearing left and ascending.

14.0 Reach **Congdon Camp,** with water from nearby brook. Ascend ridge behind cabin skirting area of former beaver activity.

14.5 Cross **Dunville Hollow Trail,** leading 5.0 mi. W to Bennington and 1.0 mi. E to the Dunville Hollow Road (which leads N 3.0 mi. to Vt. 9).

14.8 Blue-blazed side trail leads left 150 ft. to **Dunville Hollow Primitive Camping Area**. The A.T. continues NW, crosses small stream, and ascends.

15.1 Cross wide woods road, and pass through large clearing.

16.2 Cross small brook, and ascend.

16.5 Reach open summit of **Harmon Hill** (2,325 ft.). To the N are Bald and Glastenbury Mountains. The Trail veers E across clearing, enters woods, and descends.

17.6 Bear right, dropping very steeply on log and rock steps.

18.5 Reach **Bennington-Brattleboro Highway (Vt. 9),** the end of the section. To continue on Trail, cross road into woods.

Acknowledgments

Thanks to Stephen Clark, guidebook editor for the Maine Appalachian Trail Club, for his valuable advice and assistance throughout the preparation of the guide. Thanks also go to Reuben Rajala and the Appalachian Mountain Club; Earl Jette, Chuck Wooster, Emma Crane, and the Dartmouth Outing Club; Stephen Rice, Harry Peet, Ray Auger, and the Green Mountain Club; Peter Richardson for providing badly needed information and advice on the Trail; and to Earl Niewald and Fred Kacprzynski of the White Mountain National Forest.

Special thanks go to field editor, Jim Barnes of Norwich, Vt., for coordinating the 1988 revision, and to Richard B. Westlake for map revisions.

Acknowledgment should be made to the Maine Appalachian Trail Club for permission to use in revised form both "First Aid Along the Trail" (by Dr. Robert Ohler) and the material for the Mahoosuc Range in Maine from *Appalachian Trail Guide to Maine.*

Important Addresses

Appalachian Mountain Club
(AMC)
Pinkham Notch Camp
Box 298
Gorham, N.H. 03581
(603) 466-2721

Appalachian Mountain Club
5 Joy Street
Boston, Mass. 02108
(617) 523-0636

Appalachian Trail
Conference
P.O. Box 807
Harpers Ferry, W.Va. 25425
(304) 535-6331

Appalachian Trail
Conference, New England
Field Office
P.O. Box 122
3rd Floor, Aldrich House
Mechanic St.
Norwich, Vt. 05055
(802) 649-2816

Dartmouth Outing Club
Robinson Hall, Box 9
Hanover, N.H. 03755
(603) 646-2428

Green Mountain Club
Box 889
Montpelier, Vt. 05602
(802) 223-3436

Green Mountain National
Forest, Supervisor's Office
Federal Building
Rutland, Vt. 05701
(802) 775-2579

White Mountain National
Forest
P.O. Box 638, 719 Main St.
Laconia, N.H. 03247
(603) 524-6450

Emergency Numbers

AMC Pinkham Notch Camp
(603) 466-2727

Massachusetts State Police
(413) 445-5511

New Hampshire
State Police
(603) 846-5500
(800) 852-3411

Vermont State Police
(802) 773-9101

Summary of Distances

North to South From Maine-N.H. State Line		South to North From Vt.-Mass. State Line
0.0	Maine-N. H. Line	294.9
1.8	Mt. Success	293.1
4.8	Gentian Pond Campsite	290.1
5.1	Moss Pond	289.8
6.9	Dream Lake	288.0
9.8	Trident Col Tentsite	285.1
10.9	Cascade Mountain	284.0
16.4	Androscoggin River	278.5
16.7	U.S. 2, **Gorham, N.H., P.O. 03581**	278.2
18.3	Rattle River Shelter	276.6
22.4	Mt. Moriah	272.5
24.3	Imp Campsite	270.6
26.6	Mt. Lethe	268.3
28.7	Zeta Pass	266.2
30.0	Carter Dome	264.9
31.2	Carter Notch, Carter Notch Hut	263.7
31.9	Wildcat Mountain, Peak A	263.0
33.7	Wildcat Mountain, Peak D	261.2
36.7	Pinkham Notch, N.H. 16, Pinkham Notch Camp	258.2
38.5	Lowe's Bald Spot	256.4
40.4	West Branch, Peabody River	254.5
41.0	Osgood Tentsite	253.9
43.4	Mt. Madison	251.5
43.8	Madison Springs Hut, Valley Way Tentsite	251.1
44.7	Thunderstorm Junction, Lowe's Path to Mt. Adams & Gray Knob Shelter, Spur Trail to Crag Camp	250.2
45.3	Israel Ridge Path to The Perch	249.6

North to South From Maine-N.H. State Line		South to North From Vt.-Mass. State Line
46.1	Edmands Col	248.8
49.6	**Mt. Washington, N.H., P.O. 03589**	245.3
51.1	Lakes of the Clouds Hut	243.8
52.6	Mt. Franklin	242.3
55.0	Mt. Pierce (Mt. Clinton)	239.9
55.7	Mizpah Spring Hut, Nauman Tentsite	239.2
57.3	Mt. Jackson	237.6
58.6	Mt. Webster	236.3
61.5	Saco River	233.4
61.6	Crawford Notch, U.S. 302, Dry River Campground	233.3
65.1	Ethan Pond Campsite	229.8
69.2	Zealand Falls Hut	225.7
70.3	Zeacliff	224.6
73.2	Mt. Guyot, Guyot Campsite	221.7
75.3	South Twin Mountain, North Twin Spur	219.6
76.1	Galehead Hut	218.8
78.8	Garfield Ridge Campsite	216.1
79.1	Mt. Garfield	215.8
82.6	Mt. Lafayette, Greenleaf Hut	212.3
83.6	Mt. Lincoln	211.3
84.3	Little Haystack Mountain	210.6
86.4	Liberty Spring Tentsite	208.5
88.9	Franconia Notch, U.S. 3, Lafayette Campground, **North Woodstock, N.H., P.O. 03262**	206.0
91.7	Lonesome Lake Hut	203.2
93.5	Kinsman Pond Campsite	201.4
94.1	North Peak, Kinsman Mountain	200.8

North to South From Maine-N.H. State Line		South to North From Vt.-Mass. State Line
95.1	South Peak, Kinsman Mountain	199.8
97.5	Eliza Brook Shelter	197.4
99.2	East Peak, Mt. Wolf	195.7
104.4	Kinsman Notch, N.H. 112	190.5
104.6	Beaver Brook Shelter	190.3
107.6	Mt. Moosilauke	187.3
112.2	Jeffers Brook Shelter	182.7
113.3	N.H. 25, **Glencliff, N.H., P.O. 03238**	181.6
114.8	Wachipauka Pond	180.1
115.3	Mt. Mist	179.6
117.3	N.H. 25C, **Warren, N.H., P.O. 03279**	177.6
120.3	Atwell Hill Road	174.6
122.1	N.H. 25A, **Wentworth, N.H., P.O. 03282**	172.8
125.6	Mt. Cube	169.3
126.8	Mt. Cube Shelter	168.1
128.4	Quinttown, **Orford, N.H., P.O. 03777**	166.5
132.1	Firewarden's Cabin	162.8
132.2	Smarts Mountain	162.7
132.3	Smarts Mountain Shelter	162.6
138.9	Lyme-Dorchester Road, **Lyme Center, N.H., P.O. 03769**	156.0
140.4	Trapper John Shelter	154.5
143.4	Goose Pond Road	151.5
146.6	Moose Mountain Shelter	148.3
150.6	Etna-Hanover Center Road, **Etna, N.H., P.O. 03750**	144.3
152.3	Trescott Road	142.6
155.9	Velvet Rocks Shelter	139.0
157.4	Dartmouth College,	137.5

North to South From Maine-N.H. State Line		South to North From Vt.-Mass. State Line
	Hanover, N.H., P.O. 03755	
157.9	Connecticut River, N.H.-Vt. Line	137.0
158.4	I-91 Crossing	136.5
158.5	U.S. 5	136.4
158.9	**Norwich, Vt., P.O. 05055**	136.0
162.9	Happy Hill Cabin	132.0
164.8	Podunk Road	130.1
166.4	I-89 Crossing	128.5
167.0	Vt. 14, **West Hartford, Vt., P.O. 05084**	127.9
169.4	Bunker Hill	125.5
169.9	King's Highway	125.0
172.4	Cloudland Shelter	122.5
172.9	Cloudland Road	122.0
174.7	South Pomfret-Pomfret Road	120.2
176.0	Totman Hill	118.9
177.1	Woodstock Stage Road (Barnard Brook Road)	117.8
177.6	**South Pomfret, Vt., P.O. 05067**	117.3
178.6	Dana Hill	116.3
179.4	Vt. 12, **Woodstock, Vt., P.O. 05091**	115.5
179.9	Vt. 12	115.0
182.5	Wintturi Shelter	112.4
183.3	Lookout Farm Road	111.6
184.6	The Lookout	110.3
188.4	Chatauguay Road	106.5
190.2	Stony Brook Shelter	104.7
194.1	River Road	100.8
194.3	Thundering Brook Road	100.6
195.6	Kent Pond	99.3

North to South From Maine-N.H. State Line		**South to North** From Vt.-Mass. State Line
196.6	Vt. 100, Gifford Woods State Park	98.3
197.8	Junction with Long Trail	97.1
198.3	Sherburne Pass, U.S. 4, Inn at Long Trail, **Killington, Vt., P.O. 05751**	96.6
200.8	Pico Camp	94.1
203.7	Cooper Lodge, Killington Peak Trail	91.2
207.8	Governor Clement Shelter	87.1
209.2	Upper Road	85.7
210.8	Cold River Road	84.1
212.7	Lottery Road	82.2
213.1	Beacon Hill	81.8
213.6	Clarendon Shelter	81.3
214.4	Vt. 103, **North Clarendon, Vt., P.O. 05758**	80.5
214.5	Clarendon Gorge, Mill River Bridge	80.4
217.1	Minerva Hinchey Shelter	77.8
219.7	Vt. 140, **Wallingford, Vt., P.O. 05773**	75.2
220.7	Sugar Hill Road (USFS 19)	74.2
221.6	Greenwall Shelter	73.3
222.4	Trail to White Rocks Cliff	72.5
226.3	Little Rock Pond Shelter	68.6
226.4	Homer Stone Brook Trail	68.5
226.8	Little Rock Pond Campsite	68.1
227.0	Lula Tye Shelter	67.9
228.8	Danby-Landgrove Road (USFS 10), Black Branch, **Danby, Vt., P.O. 05739**	66.1
230.1	Big Branch Shelter	64.8
230.3	Old Job Trail to Old Job Shelter	64.6
231.8	Lost Pond Shelter	63.1

North to South From Maine-N.H. State Line		South to North From Vt.-Mass. State Line
233.8	Baker Peak	61.1
235.7	Griffith Lake (north end)	59.2
235.9	Griffith Lake Campsite	59.0
236.4	Peru Peak Shelter	58.5
237.7	Peru Peak	57.2
239.4	Styles Peak	55.5
240.8	Mad Tom Notch, USFS 21, **Peru, Vt. P.O. 05152**	54.1
242.5	Mad Tom Shelter	52.4
243.3	Bromley Mountain	51.6
245.3	Bromley Tenting Area	49.6
246.1	Vt. 11 & 30, **Manchester Center, Vt., P.O. 05255**	48.8
248.3	Spruce Peak	46.6
248.8	Spruce Peak Shelter	46.1
251.0	Old Rootville Road, Prospect Rock	43.9
252.1	William B. Douglas Shelter	42.8
254.5	Winhall River	40.4
256.3	Stratton Pond, North Shore Trail to Stratton View Shelter	38.6
256.4	Bigelow Shelter, Vondell Shelter	38.5
260.3	Arlington-West Wardsboro Road	34.6
262.0	Story Spring Shelter	32.9
266.7	Caughnawaga & Kid Gore Shelters	28.2
270.6	Glastenbury Mountain	24.3
270.9	Goddard Shelter	24.0
273.3	Glastenbury Lookout	21.6
275.3	Little Pond Mountain	19.6
279.2	Melville Nauheim Shelter	15.7

North to South From Maine-N.H. State Line		South to North From Vt.-Mass. State Line
280.7	Bennington-Brattleboro Highway (Vt. 9), **Bennington, Vt., P.O. 05201**	14.2
282.4	Harmon Hill	12.5
284.1	Dunville Hollow Primitive Camping Area	10.8
284.9	Congdon Camp	10.0
291.8	County Road	3.1
292.1	Seth Warner Shelter and Primitive Camping Area	2.8
294.9	Vt.-Mass. Line, south end of Long Trail	0.0

Index